Anonymus

The Case of the United States, to be laid before the Tribunal of Arbitration, convened at Geneva

Anonymus

The Case of the United States, to be laid before the Tribunal of Arbitration, convened at Geneva

ISBN/EAN: 9783742807540

Manufactured in Europe, USA, Canada, Australia, Japa

Cover: Foto ©Suzi / pixelio.de

Manufactured and distributed by brebook publishing software (www.brebook.com)

Anonymus

The Case of the United States, to be laid before the Tribunal of Arbitration, convened at Geneva

THE CASE

OF

THE UNITED STATES,

LAID BEFORE THE

𝕿𝖗𝖎𝖇𝖚𝖓𝖆𝖑 𝖔𝖋 𝕬𝖗𝖇𝖎𝖙𝖗𝖆𝖙𝖎𝖔𝖓,

CONVENED AT GENEVA

UNDER THE

PROVISIONS OF THE TREATY BETWEEN THE UNITED STATES OF AMERICA AND HER MAJESTY THE QUEEN OF GREAT BRITAIN, CONCLUDED AT WASHINGTON, MAY 8, 1871.

LEIPZIG:
F. A. BROCKHAUS.

1872.

TABLE OF CONTENTS.

I. INTRODUCTION.   Page

    Meeting of the Joint High Commission at Washington   1
    Protocol of the conferences as to the Alabama claims   2
    The Treaty of Washington 6
    What the United States will attempt to establish .   13
    Evidence and documents, and how referred to . . . 14

II. THE UNFRIENDLY COURSE PURSUED BY GREAT BRITAIN TOWARD THE UNITED STATES FROM THE OUTBREAK TO THE CLOSE OF THE INSURRECTION.

    Relations of the United States with Great Britain prior to 1860 15
    Friendly relations of the two Governments in 1860   17
    The United States in 1860 17
    Election of Mr. Lincoln 18
    Secession of South Carolina 18
    Secession of Alabama 19
    Secession of Georgia and other States 19
    Opposition to the territorial limitation of slavery the cause of secession 19
    A party in the South opposed to secession 20
    Inauguration of Mr. Lincoln 22
    The British government informed of his purposes . 22
    Lord John Russell promises to await Mr. Adams's arrival before acting 23
    The surrender of Fort Sumter 23
    The insurgents to issue letters of marque 24
    Proclamation giving notice of blockade 24
    Objects of that proclamation 24
    The joint action of France invited by Great Britain 24
    When the President's proclamation was received in Great Britain 25
    Opinion of law officers taken on an imperfect copy   27
    Her Majesty's government decide on the first of May to recognize a state of war 27
    Lord John Russell and the insurgent commissioners discuss the recognition of southern independence 28
    Communication with the French government 29

CONTENTS.

II. THE UNFRIENDLY COURSE PURSUED BY GREAT BRITAIN TOWARD THE UNITED STATES FROM THE OUTBREAK TO THE CLOSE OF THE INSURRECTION—Cont'd.

	Page
Answers of the French government	29
When the President's Proclamation was received by Great Britain	30
Effect of recognition of a state of war	31
The Queen's proclamation	32
Uncertainty of Her Majesty's government	32
Effect of the Queen's proclamation	32
Mr. Bright's views	32
The sovereign right to issue such a proclamation not denied	35
It was an unfriendly act	36
And issued with an unfriendly purpose	36
M. Rolin-Jacquemyns on the Queen's proclamation	36
Unfriendly conduct of Great Britain as to the declarations of the congress of Paris	37
The instructions to Lord Lyons might have been regarded as a cause of war	39
Former negotiations regarding the declarations of the congress of Paris	39
Lord Lyons's interview with Mr. Seward	41
Termination of negotiations with the United States	42
Great Britain desired to legalize privateering	42
Negotiations at Richmond	43
Mr. Adams's comments	45
Contrast between conduct of Great Britain toward the United States in the Trent affair, and toward violators of British neutrality in the insurgent interest	47
Mr. Rolin-Jacquemyns on British neutrality	50
Proof the unfriendly feeling of members of the British cabinet and Parliament	51
Conclusions	59

III. THE DUTIES WHICH GREAT BRITAIN, AS A NEUTRAL, SHOULD HAVE OBSERVED TOWARD THE UNITED STATES.... 61

The Queen's proclamation a recognition of obligations under the law of nations	61
Great Britain has recognized its obligations in various ways	61
The obligations recognized by the foreign enlistment act of 1819	61
Municipal laws designed to aid a government in the performance of international duties	62
History of the foreign enlistment act of 1819	62
Great Britain bound to perform the duties recognized by that act	63

III. The duties which Great Britain, as a neutral, should have observed toward the United States—Continued.

	Page
The duties recognized by that act	64
Royal commission to revise the foreign enlistment act of 1819	67
Report of that commission	68
The Foreign Enlistment act of 1870	69
Its judicial construction	69
International law is a part of the common law of England	70
Duties recognized by the Queen's proclamation of neutrality	73
Definition of neutrality	74
Duties recognized by instructions to British officials during the insurrection	75
Correspondence between the two governments in 1793–'4	76
Treaty of November 19, 1794	79
Construction of that treaty by the commissioners appointed under it	79
The neutrality laws of the United States enacted at the request of Great Britain	80
Case of the bark Maury	81
Principles thus recognized by the two governments	81
Obligation to make compensation for injuries	82
Correspondence between the United States and Portugal	82
Principles recognized in that correspondence	88
Rules in the treaty of Washington	89
What is due diligence	91
Fitting out, arming, or equipping, each an offense	97
The second clause of the first rule	97
Reasons for a change of language	98
Continuing force of the rule	100
Duty to detain offending vessels recognized by Great Britain	100
Also recognized by France	102
The second rule of the treaty	102
The third rule of the treaty	103
Duty to make compensation for injuries	104
The foregoing views in harmony with the opinions of European publicists	104
Hautefeuille	104
Bluntschli	105
Rolin-Jacquemyns	108
Ortolan	111
Pierantoni	113

III. THE DUTIES WHICH GREAT BRITAIN, AS A NEUTRAL, SHOULD HAVE OBSERVED TOWARD THE UNITED STATES—Continued.

	Page
Lord Westbury	114
The case of the Swedish vessels	114
Offending vessels not simply contraband of war	119
Opinion of Ortolan	120
Opinion of Heffter	121
Case of the Santisima Trinidad	122
Controlled by the case of the Gran Para	124
Effect of a commission of the offender as a vessel of war	124
Opinion of Sir Roundell Palmer	126
Opinion of Chief Justice Marshall	126
Decision of the Supreme Court of the United States	127
The principle recognized by France, Great Britain, Spain, Portugal, and the United States	129
Deposit of the offense	129
Résumé of principles	130

IV. WHEREIN GREAT BRITAIN FAILED TO PERFORM ITS DUTIES AS A NEUTRAL.

	Page
Admissions of British cabinet ministers	132
British ports the base of insurgent operations; a partial hospitality shown to the insurgents; a branch of their government established in Liverpool; their government vessels officially aided in evading the blockade, and in furnishing them with arms, munitions, and means for carrying on the struggle	134
The firm of Fraser, Trenholm & Co.	135
Character of the blockaded coast	137
Geographical situation of Nassau and Bermuda	138
What was done at Nassau	139
The United States denied permission to deposit coal at Nassau	142
Complaints to Earl Russell and his reply	143
Instructions as to hospitalities to the belligerents	144
Lord Palmerston's threats	145
Contraband of war fraudulently cleared at Nassau for British ports	146
Résumé for the year 1862	147
Base changed to Bermuda	148
What was done at Liverpool by Bullock	149
The Florida	149
The Alabama	150
The Sumter at Gibraltar	152
The Florida at Nassau	152
Contracts for constructing six iron-clads	153

CONTENTS.

IV. WHEREIN GREAT BRITAIN FAILED TO PERFORM ITS DUTIES AS A NEUTRAL—Continued.

	Page
The Sumter at Trinidad	153
The Florida at Nassau	154
Mr. Adams represents the foregoing facts to Earl Russell	154
Earl Russell declines to act	155
Inefficiency of the foreign enlistment act	155
Propositions to amend the foreign enlistment act	156
Propositions declined by Great Britain	156
Propositions renewed and declined	157
These proceedings were an abandonment, in advance, of "due diligence"	159
The Georgia	159
The Alexandra	160
The rulings in the Alexandra case emasculated the foreign enlistment act	162
Laird's Iron-clad rams	162
Their detention not an abandonment of the lax construction of the duties of a neutral	165
The contracts with Arman for the construction of vessels in France	166
Conduct of the French Government	167
Contrast between the conduct of France and of Great Britain	168
The Tuscaloosa at the Cape of Good Hope	168
She is released against the advice of Sir Baldwin Walker	169
The course of the governor is disapproved	170
The Tuscaloosa comes again into the waters of the Colony	170
The governor reverses his policy and seizes the vessel	170
His course is again disapproved	171
Blockade-running	171
Cotton shipments	172
The insurgent government interested in blockade-running	174
These facts brought to Earl Russell's notice	176
He sees no offense in them	176
Earl Russell's attention again called to these facts	177
He again sees no offense in them	178
Blockade-running in partnership with the insurgent government	179
Continued partiality	180
The Rappahannock	182
The Shenandoah	183

IV. **WHEREIN GREAT BRITAIN FAILED TO PERFORM ITS DUTIES AS A NEUTRAL.**—Continued.

	Page
Mr. Mountague Bernard's list of vessels detained by Great Britain	185
The charges in Mr. Fish's instructions of September 25, 1869, are sustained by this evidence	187

V. **WHEREIN GREAT BRITAIN FAILED TO PERFORM ITS DUTIES AS A NEUTRAL. THE INSURGENT CRUISERS.**

Earl Russell denounces the acts of which the United States complain as unwarranted and totally unjustifiable	194
British territory the base of the naval operations of the insurgents	194
Their arsenal	194
The systematic operations of the insurgents a violation of the duties of a neutral	195
Continuing partiality for the insurgents	196
Recapitulation of hostile acts tolerated in British Possessions	197
These facts throw suspicion upon the acts of British officials toward the insurgent cruisers	198
They show an abnegation of all diligence to prevent the acts complained of	199
They throw upon Great Britain the burden of proof to show that the acts complained of could not have been prevented	200
List of the insurgent cruisers	200
The Sumter	200
The Nashville	206
The Florida and her tenders, the Clarence, the Tacony, and the Archer	206
The Alabama and her tender, the Tuscaloosa	229
The Retribution	245
The Georgia	246
The Tallahassee, or the Olustee	258
The Chickamauga	260
The Shenandoah	262
Summary	286
The conduct of other nations contrasted with that of Great Britain	291

VI. **THE TRIBUNAL SHOULD AWARD A SUM IN GROSS TO THE UNITED STATES.**

Offer of the American Commissioners in the Joint High Commission	294
Rejection of the offer by the British Commissioners	295
Terms of the submission by the Treaty	295
General statement of the claims	295

VI. THE TRIBUNAL SHOULD AWARD A SUM IN GROSS TO THE UNITED STATES—Continued.

	Page
Claims growing out of the destruction of vessels and cargoes	295
Government vessels	296
Merchant vessel	296
Injuries to persons	296
Expenditures in pursuit of the cruisers	297
Transfer of vessels to the British flag	297
Enhanced rates of insurance	299
Prolongation of the war	300
Interest claimed to the date of payment	302
Reasons why a gross sum should be awarded	302
INDEX	303

CASE OF THE UNITED STATES.

PART I.

INTRODUCTION.

Meeting of the Joint High Commission at Washington.
In the spring of the present year (1871) five Commissioners on the part of Great Britain and five Commissioners on the part of the United States of America met at Washington in a body, which, when organized, was known as the Joint High Commission, in order to discuss, and, if possible, to arrange for, the adjustment of several causes of difference between the two Powers.

Among the subjects which were brought before that body by the United States were "the differences which arose during the rebellion in the United States, and which have existed since then, growing out of the acts committed by the several vessels, which have given rise to the claims generically known as the Alabama Claims." [1]

The sessions of the Joint High Commission were many in number, and were largely devoted to the consideration of the differences referred to in Mr. Fish's letter to Sir Edward Thornton, from which the above-cited quotation is made. The High Commissioners, in the protocol of their thirty-sixth conference, caused to be recorded a statement of their negotiations on this subject, in the following language:

---

[1] Mr. Fish to Sir Edward Thornton, January 30, 1871, Vol. VI, page 16.

INTRODUCTION.

Protocol of the conferences as to the Alabama Claims. "At the conference held on the 8th of March the American Commissioners stated that the people and Government of the United States felt that they had sustained a great wrong, and that great injuries and losses were inflicted upon their commerce and their material interests by the course and conduct of Great Britain during the recent rebellion in the United States; that what had occurred in Great Britain and her colonies during that period had given rise to feelings in the United States which the people of the United States did not desire to cherish toward Great Britain; that the history of the Alabama and other cruisers, which had been fitted out, or armed, or equipped, or which had received augmentation of force in Great Britain or in her colonies, and of the operations of those vessels, showed extensive direct losses in the capture and destruction of a large number of vessels, with their cargoes, and in the heavy national expenditures in the pursuit of the cruisers, and indirect injury in the transfer of a large part of the American commercial marine to the British flag, in the enhanced payments of insurance, in the prolongation of the war, and in the addition of a large sum to the cost of the war and the suppression of the rebellion; and also showed that Great Britain, by reason of failure in the proper observance of her duties as a neutral, had become justly liable for the acts of those cruisers and of their tenders: that the claims for the loss and destruction of private property which had thus far been presented amounted to about fourteen millions of dollars, without interest, which amount was liable to be greatly increased by claims which had not been presented; that the cost to which the Government had been put in the pursuit of cruisers could easily be ascertained by certificates of Government accounting officers; that, in the hope of an amicable settlement, no estimate was made of the indirect losses, without prejudice, however, to the right to indemnification on their account in the event of no such settlement being made.

"The American Commissioners further stated that they hoped that the British Commissioners would be able to place upon record an expression of regret by Her Majesty's Government for the depredations committed by the vessels whose acts were now under discussion. They also proposed that the Joint High Commission should agree upon a sum which should be paid by Great Britain to the United States, in satisfaction of all the claims and the interest thereon.

"The British Commissioners replied that Her Majesty's Government could not admit that Great Britain had failed to discharge toward the United States the duties imposed on her by the rules of International Law, or that she was justly liable to make good to the United States the losses occasioned by the acts of the cruisers to which the American Commissioners had referred. They reminded the American Commissioners that several vessels, suspected of being designed to cruise against the United States, including two iron-clads, had been arrested or detained by the British Government, and that that Government had, in some instances, not confined itself to the discharge of international obligations, however widely construed, as, for instance, when it acquired, at a great cost to the country, the control of the Anglo-Chinese Flotilla, which, it was apprehended, might be used against the United States.

"They added that, although Great Britain had, from the beginning, disavowed any responsibility for the acts of the Alabama and the other vessels, she had already shown her willingness, for the sake of the maintenance of friendly relations with the United States, to adopt the principle of arbitration, provided that a fitting Arbitrator could be found, and that an agreement could be come to as to the points to which arbitration should apply. They would, therefore, abstain from replying in detail to the statement of the American Commissioners, in the hope that the necessity for entering upon a lengthened controversy might be obviated by the adoption of so fair a mode of settlement as that which they were instructed to propose; and they had now to repeat, on behalf of their Government, the offer of arbitration.

"The American Commissioners expressed their regret at this decision of the British Commissioners, and said further that they could not consent to submit the question of the liability of Her Majesty's Government to arbitration unless the principles which should govern the Arbitrator in the consideration of the facts could be first agreed upon.

"The British Commissioners replied that they had no authority to agree to a submission of these claims to an Arbitrator with instructions as to the principles which should govern him in the consideration of them. They said that they should be willing to consider what principles should be adopted for observance in future; but that they were of opinion that the best mode of conducting an arbitration was to submit the facts to the Arbitrator, and leave him free to decide upon them after hearing such arguments as might be necessary.

"The American Commissioners replied that they were willing to consider what principles should be laid down for observance in similar cases in future, with the understanding that any principles that should be agreed upon should be held to be applicable to the facts in respect to the Alabama Claims.

"The British Commissioners replied that they could not admit that there had been any violation of existing principles of International Law, and that their instructions did not authorize them to accede to a proposal for laying down rules for the guidance of the Arbitrator, but that they would make known to their Government the views of the American Commissioners on the subject.

"At the respective conferences on March 9, March 10, March 13, and March 14, the Joint High Commission considered the form of the declaration of principles or rules which the American Commissioners desired to see adopted for the instruction of the Arbitrator and laid down for observance by the two Governments in future.

"At the close of the conference of the 14th of March, the British Commissioners reserved several questions for the consideration of their Government.

"At the conference on the 5th of April, the British Commissioners stated that they were instructed by Her Majesty's Government to declare that Her Majesty's Government could not assent to the proposed rules as a statement of principles of International Law which were in force at the time when the Alabama Claims arose, but that Her Majesty's Government, in order to evince its desire of strengthening the friendly relations between the two countries, and of making satisfactory provision for the future, agreed that, in deciding the questions between the two countries arising out of those claims, the Arbitrator should assume that Her Majesty's Government had undertaken to act upon the principles set forth in the rules which the American Commissioners had proposed, *viz.*:

"'That a neutral Government is bound,

"'First, to use due diligence to prevent the fitting out, arming, or equipping, within its jurisdiction, of any vessel which it has reasonable ground to believe is intended to cruise or carry on war against a Power with which it is at peace; and also to use like diligence to prevent the departure from its jurisdiction of any vessel intended to cruise or carry on war as above, such vessel having been specially adapted, in whole or in part, within such jurisdiction, to warlike use.

"'Secondly, not to permit or suffer either belligerent to make use of its ports or waters as the base of naval operations against the other, or for the purpose of the renewal or augmentation of military supplies or arms, or the recruitment of men.

"'Thirdly, to exercise due diligence in its own ports or waters, and, as to all persons within its jurisdiction, to prevent any violation of the foregoing obligations and duties.'

"It being a condition of this undertaking that these obligations should in future be held to be binding internationally between the two countries,

"It was also settled that, in deciding the matters submitted to him, the Arbitrator should be governed by the foregoing rules, which had been agreed upon as rules to be taken as applicable to the case, and by such principles of International Law, not inconsistent therewith, as the Arbitrator schould determine to have been applicable to the case.

"The Joint High Commission then proceeded to consider the form of submission and the manner of constituting a Tribunal of Arbitration.

"At the conferences on the 6th, 8th, 9th, 10th, and 12th

of April the Joint High Commission considered and discussed the form of submission, the manner of the award, and the mode of selecting the Arbitrators.

"The American Commissioners, referring to the hope which they had expressed on the 8th of March, inquired whether the British Commissioners were prepared to place upon record an expression of regret by Her Majesty's Government for the depredations committed by the vessels whose acts were now under discussion; and the British Commissioners replied that they were authorized to express, in a friendly spirit, the regret felt by Her Majesty's Government for the escape, under whatever circumstances, of the Alabama and other vessels from British ports, and for the depredations committed by those vessels.

"The American Commissioners accepted this expression of regret as very satisfactory to them and as a token of kindness, and said that they felt sure it would be so received by the Government and people of the United States.

"In the conference on the 13th of April the Treaty, Articles I to XI, were agreed to."

The Treaty of Washington. The Treaty referred to in this statement was signed at Washington on the 8th day of May, 1871 and the ratifications thereof were exchanged at London on the 17th day of the following June. The articles which relate to this subject are the following:

"ARTICLE I.

"Whereas differences have arisen between the Government of the United States and the Government of Her Britannic Majesty, and still exist, growing out of the acts committed by the several vessels which have given rise to the claims generically known as the 'Alabama Claims;'

"And whereas Her Britannic Majesty has authorized Her High Commissioners and Plenipotentiaries to express, in a friendly spirit, the regret felt by Her Majesty's Government for the escape, under whatever circumstances, of the Alabama and other vessels from British ports, and for the depredations committed by those vessels:

"Now, in order to remove and adjust all complaints and

claims on the part of the United States, and to provide for the speedy settlement of such claims, which are not admitted by Her Britannic Majesty's Government, the High Contracting Parties agree that all the said claims, growing out of acts committed by the aforesaid vessels, and generically known as the 'Alabama Claims,' shall be referred to a Tribunal of Arbitration, to be composed of five Arbitrators, to be appointed in the following manner, that is to say: One shall be named by the President of the United States; one shall be named by Her Britannic Majesty; His Majesty the King of Italy shall be requested to name one; the President of the Swiss Confederation shall requested to name one; and His Majesty the Emperor of Brazil shall be requested to name one.

"In case of the death, absence, or incapacity to serve of any or either of the said Arbitrators, or in the event of either of the said Arbitrators omitting or declining or ceasing to act as such, the President of the United States, or Her Britannic Majesty, or His Majesty the King of Italy, or the President of the Swiss Confederation, or His Majesty the Emperor of Brazil, as the case may be, may forthwith name another person to act as Arbitrator in the place and stead of the Arbitrator originally named by such Head of a State.

"And in the event of the refusal or omission for two months after receipt of the request from either of the High Contracting Parties of His Majesty the King of Italy, or the President of the Swiss Confederation, or His Majesty the Emperor of Brazil, to name an Arbitrator, either to fill the original appointment, or in the place of one who may have died, be absent, or incapacitated, or who may omit, decline, or from any cause cease to act as such Arbitrator, His Majesty the King of Sweden and Norway shall be requested to name one or more persons, as the case may be, to act as such Arbitrator or Arbitrators.

"ARTICLE II.

"The Arbitrators shall meet at Geneva, in Switzerland, at the earliest convenient day after they shall have been named, and shall proceed impartially and carefully to examine and decide all questions that shall be laid before them on the part of the Governments of the United States and Her Britannic Majesty, respectively. All questions considered by the Tribunal, including the final award, shall be decided by a majority of all the Arbitrators.

"Each of the High Contracting Parties shall also name one person to attend the Tribunal as its agent to represent it generally in all matters connected with the arbitration.

"Article III.

"The written or printed case of each of the two Parties, accompanied by the documents, the official correspondence, and other evidence on which each relies, shall be delivered in duplicate to each of the arbitrators and to the agent of the other Party as soon as may be after the organization of the Tribunal, but within a period not exceeding six months from the date of the exchange of the ratifications of this Treaty.

"Article IV.

"Within four months after the delivery on both sides of the written or printed case, either Party may, in like manner, deliver in duplicate to each of the said Arbitrators, and to the agent of the other Party, a counter-case and additional documents, correspondence, and evidence, in reply to the case, documents, correspondence, and evidence so presented by the other Party.

"The Arbitrators may, however, extend the time for delivering such counter-case, documents, correspondence, and evidence, when, in their judgment, it becomes necessary, in consequence of the distance of the place from which the evidence to be presented is to be procured.

"If in the case submitted to the Arbitrators either Party shall have specified or alluded to any report or document in its own exclusive possession, without annexing a copy, such Party shall be bound, if the other Party thinks proper to apply for it, to furnish that Party with a copy thereof; and either may call upon the other, through the Arbitrators, to produce the originals or certified copies of any papers adduced as evidence, giving in each instance such reasonable notice as the Arbitrators may require.

"ARTICLE V.

"It shall be the duty of the agent of each Party, within two months after the expiration of the time limited for the delivery of the counter-case on both sides, to deliver in duplicate to each of the said Arbitrators and to the agent of the other Party a written or printed argument, showing the points and referring to the evidence upon which his Government relies; and the Arbitrators may, if they desire further elucidation with regard to any point, require a written or printed statement or argument, or oral argument by counsel upon it; but in such case the other Party shall be entitled to reply either orally or in writing, as the case may be.

"ARTICLE VI.

"In deciding the matters submitted to the Arbitrators they shall be governed by the following three rules, which are agreed upon by the High Contracting Parties as rules to be taken as applicable to the case, and by such principles of International Law, not inconsistent therewith, as the Arbitrators shall determine to have been applicable to the case:

RULES.

"A neutral Government is bound—

"First, to use due diligence to prevent the fitting out, arming, or equipping, within its jurisdiction, of any vessel which it has reasonable ground to believe is intended to cruise or to carry on war against a Power with which it is at peace: and also to use like diligence to prevent the departure from its jurisdiction, of any vessel intended to cruise or carry on war as above, such vessel having been specially adapted, in whole or in part, within such jurisdiction, to warlike use.

"Secondly, not to permit or suffer either belligerent to make use of its ports or waters as the base of naval operations against the other, or for the purpose of the renewal or augmentation of military supplies or arms, or the recruitment of men.

"Thirdly, to exercise due diligence in its own ports and waters, and, as to all persons within its jurisdiction, to prevent any violation of the foregoing obligations and duties.

"Her Britannic Majesty has commanded her High Commissioners and Plenipotentiaries to declare that Her Majesty's Government cannot assent to the foregoing rules as a statement of principles of International Law which were in force at the time when the claims mentioned in Article I arose, but that Her Majesty's Government, in order to evince its desire of strengthening the friendly relations between the two countries, and of making satisfactory provision for the future, agrees that in deciding the questions between the two countries arising out of those claims, the Arbitrators should assume that Her Majesty's Government had undertaken to act upon the principles set forth in these rules.

"And the High Contracting Parties agree to observe these rules as between themselves in future, and to bring them to the knowledge of other maritime Powers, and to invite them to accede to them.

"ARTICLE VII.

"The decision of the Tribunal shall, if possible, be made within three months from the close of the argument on both sides.

"It shall be made in writing and dated, and shall be signed by the Arbitrators who may assent to it.

"The said Tribunal shall first determine as to each vessel separately whether Great Britain has, by any act or omission, failed to fulfill any of the duties set forth in the foregoing three rules, or recognized by the principles of International Law not inconsistent with such rules, and shall certify such fact as to each of the said vessels. In case the Tribunal find that Great Britain has failed to fulfill any duty or duties as aforesaid, it may, if it think proper, proceed to award a sum in gross to be paid by Great Britain to the United States for all the claims referred to it; and in such case the gross sum so awarded shall be paid in coin by the Government of Great Britain to the Government of the United

States, at Washington, within twelve months after the date of the award.

"The award shall be in duplicate, one copy whereof shall be delivered to the agent of the United States for his Government, and the other copy shall be delivered to the agent of Great Britain for his Government.

"ARTICLE VIII.

"Each Government shall pay its own agent and provide for the proper remuneration of the counsel employed by it and of the Arbitrator appointed by it, and for the expense of preparing and submitting its case to the Tribunal. All other expenses connected with the arbitration shall be defrayed by the two Governments in equal moieties.

"ARTICLE IX.

"The Arbitrators shall keep an accurate record of their proceedings, and may appoint and employ the necessary officers to assist them.

"ARTICLE X.

"In case the Tribunal finds that Great Britain has failed to fulfill any duty or duties as aforesaid, and does not award a sum in gross, the High Contracting Parties agree that a Board of Assessors shall be appointed to ascertain and determine what claims are valid, and what amount or amounts shall be paid by Great Britain to the United States on account of the liability arising from such failure, as to each vessel, according to the extent of such liability as decided by the Arbitrators.

"The Board of Assessors shall be constituted as follows: One member thereof shall be named by the President of the United States, one member thereof shall be named by Her Britannic Majesty, and one member thereof shall be named by the Representative at Washington of His Majesty the King of Italy; and, in case of a vacancy happening from any cause, it shall be filled in the same manner in which the original appointment was made.

"As soon as possible after such nominations the Board of Assessors shall be organized in Washington, with power to hold their sittings there, or in New York, or in Boston. The members thereof shall severally subscribe a solemn declaration that they will impartially and carefully examine and decide, to the best of their judgment and according to justice and equity, all matters submitted to them, and shall forthwith proceed, under such rules and regulations as they may prescribe, to the investigations of the claims which shall be presented to them by the Government of the United States, and shall examine and decide upon them in such order and manner as they may think proper, but upon such evidence or information only as shall be furnished by or on behalf of the Governments of the United States and of Great Britain respectively. They shall be bound to hear on each separate claim, if required, one person on behalf of each Government, as counsel or agent. A majority of the Assessors in each case shall be sufficient for a decision.

"The decision of the Assessors shall be given upon each claim in writing, and shall be signed by them respectively and dated.

"Every claim shall be presented to the Assessors within six months from the day of their first meeting, but they may, for good cause shown, extend the time for the presentation of any claim to a further period not exceeding three months.

"The Assessors shall report to each Government, at or before the expiration of one year from the date of their first meeting, the amount of claims decided by them up to the date of such report: if further claims then remain undecided, they shall make a further report at or before the expiration of two years from the date of such first meeting; and in case any claims remain undetermined at that time, they shall make a final report within a further period of six months.

"The report or reports shall be made in duplicate, and one copy thereof shall be delivered to the Secretary of State of the United States, and one copy thereof to the Representative of Her Britannic Majesty at Washington.

"All sums of money which may be awarded under this Article shall be payable at Washington in coin, within twelve months after the delivery of each report.

"The Board of Assessors may employ such clerks as they shall think necessary.

"The expenses of the Board of Assessors shall be borne equally by the two Governments, and paid from time to time, as may be found expedient, on the production of accounts certified by the Board. The remuneration of the Assessors shall also be paid by the two Governments in equal moieties in a similar manner.

"ARTICLE XI.

"The High Contracting Parties engage to consider the result of the proceedings of the Tribunal of Arbitration and of the Board of Assessors, should such Board be appointed, as a full, perfect, and final settlement of all the claims hereinbefore referred to; and further engage that every such claim, whether the same may or may not have been presented to the notice of, made, preferred, or laid before the Tribunal or Board, shall, from and after the conclusion of the proceedings of the Tribunal or Board, be considered and treated as finally settled, barred, and henceforth inadmissible."

What the United States will attempt to establish. In accordance with the provisions of Article III of the Treaty, the United States have the honor to lay before the Tribunal of Arbitration this their "Printed Case," accompanied by the documents, the official correspondence, and other evidence on which they rely. They propose to show, by a historical statement of the course pursued by the British Government toward the United States, from the outbreak of the insurrection in the Southern States of the United States, that there was on the part of the British Government a studied unfriendliness or fixed predispositon adverse to the United States, which furnished a constant motive for the several acts of omission and commission, hereinafter complained of, as inconsistent with its duty as a neutral.

Having adduced the evidence of this fact, the United States will next endeavor to indicate to the Tribunal of Arbitration what they deem to have been the duties of Great Britain toward the United States, in respect to the several cruisers which will be named in this paper.

They will then endeavor to show that Great Britain failed to perform those duties, both generally, and specifically as to each of the cruisers; and that such failure involved the liability to remunerate the United States for losses thus inflicted upon them, upon their citizens, and upon others protected by their flag.

Lastly, they will endeavor to satisfy the Tribunal of Arbitration that it can find, in the testimony which will be offered by the United States, ample material for estimating the amount of such injuries, and they will ask the Tribunal to exercise the powers conferred upon it by Article VII of the Treaty, in awarding "a sum in gross, to be paid by Great Britain to the United States, for all the claims referred to."

Evidence and documents, and how referred to. In April, 1869, the President communicated to the Senate a mass of official correspondence and other papers relating to those claims, which was printed in five volumes. These, and two additional volumes, containing further correspondence, evidence, and documents, accompany this case. The whole will form "the documents, the official correspondence, and the other evidence on which [the United States] relies," which is called for by Article III of the Treaty. Reference will be made throughout this paper to these volumes thus: "Vol. I, page 1," &c., &c., &c. The United States understand, however, that they may, under the terms of the Treaty, present hereafter "additional documents, correspondence, and evidence," and they reserve the right to do so.

PART II.

THE UNFRIENDLY COURSE PURSUED BY GREAT BRITAIN TOWARD THE UNITED STATES FROM THE OUTBREAK TO THE CLOSE OF THE INSURRECTION.

Relations of the United States with Great Britain prior to 1860. In 1860 the United States had been an independent nation for a period of eighty-four years, and acknowledged as such by Great Britain for a period of seventy-seven years.[1]

During this period, while sharing to a remarkable extent in the general prosperity of the Christian Powers, they had so conducted their relations toward those Powers as to merit, and they believed that they had secured, the good-will and esteem of all. Their prosperity was the result of honest thrift; their exceptional increase of population was the fruit of a voluntary immigration to their shores; and the vast extension of their domain was acquired by purchase and not by conquest.

From no people had they better right to expect a just judgment than from the people of Great Britain. In 1783, the War of Separation had been closed by a treaty of peace, which adjusted all the questions then pending between the two Governments. In 1794, new questions having arisen, growing out of the efforts of France to make the ports of the United States a base of hostile operations against Great Britain, a new treaty was made, at the instance of the United States, by which all the difficulties were arranged satisfactorily to Great Britain, and at the same time so as to preserve the neutrality and the honor of the United States. In the same year, also, the first neutrality act was passed by Congress,[1] prescribing rules and establishing the modes of proceeding to enable the United States to perform their duties as a neutral toward Great Britain and other belligerents. In 1812, they were forced into war with Great Britain, by the claim of that Power to impress seamen on the high seas from vessels of the United States. After three years the war ceased, and the claim has never since been practically enforced. In 1818, they met British negotiators more than halfway in arranging disputed points about the North American Fisheries. In 1827, having added to their own right of discovery the French and Spanish titles to the Pacific coast, they voluntarily agreed to a joint occupation of a disputed portion of this territory, rather than resort to the last arbitrament of nations. In 1838, when a serious rebellion prevailed in Canada, the Congress of the United States, at the request of Great Britain, passed an act authorizing the Government to exercise exceptional powers to maintain the national neutrality. In 1842, the Government of the United States met a British Envoy in a spirit of conciliation, and adjusted by agreement the disputed boundary between Maine and the British Possessions. In 1846, they accepted the proposal of Great Britain, made at their own suggestion, to adopt the forty-ninth parallel as a compromise-line between the two Columbias, and to give to Great Britain the whole of Vancouver's Island. In 1850 they waived, by the Clayton-Bulwer Treaty, the right of acquisition on the Isthmus, across which for many years the line of communication from one part of their dominions to the other must run. In 1854, they conferred upon the people of the British Possessions in North America the advantages of a free, full commercial intercourse with the United States for their products, without securing corresponding benefits in return. Thus a series of difficult questions, some of which might have led to war, had been peaceably arranged by negotiations, and the increasing intercourse of the two nations was constantly fostered by continuing acts of friendliness on the part of the Government of the United States.

---

[1] For an abstract of this act see Vol. IV, pp. 102—103.

Friendly relations of the two Governments in 1860. All the political relations of the United States with England, with the exception of the episode of the war of 1812, had been those of increasing amity and friendship, confirmed by a repeated yielding of extreme rights, rather than imperil the cordial relations which the United States so much desired to maintain with their nearest neighbors, their best customers, and their blood-relations.. They had good right, therefore, to believe, and they did believe, that, by virtue of this friendly political understanding, and in consequence of the gradual and steady assimilation of the commercial interests and the financial policies of the two Governments, there was in Great Britain, in the summer of 1860, sympathy for the Government and affection for the people of the United States. They had equal reason to think that neither the British Government nor people would look with either ignorance or unconcern upon any disaster to them. Above all, they had at that time a right to feel confident, that in any controversy which might grow out of the unhappy existence of African slavery in certain of the Southern States, the British Government would not exercise its sovereign powers, questionably or unquestionably, in favor of the supporters of slavery.

The United States in 1860. On the 6th day of November, in that year, the jurisdiction of the Government of the United States extended unquestioned over eighteen States from which African slavery was excluded;[1] over fifteen States in which it was established by law;[2] and over a vast territory in which, under the then prevailing laws, persons with African blood in their veins could be held as slaves.

This large unsettled or partially settled territory, as it might become peopled, was also liable to be divided into

---

[1] Maine, New Hampshire, Vermont, Massachusetts, Rhode Island, Connecticut, New York, New Jersey, Pennsylvania, Ohio, Indiana, Illinois, Michigan, Iowa, Wisconsin, California, Minnesota, Oregon.

[2] Delaware, Maryland, Virginia, North Carolina, South Carolina, Georgia, Kentucky, Tennessee, Louisiana, Mississippi, Alabama, Missouri, Arkansas, Florida, Texas.

new States, which, as they entered the Union, might, as the law then stood, become "Slave States," thus giving the advocates of slavery an increased strength in the Congress of the nation, and more especially in the Senate, and a more absolute control of the National Government.

Since the date named three new States, entitled to a representation of six Senators in the National Senate, have been admitted into the Union from this territory;[1] and the remainder of the great dominions of the United States is now divided into ten incipient political organizations, known as Territories, which, with one exception, may at some future time become States.[2]

Election of Mr. Lincoln. The general election for President of the United States, which took place on the 6th of November, 1860, was conducted in strict conformity with the provisions of the Constitution and laws of the country, and resulted in the choice of Abraham Lincoln. The party which elected him was pledged in advance to maintain "that the normal condition of all the territory of the United States is that of freedom," and to "deny the authority of Congress, of a Territorial Legislature, or of any individuals, to give legal existence to slavery in any Territory of the United States."[3] The word "Territory" is here used in the above-mentioned sense of an incipient political organization, which may at some future time become a State.

Secession of South Carolina. This decision of the people of the United States was resisted by some of the inhabitants of the States where slavery prevailed. The people of South Carolina, with an undoubted unanimity, commenced the hostile

---

[1] Nevada, Nebraska, Kansas. West Virginia was formed from a portion of the territory of Virginia, and for this reason does not come within the meaning of the text, though it became a State after the date mentioned.

[2] New Mexico, Utah, Washington, Dakota, Colorado, Arizona, Idaho, Montana, Wyoming, District of Columbia. The territory known as the Indian Territory is without political organization, having neither Governor nor Delegate in Congress. It cannot be considered as coming within the meaning of the text.

[3] Greeley's American Conflict, Vol. I, page 320.

movement. In the following month they proclaimed, through a State Convention, their purpose to secede from the Union, because the party about to come into power had "announced that the South shall be excluded from the common terri-
Of Alabama. tory."[1] The State of Alabama, on the 11th of January, with much less unanimity, (the vote in the Convention being 61 ayes to 39 nays,[2]) followed the example of South Carolina, giving as their reason that the election of Mr. Lincoln, "by a sectional party, avowedly hostile to the domestic institutions [*i. e.*, slavery] of Alabama," was "a political wrong of an insulting and menacing character."[3]

Of Georgia and other States. The State of Georgia followed after a much greater struggle, in which the party in favor of remaining in the Union resisted to the last, the final vote being 208 ayes to 89 nays.[4] Florida, Mississippi, Louisiana, and Texas each framed an ordinance of secession from the Union before the 4th of February, in each case with more or less unanimity.

Opposition to the territorial limitation of slavery the cause of secession. On the 4th of February, 1861, representatives from some of the States which had attempted to go through the form of secession, and representatives from the State of North Carolina, which had not at that time attempted it, met at Montgomery,[5] in the State of Alabama, for the purpose of organizing a provisional government, and having done so, elected Mr. Jefferson Davis as the Provisional President, and Mr. Alexander H. Stephens as the Provisional Vice-President of the proposed Confederation. In accepting this office, on the 18th of February, Mr. Jefferson Davis said: [6]"We have vainly endeavored to secure tranquillity and obtain respect for the rights to which we were entitled," [*i. e.*, the right to extend the domains of slavery.] "As a necessity, and not a choice, we have resorted to the remedy of separation." * *

---

[1] McPherson's History of the Rebellion, page 16.
[2] McPherson's History of the Rebellion, page 4.
[3] Appleton's Annual Cyclopædia, 1861, page 10.
[4] McPherson's History of the Rebellion, page 3.
[5] Appleton's Annual Cyclopædia, 1861, Vol. 1, page 126.
[6] Appleton's Annual Cyclopædia, 1861, page 613.

"Our industrial pursuits have received no check; the cultivation of our fields progresses as heretofore; and even should we be involved in war, there would be no considerable diminution in the production of the staples which have constituted our exports, in which the commercial world has an interest scarcely less than our own. This common interest of producer and consumer can only be intercepted by an exterior force, which should obstruct its transmission to foreign markets—a course of conduct which would be detrimental to the manufacturing and commercial interests abroad."

Mr. Stephens spoke with still more explicitness. He said [1] the "foundations [of the new government] are laid. Its corner-stone rests upon the great truth that the negro is not equal to the white man; that slavery—subordination to the superior race—is his natural and moral condition."

Having thus formally declared that the contemplated limitation of the territory within which negro slavery should be tolerated was the sole cause of the projected separation, and having appealed to the world to support them, the seceding States made efforts, which proved vain, to induce the other slave States to join them. No other States passed ordinances of secession until after the fall of Fort Sumter. On the contrary, the people of the States of Tennessee [2] and Missouri [3] before that time voted by large majorities against secession; and in the States of North Carolina and Virginia conventions were called and were in session when some of the events hereinafter referred to took place; and these bodies were known to be opposed to the revolutionary movements in South Carolina and the six States bordering on the Gulf of Mexico.

A party in the South opposed to secession.
A large minority, if not a majority, of the people of the slave States known as Border States, and of the mountainous parts of the six States known as the Gulf States, did not desire separation. They were attached to the Union, which had fostered and

---

[1] Appleton's Annual Cyclopædia, 1861, page 129.
[2] McPherson's History of the Rebellion, page 5.
[3] Appleton's Annual Cyclopædia, 1861, page 478.

protected their interests, and they expressed no dissatisfaction, except with the proposed policy as to the extension of slavery, and in many cases not even with that. Their feelings were forcibly expressed by the distinguished Alexander H. Stephens, Provisional Vice-President of the Montgomery Government, in a speech made in the Convention in Georgia before that State passed the ordinance of secession, and about two months before he accepted office at Montgomery. He said, [1] "This step [of secession] once taken can never be recalled; and all the baleful and withering consequences that must follow will rest on the Convention for all coming time. When we and our posterity shall see our lovely South desolated by the demon of war, which this act of yours will inevitably invite and call forth; when our green fields of waving harvest shall be trodden down by the murderous soldiery and fiery car of war sweeping over our land; our temples of justice laid in ashes; all the horrors and desolations of war upon us, who but this Convention will be held responsible for it, and who but him who shall have given his vote for this unwise and illtimed measure, as I honestly think and believe, shall be held to strict account for this suicidal act by the present generation, and probably cursed and execrated by posterity for all coming time, for the wide and desolating ruin that will inevitably follow this act you now propose to perpetrate? Pause, I entreat you, and consider for a moment what reasons you can give that will even satisfy yourselves in calmer moments; what reasons you can give to your fellow-sufferers in the calamity that it will bring upon us. What reasons can you give to the nations of the earth to justify it? They will be the calm and deliberate judges in the case, and what cause or one overt act can you name or point to, on which to rest the plea of justification? What right has the North assailed? What interest of the South has been invaded? What justice has been denied? And what claim founded in justice and right has been withheld? Can either of you to-day name one governmental act of wrong, deliberately and purposely

---

[1] McPherson's History of the Rebellion, page 25.

done by the Government of Washington, of which the South has a right to complain? I challenge the answer."

All the facts above referred to in this paper were patent to the whole world, were ostentatiously put forth by the insurgents, and were openly commented upon by the public press throughout the United States. It is, therefore, not unreasonable to presume that the British Government received from its representatives and agents in the United States full information concerning them as they took place. To suppose the contrary would be to ignore the well-known fidelity of those officers.

Inauguration of Mr. Lincoln. Mr. Lincoln entered upon the duties of his office on the 4th of March, 1861. He found the little Army of the United States scattered, and disintegrated; the Navy sent to distant quarters of the globe; the Treasury bankrupt; the credit of the United States seriously injured by forced sales of Government securities; the public service demoralized; the various Departments of the Government filled with unfaithful clerks and officers, whose sympathies were with the South, who had been placed in their positions for the purpose of paralyzing his administration. These facts, which were known to the world, must have attracted the attention of the observant Representative of Great Britain at Washington, and must have enabled him to make clear to his Government the reasons why the Cabinet at Washington must pause before asserting its rights by force.

The British Government informed of his purposes. The new Government took an early opportunity to inform the British Government of its purposes.[1] On the 9th of March, four days after the installment of Mr. Lincoln, Mr. Dallas, the Minister of the United States at London, was instructed to communicate to Lord Russell the Inaugural Address of the President, and to assure him that the President entertained full confidence in the speedy restoration of the harmony and unity of the Government. He was further told that "the United States have had too many assurances and manifestations of the friendship and good-will of Great Britain, to entertain any doubt

---

[1] Seward to Dallas, Vol. I, page 8.

that these considerations will have their just influence with the British Government, and will prevent that Government from yielding to solicitations to intervene in any unfriendly way in the domestic concerns of our country."

[1]Mr. Dallas, in complying with his instructions, (April 9, 1861,) pressed upon Lord Russell the importance of England and France abstaining, "at least for a considerable time, from doing what, by encouraging groundless hopes, would widen a breach still thought capable of being closed." Lord Russell replied that the coming of Mr. Adams (Mr. Dallas's successor)[1] "would doubtless be regarded as the appropriate and natural occasion for finally discussing and determining the question."

Lord John Russell promises to await Mr. Adams's arrival before acting.

The United States therefore had reasonable ground to believe, not only in view of the great moral interests of which they were the exponents, and of the long-standing friendship between them and Great Britain, but also in consequence of the voluntary promise of Lord Russell, that an opportunity would be afforded them to explain their views and purposes through their newly selected and specially trusted representative; and least of all had they cause to anticipate that a government which they supposed to be in sympathy with their policy as to African slavery, would precipitate a decision as to the insurgents, which was so obviously injurious to the United States, as to almost appear to have been designedly so.

Surrender of Fort Sumter.

The delay upon which the Government of the United States relied to firmly secure the loyalty of the Border States, and their aid in inducing the peaceable return of the Gulf States, was interrupted by the attack upon Fort Sumter, made by order of the Government at Montgomery. This attack ended in the surrender of the garrison on the 13th of April. This was followed on the 15th of April by a [2]Proclamation of the President, calling out the militia, and convening an extra session of Congress on the 4th day of the next July.

---

[1] Dallas to Seward, Vol. I, page 12.
[2] Vol. I, page 16.

UNFRIENDLINESS OF GREAT BRITAIN.

The insurgents to issue letters of marque. On the 17th of April, Mr. [1] Jefferson Davis gave notice that letters of marque would be granted by the persons who had attempted to establish a Government at Montgomery, by usurping the authority of the United States.

Proclamation giving notice of blockade. On the 19th of April, President Lincoln issued a Proclamation, declaring that a blockade of the ports within the States of South Carolina, Georgia, Alabama, Florida, Mississippi, Louisiana, and Texas would be established for the purpose of collecting the revenue in the disturbed part of the country, and for the protection of the public peace, and of the lives and properties of quiet and orderly citizens, until Congress should assemble. That body was summoned to assemble on the fourth day of the following July.

Objects of that proclamation.

The full text of this Proclamation will be found in Vol. I, page 21.

In the course of the discussion between the two Governments growing out of the war, it has been repeatedly asserted that Her Majesty's Government was induced to confer upon the insurgents in the South the status of belligerents, in consequence of the receipt of the news of the President's Proclamation of April 19. The United States are therefore forced to invite the patience of the Board of Arbitrators, while they establish, from conclusive proof, that Her Majesty's Government is mistaken in that respect.

The joint action of France invited by Great Britain. Before any armed collision had taken place, there existed an understanding between Her Majesty's Government and the Government of the Emperor of the French, with a view to securing a simultaneous and identical course of action of the two Governments on American questions. It is within the power of the British Government to inform the Arbitrators when that understanding was reached. The fact that it had been agreed to by the two governments was communicated to Mr. Dallas, by Lord John Russell, on the 1st day of May, 1861.[2]

There was nothing in the previous relations between Great

---

[1] Appleton's Annual Cyclopædia, 1861, page 137.
[2] Mr. Dallas to Mr. Seward, May 2, 1861. Vol. I, p. 33—34.

UNFRIENDLINESS OF GREAT BRITAIN.

Britain and the United States, which made it necessary for Her Majesty's Government to seek the advice, or to invite the support of the Emperor of the French, in the crisis which was threatened. The United States are at a loss to conjecture what inducement could have prompted such an act, unless it may have been the perception on the part of Her Majesty's Government that it was in its nature not only unfriendly, but almost hostile to the United States.

When the news of the bloodless attack upon Fort Sumter became known in Europe, Her Majesty's Government apparently assumed that the time had come for the joint action which had been previously agreed upon; and, without waiting to learn the purposes of the United States, it announced its intention to take the first step by recognizing the insurgents as belligerents.

When the President's Proclamation was received in Great Britain. The President's Proclamation, which has since been made the ostensible reason for this determination, was issued on the 19th of April, and was made public in the Washington newspapers of the morning of the 20th. An imperfect copy of it was also telegraphed to New York, and from thence to Boston, in each of which cities it appeared in the newspapers of the morning of the 20th.

The New York papers of the 20th gave the substance of the Proclamation, without the official commencement and close, and with several errors of more or less importance.

The Boston papers of the same date, in addition to the errors in the New York copy, omitted the very important statement in regard to the collection of the revenue, which appears in the Proclamation as the main cause of its issue.

During the morning of the 19th of April, a riot took place in Baltimore, which ended in severing direct communication, by rail or telegraph, between Washington and New York. Telegraphic communication was not restored until the 30th of the month. The regular passage of the mails and trains was resumed about the same time. It appears by a dispatch from Lord Lyons to Lord John Russell that the mails had not been resumed on the 27th.[1]

---

[1] Blue Book, North America, No. 1, 1862, page 26.

It is absolutely certain that no full copy of the text of the Proclamation could have left Washington by the mails of the 19th, and equally certain that no copy could have reached New York from Washington after the 19th for several days.

On the 20th the steamer Canadian sailed from Portland, taking the Boston papers of that day, with the imperfect copy of the Proclamation, in which the clause in regard to the collection of the revenue was suppressed. This steamer arrived at Londonderry on the 1st of May, and the "Daily News" of London, of the 2d of May, published the following telegraphic items of news: "President Lincoln has issued a Proclamation, declaring a blockade of all the ports in the seceded States. The Federal Government will condemn as pirates all privateer-vessels which may be seized by Federal ships." The Canadian arrived at Liverpool on the 2d of May, and the "Daily News," of the 3d, and the "Times," of the 4th of May, published the imperfect Boston copy of the Proclamation in the language as shown in the note below.[1]

---

[1] The following is the President's Proclamation of the blockade of the Southern ports:

"An insurrection against the Government of the United States has broken out in the States of South Carolina, Georgia, Alabama, Florida, Mississippi, Louisiana, and Texas, and the laws of the United States cannot be executed effectually therein conformably to that provision of the Constitution which requires duties to be uniform throughout the United States; and further, a combination of persons, engaged in such insurrection, have threatened to grant pretended letters of marque to authorize the bearers thereof to commit assaults on the lives, vessels, and property of good citizens of the country lawfully engaged in commerce on the high seas and in the waters of the United States; and whereas an Executive Proclamation has already been issued, requiring the persons engaged in these disorderly proceedings to desist, and therefore calling out the militia force for the purpose of repressing the same, and convening Congress in extraordinary session to deliberate and determine thereon, the President, with a view to the same purposes before mentioned, and to the protection of the public peace and the lives and property of its orderly citizens pursuing their lawful occupations, until Congress shall have assembled and deliberated on said unlawful proceedings, or until the same shall have

No other than the Boston copy of the Proclamation appears to have been published in the London newspapers. It is not likely that a copy was received in London before the 10th, by the Fulton from New York.

Opinion of Law Officers taken on an imperfect copy. It was on this meager and incorrect information that the advice of the British Law Officers was based, upon which that Government acted. On the evening of the 2d of May, Lord John Russell stated in the House of Commons that [1] "Her Majesty's Government heard the other day that the Confederated States have issued letters of marque, and to-day we have heard that it is intended there shall be a blockade of all the ports of the Southern States. As to the general provisions of the law of nations on these questions, some of the points are so new, as well as so important, that they have been referred to the Law Officers of the Crown for their opinions."

Her Majesty's Government decide on the 1st of May to recognize a state of war. It is with deep regret that the United States find themselves obliged to lay before the Tribunal of Arbitration the evidence that, when this announcement was made in the House of Commons, Her Majesty's Government had already decided to recognize the right of the Southern insurgents to attack and destroy the commerce of the United States on the high seas. On the 1st day of May, 1861, (two days before they could have heard of the issue of the President's Proclamation,) Lord

---

ceased, has further deemed it advisable to set on foot a blockade of the ports within the States aforesaid, in pursuance of the laws of the United States and the laws of nations in such cases provided. For this purpose a competent force will be posted, so as to prevent the entrance and exit of vessels from the ports aforesaid. If, therefore, with a view to violate such blockade, any vessel shall attempt to leave any of the said ports, she will be duly warned by the commander of one of said blockading vessels, who will indorse on her register the fact and date of such warning; and if the same vessel shall again attempt to enter or leave a blockaded port, she will be captured and sent to the nearest convenient port for such proceedings against her and her cargo as may be deemed advisable."

[1] Vol. IV, page 462.

John Russell wrote as follows to the Lords Commissioners of the Admiralty:[1]

"The intelligence which reached this country by the last mail from the United States gives reason to suppose that a civil war between the Northern and Southern States of that Confederacy was imminent, if indeed it might not be considered to have already begun.

"Simultaneously with the arrival of this news, a telegram, purporting to have been conveyed to Halifax from the United States, was received, which announced that the President of the Southern Confederacy had taken steps for issuing letters of marque against the vessels of the Northern States."

*   *   *   *   *   *   *

"I need scarcely observe to Your Lordships that it may be right to apprise the Admiral that, much as Her Majesty regrets the prospect of civil war breaking out in a country in the happiness and peace of which Her Majesty takes the deepest interest, *it is Her Majesty's pleasure that nothing should be done by her naval forces which should indicate any partiality of preference for either party in the contest that may ensue.*"

Lord John Russell and the insurgent commissioners discuss the recognition of Southern Independence.

On the 4th of May[2] Lord John Russel held an interview with some individuals, whom he described as "the three gentlemen deputed by the Southern Confederacy to obtain their recognition as an independent State." Although he informed them that he could hold no official communication with them, he did discuss with them the question of recognition, and he indicated to them the points to which they must direct their attention in the discussion of the subject. He also listened to their views in response thereto; and when, on the termination of the interview they informed him "that they should remain in London for the present, in the hope that the recognition of the Southern Confederacy would not be long delayed," he interposed no objections to such a course, and suggested no improbability of such a recognition.

---

[1] Vol. I, page 33.   [2] Vol. I, page 37.

UNFRIENDLINESS OF GREAT BRITAIN. 29

Communication with the French Government.
On the 5th of May the steamship Persia arrived at Liverpool with advices from New York to the 25th of April. Lord John Russell stated on Monday, the 6th of May, in a communication to Lord Cowley,[1] "that Her Majesty's Government received no dispatches from Lord Lyons by the mail which has just arrived, [the Persia,] the communication between Washington and New York being interrupted."

In the same dispatch Lord Cowley is informed "that Her Majesty's Government cannot hesitate to admit that such Confederacy is entitled to be considered as a belligerent, and as such invested with all the rights and prerogatives of a belligerent," and he is instructed to invite the French Government to a joint action, and a line of joint policy with the British Government, toward the United States. Lord Cowley, under these instructions, had an interview on the 19th of May with the French Minister for Foreign Affairs. The Tribunal may infer from the published correspondence that is was assumed at this interview that the two Governments should act together, and that the letters of marque which might be issued by the insurgents should be respected. Lord Cowley reported

Answer of the French Government.
that[2] "His Excellency said further that in looking for precedents it had been discovered that Great Britain, although treating at the commencement of the American war letters of marque as piracy, had, after a time, recognized the belligerent rights of the States in rebellion against her." The answer to these instructions was received at the Foreign Office on the 11th of May. The United States are firmly convinced that no correct or complete copy of the President's Proclamation could have been received there in advance of it. It is known that the official copy forwarded by Lord Lyons to his Government reached London on the 14th of May.[3] The official copy sent by Mr. Seward to Mr. Dallas reached Southampton on the evening of the 9th of May, and London on the 10th. It is stated in the British notes on Mr. Fish's

---

[1] Vol. I, page 36; see also same volume, page 48.
[2] Vol. I, page 49.
[3] British Blue Book on the Blockade, 1861, page 1.

instruction of September 25th, 1869, to Mr. Motley, that the Proclamation was communicated officially by Mr. Dallas to Lord John Russell on the 11th. There is no evidence of this fact in the archives of the Legation of the United States at London, or at the Department of State at Washington. But even if the statement in the notes be correct, still the British Government received, in the afternoon of the 11th of May, 1861, its first complete and official copy of the President's Proclamation, ten days after Lord John Russell had decided to award the rights of belligerency on the ocean to the insurgents, eight days after the subject had been referred to the Law Officers for their opinion, and five days after the decision of Her Majesty's Government upon that opinion had been announced in the House of Commons, as hereinafter set forth.

<small>When the President's Proclamation was received by Great Britain.</small>

On the same day on which Lord John Russell wrote Lord Cowley (May 6th) he wrote to Lord Lyons,[1] calling the United States "the northern portion of the late Union," and reiterating that Her Majesty's Government "cannot question the right of the Southern States to be recognized as a belligerent;" and in the House of Commons, on the same evening, he announced that the Attorney and Solicitor General, the Queen's Advocate, and the Government had come to the conclusion that the Southern Confederacy of America must be treated as a belligerent. On the same evening, Lord Palmerston said in the House of Commons,[2] "No one can regret more than I do the intelligence which has been received within the last few days from America; but at the same time, any one must have been short-sighted and little capable of anticipating the probable course of human events, who had not for a long time foreseen events of a similar character to those we now deplore. From the commencement of this unfortunate quarrel between the two sections of the United States, it was evident that the causes of disunion were too deeply seated to make it possible that separa-

---

[1] Vol. I, pages 36, 37.
[2] Hansard's Debates, 3d series, Vol. CLXII, pages 1622—23.

tion would not take place, and it was also obvious that passions were so roused on both sides as to to make it highly improbable that such separation could take place without a contest."

Effect of recognition of a state of war.
A question was asked in the House of Commons on the 7th of May,[1] the next evening, as to the extent of the belligerent rights at sea which would be acquired by the South, to which Lord Palmerston declined to make answer "until the Government should be in a condition, after consulting its legal advisers, to make some distinct communication on the subject."

On the 9th of May,[1] Sir George Lewis announced that a proclamation would be issued, stating "the general effect of the common and statute law on the matter;" and on the 10th, Lord Granville repeated the declaration in the House of Lords. In the discussion there it was assumed by all the speakers that the insurgent Government might lawfully issue letters of marque.

It is believed by the United States that it was well known to Her Majesty's Government during all this time, that Mr. Adams was about to arrive with instruction from the new administration, and that he came possessed of its most confidential views on these important questions. On the 2d May Mr. Dallas wrote Mr. Seward thus:[2] "The solicitude felt by Lord John Russell as to the effect of certain measures represented as likely to be adopted by the President, induced him to request me to call at his private residence yesterday. * * * * I informed him that Mr. Adams had apprised me of his intention to be on his way hither in the steamship Niagara, which left Boston on the 1st May, and that he would probably arrive in less than two weeks, by the 12th or 15th instant. His Lordship acquiesced in the expediency of disregarding mere rumor, and waiting the full knowledge to be brought by my successor." The United States, for reasons already given, have no doubt that, before that interview, Her Majesty's Government had already decided upon their course of action. Mr. Adams did actually arrive in

---

[1] Vol. IV, page 464. [2] Vol. IV, page 486. [3] Vol. I, page 34.

The Queen's Proclamation.

London on the evening of the 13th of May. The Queen's Proclamation of neutrality was issued on the morning of that day.

Uncertainty of Her Majesty's Government.

A careful examination of the published correspondence and speeches of Lord John Russel shows that Her Majesty's Government was at that time by no means certain that there was a war in the United States. On the 1st of May,[1] he directs the Admiralty as to the course to be pursued with reference to the insurgent cruisers in the war which, he thinks, *may* "have already begun." On the 2d of May[2] he asks the Law Officers of the Crown what course the Government shall pursue. On the 1st of June, however, he is in doubt on the subject, and he writes to the Lord Commissioners of the Admirality, informing them of the rules to be observed by the British naval[3] forces "in the contest *which appears to be imminent* between the United States and the so-styled Confederate States of North America." It would seem, therefore, that on the 1st of June, 1861, Her Majesty's Government regarded only as "imminent" the hostilities which Her Majesty's Proclamation of the 13th of the previous May alleged had "unhappily commenced between the United States of America and certain States styling themselves the Confederate States of America." In point of fact, Lord John Russell's dispatch of the 1st of June described with fidelity the condition of things so far as then known in London; for at that time the intelligence of the exhilarating effect of the Queen's Proclamation upon the insurgents, and its depressing effect upon the Government and loyal population of the United States, had not reached Europe.

Effect of the Queen's Proclamation.

Whatever Lord John Russell, and his colleagues in the Government, when decided to counsel Her Majesty to issue the Proclamation of May 13th, may have thought, the debates in Parliament removed any excuse for ignorance as to the effect of that instrument.

As early as the 29th of April, in the House of Com-

---

[1] Vol. I, page 33.   [2] Vol. IV, page 482.   [3] Vol. I, page 335.

mons, an opposition member had said that "there could be no doubt that if the war should be continued in that country [the United States] *there would be thousands of privateers hovering about those coasts;*"[1] to which the Chancellor of the Exchequer (Mr. Gladstone) immediately replied: "All that relates to the dangers which may arise between British merchant-ships and American or other privateers * * * I shall pretermit, not because I presume to say or think that they are insignificant, but because I feel it my duty to address myself to those points which touch more directly and more practically [the Budget] the matter in hand,"[2]

In a debate in the House of Lords, on the 10th of May, Lord Hardwicke[3] said that he "was anxious that the House should not enter too strong a protest against that which was a natural consequence of war, namely, that vessels should be fitted out by private individuals under letters of marque. That was, no doubt, privateering, but it did not by any means follow that privateering was piracy. He believed that if privateering-ships were put in the hands of proper officers, they were not engaged in piracy any more than men-of-war. He thought that a feeble State engaged in a war with a powerful one had a right to make use of its merchant-vessels for the purpose of carrying on the contest, and there was no violation of the law of nations in such a proceeding."

In the more elaborate discussion which followed on the 16th of the same month in the House of Lords, the Lord Chancellor[4] said: "If, after the publishing of the present Proclamation, any English subject were to enter into the service of either of the belligerents on the other side of the Atlantic, there could be no doubt that the person so acting would be liable to be punished for a violation of the laws of his own country, and would have no right to claim any interference on the part of his Government to shield him

---

[1] Hansard's Debates, 3d series, Vol. CLXII, page 1276.
[2] Hansard's Debates, 3d series, Vol. CLXII, page 1277.
[3] Vol. IV, page 486.   [4] Vol. IV, page 490.

from any consequences which might arise. There could, however, at the same time, be no doubt that, although he would be guilty of a breach of the laws of his own country, he ought not to be regarded as a pirate for acting under a commission from a State admitted to be entitled to the exercise of belligerent rights, and carrying on what might be called a *justum bellum*. Anybody dealing with a man under those circumstances as a pirate, and putting him to death, would, he contended, be guilty of murder."

The distinguished jurist, who then sat upon the woolsack, described in that speech one legal effect of this hastily issued Proclamation with undoubted correctness. It relieved Englishmen or foreigners in England, and Englishmen on insurgent cruisers carrying on war against the United States, from the penalties of a high class of felonies. Lord Lyndhurst, one of the most eminent predecessors of Lord Campbell, in an opinion in the House of Lords in 1853, cited with respect by Sir George Cornwall Lewis, (himself one of Lord Palmerston's Cabinet), said: "If a number of British subjects were to combine and conspire together to excite revolt among the inhabitants of a friendly State, * * * and these persons, in pursuance of that conspiracy, were to issue manifestoes and proclamations for the purpose of carrying that object into effect; above all, *if they were to subscribe money for the purpose of purchasing arms to give effect to that intended enterprise*, I conceive, and I state with confidence, that such persons would be guilty of a misdemeanor, and liable to suffer punishment by the laws of this country, inasmuch as their conduct would tend to embroil the two countries together, to lead to remonstrances by the one with the other, and ultimately, it might be, to war. * * * Foreigners residing in this country, as long as they reside here under the protection of this country, are considered in the light of British subjects, or rather subjects of Her Majesty, and are punishable by the criminal law precisely in the same manner, to the same extent, and under the same conditions, as natural-born subjects of Her Majesty. * * * The offence of endeavoring to excite revolt against a neighboring State is an offence against the law of nations. No writer on the law of nations states otherwise. But the law of nations, according to the decision of our greatest judges, is part of the law of England." [1]

Mr. Bright's views. The United States will close this branch of the examination by citing the language of Mr. Bright, in the House of Commons, on the 13th of March, 1865. [2] "Going back nearly four years, we recollect what occurred when the news arrived of the first shot having been fired at Fort Sumter. That, I think, was about the 12th of April. Immediately after that time it was announced that a new minister was coming to this country. Mr. Dallas had intimated to the Government that, as he did not represent the new President, he would rather not undertake anything of importance; but that his successor was on his way, and would arrive on such a day. When a man leaves New York on a given day you can calculate to about twelve hours when he will be in London. Mr. Adams, I think, arrived in London about the 13th of May, and when he opened his newspaper next morning he found the Proclamation of Neutrality, acknowledging the belligerent rights of the South. I say that the proper course to have taken would have been to wait till Mr. Adams arrived here, and to have discussed the matter with him in a friendly manner, explaining the ground upon which the English Government had felt themselves bound to issue that proclamation, and representing that it was not done in any manner as an unfriendly act toward the United States Government. But no precaution whatever was taken. It was done with unfriendly haste, and had this effect: that it gave comfort and courage to the conspiracy at Montgomery and at Richmond, and caused great grief and irritation among that portion of the people of America most strongly desirous of maintaining amicable and friendly relations between their country and England."

The sovereign right to issue such a proclamation not denied. The United States have made this review of the course pursued by Great Britain in recognizing the insurgents as belligerents, with

---

[1] On Foreign Jurisdiction and the Extradition of Criminals; by the Right Hon. Sir George Cornwall Lewis, Bart., M. P., London, 1859, page 66.
[2] Vol. V, pages 639, 640.

no purpose of questioning the sovereign right of that Power to determine for itself whether the facts at that time justified such a recognition. Although the United States strenuously deny that the facts as they then were known to Her Majesty's Government did justify that Government in conferring upon the rebellious citizens of the United States the privilege of belligerents, and still less justified it in counselling France to do the same thing, yet they recognize and insist that (in the language of the President to Congress on the 6th day of December, 1869) a "nation is its own judge when to accord the rights of belligerency, either to a people struggling to free themselves from a government they believe to be oppressive, or the independent nations at war with each other."[1]

It was an unfriendly act. But while thus firmly insisting upon the sovereign rights of independent nationality, they also maintain "that the rightfulness of such an act depends upon the occasion and the circumstances, and it is an act, like the sovereign act of war, which the morality of the public law and practice requires should be deliberate, seasonable, and just in reference to surrounding facts;"[2] and "they regard the concession of belligerency by Great Britain as a part of this case only so far as it shows the beginning and animus of that course of conduct which resulted so disastrously to the United States."[3]

And issued with an unfriendly purpose. Viewed in this light, the United States, with deep and unfeigned regret, have been forced to conclude, from all the circumstances, that Her Majesty's Government was actuated at that time by a conscious unfriendly purpose toward the United States.

M. Rolin-Jacquemyns on the Queen's Proclamation. In the language of a continental publicist, "L'Angleterre a été bien pressée de faire usage de son droit strict pour constater solennellement que l'Union Américaine était ébranlée, et donner aux insurgés ce que le monde entier a considéré tout au moins comme un appui moral; * * l'acte a été posé la veille

---

[1] Annual Message of the President to Congress, 1869.
[2] Mr. Fish to Mr. Motley, September 25, 1869. Vol. VI, page 4.
[3] Mr. Fish to Mr. Motley, May 15, 1869. Vol. VI, page 1

du jour où le nouvel ambassadeur américain, M. Adams, devait débarquer à Londres, et au moment où positivement les insurgés n'existaient pas comme puissance navale, où ils n'avaient de marine et de tribunaux de prise que sur le papier."[1]

Unfriendly conduct of Great Britain as to the declarations of the Congress of Paris. This precipitate and unfriendly act of Great Britain did not go forth alone. On the 6th of May, 1861, five days before the receipt of the authentic copy of the President's Proclamation, Lord John Russell instructed Lord Cowley, the British Ambassador at Paris, to ascertain whether the Imperial Government was disposed to make a joint endeavor with Her Majesty's Government "to obtain from each of the belligerents [*observe that the insurgents were styled "belligerents" seven days in advance of the Queen's proclamation*] a formal recognition of the second and third articles of the Declaration of Paris."

Lord Cowley, on the 9th of May, informed Lord John Russell that "the Imperial Government concurred entirely in the views of Her Majesty's Government and would be prepared to join Her Majesty's Government in endeavoring to obtain of the belligerents a formal recognition of the second and third articles of the Declaration of Paris."[2]

This proposition to open direct negotiations with the insurgents was the second step in the joint action which had been agreed upon. For reasons which Her Majesty's Government is in a position to explain, but which can only be conjectured by the United States and by the Tribunal, care appears to have been taken to prevent the knowledge of it from reaching the Government of the United States.

On the receipt of the information from Lord Cowley, Lord John Russell prepared at once a draught of instructions to Lord Lyons, the British Minister at Washington, and, on the 16th of May, sent them to Lord Cowley to be submitted to the Emperor's Government.[3]

---

[1] De la neutralité de la Grande-Bretagne pendant la guerre civile américaine d'après M. Montague Bernard, par G. Rolin-Jacquemyns, page 11.
[2] Vol. I, page 49.   [3] Vol. I, page 60.

On the next day, Lord Cowley replied that he had seen M. Thouvenel, the Minister for Foreign Affairs, and added: "M. Thouvenel had already written to M. Mercier [the French Minister at Washington] in the same terms as your Lordship proposes to address your instructions to Lord Lyons. I need hardly add that His Excellency concurs entirely in the draught."[1]

On the 18th of May, Lord John Russell hastened to send his instructions to Lord Lyons.[1] He told him "to encourage the Government" of the United States "in any disposition which they might evince to recognize the Declaration of Paris in regard to privateering;" and he added that "Her Majesty's Government do not doubt that they will, without hesitation, recognize the remaining articles of the declaration." He continued: "You will clearly understand that Her Majesty's Government cannot accept the renunciation of privateering on the part of the Government of the United States, if coupled with the condition that they should enforce its renunciation on the Confederate States, either by denying their right to issue letters of marque, or by interfering with the belligerent operations of vessels holding from them such letters of marque;" and he closed by instructing Lord Lyons to take such means as he might judge most expedient to transmit to Her Majesty's Consul at Charleston or New Orleans a copy of a previous dispatch of the same day, in order that it might be communicated to Mr. Jefferson Davis at Montgomery. Lord Lyons had no instructions to show to Mr. Seward the dispatch from which these citations have been made, and it evidently was contemplated that he should not exhibit it.

He was, however, to read to him the previous instructions of the same date referred to in that dispatch, and to leave a copy with him, if desired. These previous instructions, numbered 136, may be found on the 107th page of the first of the accompanying volumes. It was not only to be shown to Mr. Seward, but a copy of it was to be shown to Mr. Jefferson Davis.[2] The attention of the Tribunal of Arbitration is, in this connection, particularly invited to the fact that these instructions, numbered 136, contain nothing

---

[1] Vol. I, page 61.   [2] Vol. I, page 51.

indicating a design on the part of the British Government to put itself in communication with the insurgent authorities, nothing to induce Mr. Seward to think that they were other than what, on their face, they purported to be, a communication from the Government of Great Britain to the Government of the United States, through the ordinary diplomatic channel.

The instructions to Lord Lyons might have been regarded as a cause of war.

It is not improbable that the Arbitrators may be of opinion that the use of the British Legation at Washington for such a purpose was an act which the United States would have been justified in regarding as a cause of war. It was, to say the least, an abuse of diplomatic privilege, and a violation, in the person of Her Majesty's principal Secretary of State for Foreign Affairs, of the duties of neutrality which Her Majesty's Government was about to impose upon her subjects.

Before relating what Lord Lyons did, under these instructions, it is necessary to pause in order that the Tribunal may be informed what Mr. Seward and Mr. Adams had been doing in the same matter simultaneously with the proceedings which have been detailed.

Former negotiations regarding the Declaration of the Congress of Paris.

In the year 1854 the Government of the United States submitted to the principal maritime nations two propositions, soliciting their assent to them as permanent principles of international law. These propositions were, that free ships should make free goods; and that neutral property on board an enemy's vessel should not be subject to confiscation unless contraband of war.

Great Britain, being then at war with Russia, did not act upon these propositions; but in the Congress which assembled at Paris when the peace of 1856 was made, Great Britain and the other nations, parties to the Congress, gave their assent to them, and to two other propositions—the abolition of privateering, and the necessity of efficiency to the legalization of a blockade. It was also agreed that the four propositions should be maintained as a whole and indivisible, and that the Powers who might accede to them should accede to them as such.[1]

---

[1] 24th Protocol, April 16, 1856, Congress of Paris.

Great Britain then joined in inviting the United States to give its adhesion to the four indivisible points. The Washington Cabinet of that day replied that the United States was willing to assent to all the propositions, except the one relating to privateering, as being, in fact, recognitions of principles which had always been maintained by them; but that they could not consent to abolish privateering without a further agreement to exempt private property from capture on the high seas; and they proposed to amend the declaration of the Congress of Paris in that sense, and offered to give their adhesion to it when so amended.

In January, 1857, the proposals of the United States not having been acted upon, their Minister at London was directed to suspend negotiations until the new President, Mr. Buchanan, could examine the subject; and the suspension continued until after Mr. Lincoln was inaugurated.

On the 24th April, 1861, less than two months after Mr. Lincoln's accession to power, Mr. Seward resumed the suspended negotiations by instructing Mr. Adams[1] (similar instructions being given to the Ministers of the United States to the other maritime powers) to give an unqualified assent to the four propositions, and to bring the negotiation to a speedy and satisfactory conclusion.

Owing, probably, to the interruption in the communications between Washington and New York when the dispatch of April 24 was written, Mr. Adams does not appear to have been able to communicate his instructions to Lord John Russell before the 21st of May. He then informed Lord John that he had received instructions to negotiate, which he would "submit to his consideration if there was any disposition to pursue the matter further." Lord John Russell "expressed the willingness of Great Britain to negotiate, but he seemed to desire to leave the subject in the hands of Lord Lyons, to whom he intimated that he had already transmitted authority to assent to any modification of the only point in issue which the Government of the United States might prefer."[2] He did not inform Mr. Adams that he also proposed to open

---

[1] Vol. I, page 44. [2] Vol. I, page 52.

negotiations with the insurgents, nor had Mr. Adams reason to suspect that fact.

Matters were thus suspended in London, to enable Lord Lyons to work out Lord John Russell's instructions at Washington and in Richmond.

Lord Lyons received the dispatches of the 18th of May on the 2d of June,[1] and at once conferred with Mr. Mercier. It was agreed that they should try to manage the business so as to prevent "an inconvenient outbreak from the Government"[2] of the United States. He then notified Earl Russell of what they proposed to do, and informed him of the instructions to Mr. Adams on this subject. He also intimated that it would be unreasonable to expect that the insurgents should abandon privateering, unless "in return for some great concession." What concession remained to be given except recognition of national independence?

Lord Lyon's Interview with Mr. Seward. It was not until the 15th of June that Lord Lyons and Mr. Mercier communicated the purport of their instructions to Mr. Seward in a joint interview, of which we have Mr. Seward's account[3] and Lord Lyons's account,[4] both dated the 17th of June. These accounts do not differ materially. The action as to the British Minister was this: Lord Lyons stated that he was instructed to read a dispatch to Mr. Seward and to leave a copy with him if he desired. Mr. Seward refused to permit the dispatch to be read officially, unless he could first have an opportunity to acquaint himself with its contents. Lord Lyons handed him Lord John Russell's No. 136 for the purpose of unofficial examination. Mr. Seward saw that it spoke of the insurgents as belligerents, and on that ground refused to permit it do be officially communicated to him. He added that he preferred to treat the question in London, and Lord Lyons left with him, unofficially, a copy of Lord John Russell's 136, in order that he might more intelligently instruct Mr. Adams.

The instructions thereupon written to Mr. Adams are in

---

[1] Vol. I, page 55.   [2] Vol. I, page 56.
[3] Vol. I, page 60.   [4] Vol. I, page 62.

the same tone.¹ Mr. Seward expresses regret that the British and French governments should have seen fit to take joint action in the matter; he refuses to admit that there are two belligerent parties to the struggle; he expresses regret that Great Britain did not await the arrival of Mr. Adams before instructing Lord Lyons, as Mr. Adams's instructions covered the whole ground; but he nowhere manifests a knowledge of the purpose of Great Britain to enter into communications with the insurgents at Richmond. That was studiously concealed from him.

Termination of negotiations with United States. The negotiations were then transferred again to London, to the "profound surprise"² of Mr. Adams. They were protracted there until the 19th of August, when Lord Russell informed Mr. Adams that Great Britain could only receive the assent of the United States to the Declaration of Paris, upon the condition that Her Majesty should not thereby "undertake any engagement which should have any bearing, direct or indirect," upon the insurrection. The United States declined to be put upon a different footing from that of the forty-two independent Powers enumerated in Lord Russell's No. 136 to Lord Lyons, whose assent had been received without conditions, and the negotiations dropped.

Great Britain desired to legalize privateering. The arbitrators will thus perceive that Her Majesty's Government, having recognized the insurgents as belligerents, felt itself bound to receive the assent of the United States to the declarations of the Congress of Paris only conditionally, so as to have no bearing upon letters of marque that might be issued by the insurgents. But they will also observe that the two steps of the recognition of belligerency and the invitations to assent to the second and third clauses in the declarations, were taken simultaneously, in accordance with a previous arrangement for joint action; and it is not impossible that they may come to the conclusion that Her Majesty's Government, when the insurgents were recognized as belligerents, contemplated that they would proceed to issue letters of

---

¹ Vol. I, page 205. ² Vol. I, page 71.

marque, and intended to legalize those letters in the eye of British law, and to countenance the bearers of them in the destruction of American commerce.

Meanwhile Lord Lyons had not forgotten his instructions to secure the assent of Mr. Jefferson Davis to the second and third rules of the Declaration of Paris.

Negotiations at Richmond. On the 5th of July he sent instructions to Mr. Bunch, British Consul at Charleston, to "obtain from the existing government in those [the insurgent] States securities concerning the proper treatment of neutrals."[1] He inclosed a copy of Lord Russell's 136. He advised Mr. Bunch not to go to Richmond, but to communicate through the governor of the State of South Carolina; and he accompanied this with "a long private letter on the same subject."[2] The nature of that private letter may be gathered from what Mr. Bunch did.

He put himself and his French colleague at once in communication with a gentleman who was well qualified to serve his purpose, but who was not the governor of South Carolina. They showed to this agent Lord John Russell's dispatch to Lord Lyons, and Lord Lyons's official and private letters to Mr. Bunch, and they told him that the step to be taken was one of "very great significance and importance." The agent asked them whether they "were prepared to receive an official act which should be based upon their request, thus giving to the Confederate Government the advantage before the world of such an implied recognition as this would afford." [2] They replied that they "wished a spontaneous declaration;" "that to make this request the declared basis of the act would be to proclaim this negotiation, and the intense jealousy of the United States was such that this would be followed by the revocation of their exequaturs," which they wished to avoid; that "they could only look upon this step as the initiative toward a recognition, yet the object of their Government being to reach that recognition gradually, so as not to give good ground for a breach, this indirect way was absolutely necessary." And

---

[1] Vol. 1, page 123.
[2] Manuscript in Department of State.

they added, "All we have a right to ask is that you shall not give publicity to this negotiation: that we nor our Governments should be upon the record."[1]

Their agent, being thus possessed of their views, went to Richmond, with Lord Lyons's letters and Lord Russell's dispatch, and while there he secured the passage, in the insurgent congress, of resolutions partially draughted by Mr. Jefferson Davis, which declared their purpose to observe principles towards neutrals similar to the second and third rules of the Declaration of Paris: that blockades to be binding must be effectual; and that they "*maintained the right of privateering.*"[2] In communicating this result to Lord Lyons, Mr. Bunch said, "*The wishes of Her Majesty's Government would seem to have been fully met, for, as no proposal was made that the Confederate Government should abolish privateering, it could not be expected that they should do so of their own accord, particularly as it is the arm upon which they most rely for the injury of the extended commerce of their enemy.*"[3] The United States think that the Tribunal of Arbitration will agree with Mr. Bunch, that it was not expected that the insurgents would abolish privateering.

The Tribunal of Arbitration cannot fail to observe that the propositions which were made in these negotiations to the Government of the United States were communicated to the insurgents, while pains were taken to conceal from the United States the fact that negotiations were opened at Richmond; that Earl Russell refused to receive the assent of the United States to the Declaration of Paris, except upon conditions derogatory to their sovereignty; and that Lord Lyons was instructed to secure the assent of the Government of the United States to the four principles laid down by the Declaration of Paris, while he was instructed, as to the insurgents, to secure their assent only to the second, third, and fourth propositions; and had no instructions to take steps to prevent privateering or to induce the insurgents to accept the first

---

[1] Unpublished manuscript in the Department of State at Washington.
[2] Vol. I, page 137. [3] Vol. I, page 136.

rule in the Declaration of Paris, although it had been agreed that the rules should be maintained as a whole and indivisible, and that the Powers who might accede to them should accede to them as such. The practical effect of this diplomacy, had it been successful, would have been the destruction of the commerce of the United States, (or its transfer to the British flag,) and the disarming a principal weapon of the United States upon the ocean, should a continuation of this course of insincere neutrality unhappily force the United States into a war. Great Britain was thus to gain the benefit to its neutral commerce of the recognition of the second and third articles, and their devastation legalized, while the United States were to be deprived of a dangerous weapon of assault upon Great Britain.

Mr. Adams's comments. When the whole story of these negotiations was understood by Mr. Adams, he wrote to his Government as follows:[1]

"It now appears plainly enough that he wanted, from the first, to get the first article of the Declaration of Paris out of the negotiation altogether, if he could. But he did not say a word of this to me at the outset, neither was it consistent with the position heretofore taken respecting the necessity of accepting the declaration 'pure and simple.' What I recollect him to have said on the 18th of May was, that it had been the disposition of his Government, as communicated to Lord Lyons, to agree upon almost any terms, respecting the first article, that might suit the Government of the United States. When reminded of this afterward, he modified the statement to mean that the article might be omitted altogether. It now turns out, if we may judge from the instructions, that he did not precisely say either the one thing or the other. Substantially, indeed, he might mean that the general law of nations, if affirmed between the two Governments, would, to a certain extent, attain the object of the first article of the Declaration of Paris, without the adoption of it as a new principle. But he must have known, on the day of the date of these instructions, *which is the very day of his first con-*

---

[1] Vol. I, page 103.

ference with me, and four days after the issue of the Queen's Proclamation, that the Government of the United States contemplated, in the pending struggle, neither encouraging privateers nor issuing letters of marque; hence that such a proposition would only complicate the negotiation for no useful purpose whatever. Besides which, it should be borne in mind that the effect, if adopted, would have been, instead of a simple adhesion to the Declaration of Paris, to render it necessary to reopen a series of negotiations for a modification of it between all the numerous parties to that instrument. Moreover, it is admitted by his Lordship that no powers had been given to make any convention at all—the parties could only agree. Yet, without such powers, what was the value of an agreement? For the Declaration of Paris was, by its very terms, binding only between parties who acceded to it as a whole. Her Majesty's Government thus placed themselves in the position of a party which proposes what it gives no authority to perform, and which negotiates upon a basis on which it has already deprived itself of the power to conclude.

"How are we to reconcile these inconsistencies? By the terms of the Queen's Proclamation his lordship must have been aware that Great Britain had released the United States from further responsibility for the acts of its new-made belligerent that was issuing letters of marque, as well as from the possible offences of privateers sailing under its flag; and yet, when the Government of the United States comes forward and declares its disposition to accept the terms of the Declaration of Paris, pure and simple, the Government of Her Majesty cannot consent to receive the very thing that they have been all along asking for, because it might possibly compel them to deny to certain privateers the rights which may accrue to them by virtue of their voluntary recognition of them as belonging to a belligerent power. Yet it now appears that, on the 18th of May, the same Government was willing to reaffirm the law of nations, which virtually involved the very same difficulty on the one hand, while on the other it had given no powers to negotiate a new convention, but contemplated a simple adhesion to the old declaration on the part of the United States. The only way by which I can explain these various involutions of policy with a proper regard to Lord Russell's character for straightforwardness, which I have no disposition to impugn, is this: He may have instructed Lord Lyons prior to the 18th of May, the day of our first conference. I certainly received the impression that he had done so. Or he may have written the paper before one o'clock of that day, and thus have referred to the act as a thing completed, though still within his power, in order to get rid of the propositions to negotiate directly here. Of that I do not pretend to judge. But neither in one case nor in the other was there the smallest intimation of a desire to put in any caveat whatever of the kind proposed in his last declaration. That seems to have been an afterthought, suggested when all other obstacles to the success of a negotiation had been removed.

"That it originated with Lord Russell I cannot credit consistently with my great respect for his character.

"That it was suggested after his proposed consultation with his colleagues, and by some member who had in view the defeat of the negotiation in the interests of the insurgents, I am strongly inclined to believe. The same influence may have been at work in the earlier stages of the business as well as the latest, and have communicated that uncertain and indirect movement which I have commented on, not less inconsistent with all my notions of his lordship's character than with the general reputation of British policy."

Contrast between conduct of Great Britain toward the United States, in the Trent affair, and toward violators of British neutrality, in the insurgent interest.

The partial purpose which was thus disclosed in the first official act of the Queen's Government, after the issue of the proclamation of neutrality, appears often in the subsequent conduct of that Government. Thus, when, a few months later, an officer of the Navy of the United States had taken from the deck of a British vessel on the high seas four prominent agents traveling on an errand that, if successful, would result in disaster to the United States, against which they were in rebellion, the course of the British Cabinet indicated an unfriendliness so extreme as to approach to a desire for war. The news of this reached both countries at about the same time. In the United States, while there was some excitement and some manifestation of pleasure, Lord Lyons bears witness to the moderation of the tone of the press.[1] Mr. Seward immediately wrote Mr. Adams to acquaint him that the act of Captain Wilkes was unauthorized, and Mr. Adams communicated this fact to Lord Russell.[2]

The excitement in England, on the contrary, was intense, and was fanned into animosity by the press. Although without information as to the purpose of the Government of the United States, peremptory instructions were immediately sent to Lord Lyons to demand the release of the four gentlemen, and to leave Washington with all the members of the legation, if the demand was not complied with in seven days.[3]

In anticipation of a refusal, vessels of war were hurriedly fitted out at the naval stations, and troops were pressed forward to Canada. In the midst of this preparation Lord Russell received from Mr. Adams official information that the act had not been authorized by the Government of the United States; but this intelligence was suppressed, and public opinion was encouraged to drift into a state of hostility toward the United States. The arming continued with ostentatious publicity; the warlike preparations went on, and the peremptory instructions to Lord Lyons were neither revoked nor in any sense modified.

Contrast this conduct of Great Britain with reference to a violation of British sovereignty that had not been authorized or assumed by the Government of the United States, and that, to say the least, could be plausibly defended by reference to the decisions of Sir William Scott,[4] with its course

---

[1] Lord Lyons to Earl Russell, Nov. 25, 1861, Blue Book No. 5, North America, 1862, page 10.

[2] Earl Russell to Lord Lyons. Same, page 11.

[3] Earl Russell to Lord Lyons. Blue Book No. 5, North America, 1862, page 3.

[4] The Atlanta, 6 Charles Robinson's Reports, page 440. On the receipt of the news in London, the Times of November 28, 1861, published a leading article which contained some statements worthy of note. Among other things it said: "Unwelcome as the truth may be, it is nevertheless a truth, that we

concerning the open, undisguised, oft-repeated, flagrant, and indefensible violations of British sovereignty by the agents of the insurgents in Liverpool, in Glasgow, in London, in Nassau, in Bermuda, it may almost be said wherever the British flag could give them shelter and protection. When the information as to the Florida was conveyed to Her Majesty's Principal Secretary of State for Foreign Affairs, he interposed no objection to her sailing from Liverpool. When the overwhelming proof of the complicity of the Alabama was laid before him, he delayed to act until it was too late, and then, by his neglect to take notice of the notorious criminals, he encouraged the guilty Laird to construct the two rebel rams—the keel of one of them being laid on the same stocks from which the Alabama had just been launched.[1] When the evidence of the character and destination of those rams was brought to his notice, he held it

have ourselves established a system of International Law which now tells against us. In high-handed and almost despotic manner we have, in former days, claimed privileges over neutrals which have at different times banded all the maritime powers of the world against us. We have insisted even upon stopping the ships of war of neutral nations, and taking British subjects out of them; and an instance is given by Jefferson in his Memoirs in which two nephews of Washington were impressed by our cruisers as they were returning from Europe, and placed as common seamen under the discipline of ships of war. We have always been the strenuous asserters of the rights of belligerents over neutrals, and the decisions of our courts of law as they must now be cited by our law officers, have been in confirmation of these unreasonable claims, which have called into being confederations and armed neutralities against us, and which have always been modified in practice when we were not supreme in our dominion at sea. Owing to these facts the authorities which may be cited on this question are too numerous and too uniform as to the right of search by belligerent ships of war over neutral merchant vessels to be disputed. * * * * * * *

"It is, **and** it always has been, vain to appeal to old folios and bygone authorities in justification of acts which every Englishman and every Frenchman cannot but feel to be injurious and insulting." See also the case of Henry Laurens, Dip. Cor. of Revolution, Vol. I, page 708, et seq.

[1] Mr. Dudley to Mr. Seward, Vol. II, page 315.

for almost two months, although they were then nearly ready to go to sea, and then at first refused to stop them. Wiser and more just counsels prevailed four days later.[1] And when Mr. Adams, under instructions from his Government, transmitted to Earl Russell convincing proof of "a deliberate attempt to establish within the limits of this kingdom [Great Britain] a system of action in direct hostility to the Government of the United States,"[2] embracing "not only the building and fitting out of several ships of war under the direction of agents especially commissioned for the purpose, but the preparation of a series of measures under the same auspices for the obtaining from Her Majesty's subjects the pecuniary means essential to the execution of those hostile projects,"[3] Lord Russell refused to see in the inclosed papers any evidence of those facts worthy of his attention, or of the action of Her Majesty's Government.[4]

It is not surprising that the consistent course of partiality towards the insurgents, which this Minister evinced throughout the struggle, should have drawn from Mr. Adams the despairing assertion that he was "permitting himself to be deluded by what I cannot help thinking the willful blindness and credulous partiality of the British authorities at Liverpool. *From experience in the past I have little or no confidence in any application that may be made of the kind.*"[4] The probable explanation of Lord Russell's course is to be found in his own declaration in the House of Lords: "There may be one end of the war that would prove a calamity to the United States and to the world, and especially calamitous to the negro race in those countries, and that would be the subjugation of the South by the North."[5] He did not desire that the United States should succeed in their efforts to obtain that result. The policy of Great Britain, under his guidance, but for the exertions and sacrifices of the people of the United States, might have prevented it.

<small>M. Rolin-Jacquemyns on the British neutrality.</small>   The insincere neutrality which induced the Cabinet of London to hasten to issue the Queen's Proclamation upon the eve of the

---

[1] Vol. II, page 363.   [2] Vol. I, page 562.   [3] Vol. I, page 578.
[4] Vol. I, page 529.   [5] Vol. IV, page 535.

day that Mr. Adams was to arrive in London, and which prompted the counselings with France, and the tortuous courses as to the Declaration of the Congress of Paris which have just been unraveled, has been well described by Mr. Rolin-Jacquemyns: "L'idéal du personnage *neutrarum partium*, c'est le juge qui, dans l'apologue de l'huitre et les plaideurs, avale le contenu du mollusque, et adjuge les écailles aux deux belligérents. Il n'est d'aucun parti, mais il s'engraisse scrupuleusement aux dépens de tous deux. Une telle conduite de la part d'un grand peuple peut être aussi conforme aux précédents que celle du vénérable magistrat dont parle le fable. Mais quand elle se fonde sur une loi positive, sur une règle admise, c'est une preuve que cette règle est mauvaise, comme contraire à la science, à la dignité et à la solidarité humaine."[1]

This feeling of personal unfriendliness towards the United States in the leading members of the British Government continued during a long portion or the whole of the time of the commission or omission of acts hereinafter complained of.

Proof of unfriendly feeling of members of the British Cabinet.

Thus, on the 14th day of October, in the year 1861, Earl Russell[2] said, in a public speech made at Newcastle: "We now see the two parties (in the United States) contending together, not upon the question of slavery, though that I believe was probably the original cause of the quarrel, not contending with respect to free trade and protection, but contending, as so many States in the Old World have contended, the one side for empire and the other for independence. [Cheers.] Far be it from us to set ourselves up as judges in such a contest. But I cannot help asking myself frequently, as I trace the progress of the contest, to what good end can it tend? [Hear! Hear!] Supposing the contest to end in the reunion of the different States; supposing that the South should agree to enter again the Federal Union with all the rights guaranteed to her by the Constitution,

---

[1] De la neutralité de la Grande-Bretagne pendant la guerre civile américaine, d'après M. Montague Bernard, par G. Rolin-Jacquemyns, page 13.
[2] London Times, October 16, 1861.

should we not then have debated over again the fatal question of slavery, again provoking discord between North and South? * * * But, on the other hand, supposing that the Federal Government completely conquer and subdue the Southern States; supposing that be the result of a long military conflict and some years of civil war, would not the national prosperity of that country, to a great degree, be destroyed? * * * If such are the unhappy results which alone can be looked forward to from the reunion of these different parts of the North American States, is it not then our duty, though our voice, and, indeed, the voice of any one in this country, may be little listened to—is it not the duty of men who were so lately fellow-citizens—is it not the duty of men who profess a regard for the principles of Christianity—is it not the duty of men who wish to preserve in perpetuity the sacred inheritance of liberty, to endeavor to see whether this sanguinary conflict cannot be put an end to?"

Mr. Gladstone also spoke at Newcastle on the 7th day of October, 1862. It is scarcely too much to say that his language, as well as much of the other language of members of Her Majesty's Government herein quoted, might well have been taken as offensive by the United States. He said:[1] "We may have our own opinions about slavery; we may be for or against the South; but there is no doubt that Jefferson Davis and other leaders of the South have made an army. They are making, it appears, a navy; and they have made what is more than either—they have made a nation. [Loud cheers.] * * * We may anticipate with certainty the success of the Southern States so far as regards their separation from the North. [Hear! Hear!] I cannot but believe that that event is as certain as any event yet future and contingent can be." [Hear! Hear!]

In a debate in the House of Lords, on the 5th of February, 1863, Lord Russell said:[2]

"There is one thing, however, which I think may be the result of the struggle, and which, to my mind, would be a great calamity. That is the subjugation of the South by

---

[1] London Times, October 9, 1862.
[2] Vol IV, page 535.

the North. If it were possible that the Union could be re-formed; if the old feelings of affection and attachment toward it could be revived in the South, I, for one, would be glad to see the Union restored. If, on the other hand, the North were to feel that separation was finally decreed by the events of the war, I should be glad to see peace established upon those terms. But there may be, I say, one end of the war that would prove a calamity to the United States and to the world, and especially calamitous to the negro race in those countries, and that would be the subjugation of the South by the North."

In a spirited debate in the House of Commons on the 27th of March, 1863, Mr. Laird, the builder of the Alabama, and of the rams which were afterward seized, arose and attempted to justify his course in a speech which was received with prolonged cheering and satisfaction by a large portion of the House. Among other things which he then said, and which were received as expressive of the views and sentiments of those who cheered him, was the following:[1]

"I will allude to a remark which was made elsewhere last night — a remark, I presume, applying to me, or to somebody else, which was utterly uncalled for. [Hear!] I have only to say that I would rather be handed down to posterity as the builder of a dozen Alabamas than as the man who applies himself deliberately to set class against class [loud cheers] and to cry up the institutions of another country, which, when they come to be tested, are of no value whatever, and which reduced liberty to an utter absurdity." [Cheers.]

Two years later, on the 13th day of March, 1865, the course of this member of the British House of Commons, and this extraordinary scene, were thus noticed by Mr. Bright:[2]

"Then I come to the last thing I shall mention — to the question of the ships which have been preying upon the commerce of the United States. I shall confine myself to that one vessel, the Alabama. She was built in this country;

---

[1] London Times, March 28, 1863.
[2] Vol. V, page 641.

all her munitions of war were from this country; almost every man on board her was a subject of Her Majesty. She sailed from one of our chief ports. She is reported to have been built by a firm in whom a member of this House was, and, I presume is, interested. Now, sir, I do not complain. I know that once, when I referred to this question two years ago, when my honorable friend, the member for Bradford, brought it forward in this House, the honorable member for Birkenhead [Mr. Laird] was excessively angry. I did not complain that the member for Birkenhead had struck up a friendship with Captain Semmes, who may be described as another sailor once was of similar pursuits, as being 'the mildest-mannered man that ever scuttled ship.' Therefore I do not complain of a man who has an acquaintance with that notorious person, and I do not complain, and did not then, that the member for Birkenhead looks admiringly upon the greatest example which men have ever seen of the greatest crime which men have ever committed. I do not complain even that he should applaud that which is founded upon a gigantic traffic in living flesh and blood, which no subject of this realm can enter into without being deemed a felon in the eyes of our law and punished as such. But what I do complain of is this: that the honorable gentleman, the member for Birkenhead, a magistrate of a county, a deputy lieutenant — whatever that may be — a representative of a constituency, and having a seat in this ancient and honorable assembly — that he should, as I believe he did, if concerned in the building of this ship, break the law of his country, driving us into an infraction of International Law, and treating with undeserved disrespect the Proclamation of Neutrality of the Queen. I have another complaint to make, and in allusion to that honorable member. 'It is within your recollection that when on the former occasion he made that speech and defended his course, he declared that he would rather be the builder of a dozen Alabamas than do something which nobody had done. That language was received with repeated cheering from the opposition side of the House. Well, sir, I undertake to say that that was at least a very unfortunate circumstance, and I beg to tell the honorable gentleman that at the end of the last session, when the great debate took place on the question of Denmark, there were many men on this side of the House who had no objection whatever to see the present Government turned out of office, for they had many grounds of complaint against them; but they felt it impossible that they should take the responsibility of bringing into office the right honorable member for Buckinghamshire or the party who could utter such cheers on such a subject at that."

On the 27th of March, 1863, in a debate in the House of Commons on the fitting out of these piratical cruisers, Lord Palmerston said:[1]

"There is no concealing the fact, and there is no use in disguising it, that whenever any political party, whether in or out of office, in the United States, finds itself in difficulties, it raises a cry against England as a means of creating what, in American language, is called 'political capital.' That is a practice, of course, which we must deplore. As long as it is confined to their internal affairs we can only hope that, being rather a dangerous game, it will not be carried further than is intended. When a government or a large party excite the passions of one nation against another, especially if there be no just cause, it is manifest that such a course has a great tendency to endanger friendly relations between the two countries. We understand, however, the object of these proceedings in the present instance, and therefore we do not feel that irritation which might otherwise be excited. But if this cry is raised for the purpose of driving Her Majesty's Government to do something which may be contrary to the laws of the country, or which may be derogatory to the dignity of the country, in the way of altering our laws for the purpose of pleasing another government, then all I can say is that such a course is not likely to accomplish its purpose."

On the 30th of June, 1863, Mr. Gladstone, in the course of a long speech, said:[2]

"Why, sir, we must desire the cessation of this war. No

---

[1] Vol. IV, page 530.   [2] Vol. V, page 666.

man is justified in wishing for the continuance of a war unless that war has a just, an adequate, and an attainable object, for no object is adequate, no object is just, unless it also be attainable. We do not believe that the restoration of the American Union by force is attainable. I believe that the public opinion of this country is unanimous upon that subject. [No!] Well, almost unanimous. I may be right or I may be wrong—I do not pretend to interpret exactly the public opinion of the country. I express in regard to it only my private sentiments. But I will go one step further, and say I believe the public opinion of this country bears very strongly on another matter upon which we have heard much, namely, whether the emancipation of the negro race is an object that can be legitimately pursued by means of coercion and bloodshed. I do not believe that a more fatal error was ever committed than when men—of high intelligence I grant, and of the sincerity of whose philanthropy I, for one, shall not venture to whisper the smallest doubt—came to the conclusion that the emancipation of the negro race was to be sought, although they could only travel to it by a sea of blood. I do not think there is any real or serious ground for doubt as to the issue of this contest."

In the same debate, Lord Palmerston, with an unusual absence of caution, lifted the veil that concealed his feelings, and said:[1]

"Now, it seems to me that that which is running in the head of the honorable gentleman, [Mr. Bright,] and which guides and directs the whole of his reasoning, is the feeling, although perhaps disguised to himself, that the Union is still in legal existence; that there are not in America two belligerent parties, but a legitimate government and a rebellion against that government. Now, that places the two parties in a very different position from that in which it is our duty to consider them."

As late as the 9th of June, 1864, Earl Russell said[2] in the House of Lords:

"It is dreadful to think that hundreds of thousands of men

---

[1] Vol. V, page 695.   [2] Vol. V, page 507.

are being slaughtered for the purpose of preventing the Southern States from acting on those very principles of independence which in 1776 were asserted by the whole of America against this country. Only a few years ago the Americans were in the habit, on the 4th of July, of celebrating the promulgation of the Declaration of Independence, and some eminent friends of mine never failed to make eloquent and stirring orations on those occasions. I wish, while they keep up a useless ceremony—for the present generation of Englishmen are not responsible for the War of Independence—that they had inculcated upon their own minds that they should not go to war with four millions, five millions, or six millions of their fellow-countrymen who want to put the principles of 1776 into operation as regards themselves."

The United States have thus presented for the consideration of the Tribunal of Arbitration the publicly expressed sentiments of the leading members of the British Cabinet of that day. Lord Palmerston was the recognized head of the Government. Earl Russell, who, at the commencement of the insurrection, sat in the House of Commons as Lord John Russell, was during the whole time Her Majesty's Principal Secretary of State for Foreign Affairs, specially charged with the expression of the views and feelings of Her Majesty's Government on these questions. Both were among the oldest and most tried statesmen of Europe. Mr. Gladstone, the present distinguished chief of the Government, was then the Chancellor of the Exchequer; and Lord Campbell, well known in both hemispheres as a lawyer and as a lover of letters, sat upon the woolsack when the contest began. Lord Westbury, who succeeded him in June, 1861, was the chief counselor of the policy pursued by the British Government. These gentlemen were entitled to speak the voice of the governing classes of the Empire; and the United States have been forced with sincere regret to the conviction that they did express the opinions and wishes of much of the cultivated intellect of Great Britain.

The United States would do great injustice, however, to the sentiments of their own people did they fail to add, that some of the most eloquent voices in Parliament were raised in behalf of the principles of freedom which they represented in the contest; and that members of the governing classes most elevated in rank and distinguished in intellect, and a large part of the industrial classes, were understood to sympathize with them. They cannot, however, shut their eyes to the fact, and they must ask the Tribunal of Arbitration to take note, that, with the few exceptions referred to, the leading statesmen of that country, and nearly the whole periodical press and other channels through which the British cultivated intellect is accustomed to influence public affairs, sustained the course of the existing Government in the unfriendly acts and omissions which resulted so disastrously to the United States. The United States complain before this Tribunal only of the acts and omissions of the British Government. They refer to the expressions and statements from unofficial sources as evidence of a state of public opinion, which would naturally encourage the members of that Government in the policy and acts of which the United States complain.

It is not worth while to take up the time of the Tribunal of Arbitration, by an inquiry into the reasons for this early and long-continued unfriendliness of the British Government, toward a government which was supposed to be in sympathy with its political and moral ideas, and toward a kindred people with whom it had long maintained the attitude of friendship. They may have been partly political, as expressed in Parliament by an impetuous member, who spoke of the bursting of the bubble republic,[1] (for which he received a merited rebuke from Lord John Russell)[2]; or they may have been those declared without rebuke at a later date in the House of Commons by the present Marquis of Salisbury, then Lord Robert Cecil, when he said[3] that "they [the people of the Southern States] were the natural allies of this country, as great producers of the articles we needed and great consumers of the articles we supplied. The North, on the other hand, kept an opposition-shop in the same departments of trade as ourselves;" or they may have been those announced by Earl Russell last year, when saying,[4] "It was

---

[1] Hansard, 3d series, Vol. 163, page 134.
[2] Same, page 276.   [3] Vol. V, page 671.
[4] Earl Russell's Speeches and Dispatches, Vol. II, page 266.

the great object of the British Government to preserve for the subject the security of trial by jury, and for the nation the legitimate and lucrative trade of ship-building."

Conclusions. Without pursuing an inquiry in this direction, which, at the best, would be profitless, the United States invite the careful attention of the Arbitrators to the facts which appear in the previous pages of this Case. In approaching the consideration of the third branch of the subjects herein discussed, in which the United States will endeavor to show that Great Britain failed in her duties toward the United States—as those duties will be defined in the second branch thereof—the Tribunal of Arbitration will find in these facts circumstances which could not but influence the minds of the members of Her Majesty's Government, and induce them to look with disfavor upon efforts to repress the attempts of British subjects, and of other persons, to violate the neutrality of British soil and waters in favor of the rebels.

Some of the members of the British Government of that day seem to have anticipated the conclusion which must inevitably be drawn from their acts, should the injuries and wrongs which the United States have suffered ever be brought to the adjudication of an impartial tribunal.

Lord Westbury, (appointed Lord High Chancellor on the death of Lord Campbell, in June, 1861,) declared, in the House of Lords, in 1868, that "*the animus with which the neutral Powers acted was the only true criterion.* The neutral Power might be mistaken; it might omit to do something which ought to be done, or direct something to be done which ought not to be done; but the question was whether, from beginning to end, it had acted with sincerity and with a real desire to promote and preserve a spirit of neutrality. * * * He [Mr. Seward] said, in effect, 'Whether you were a sincere and loyal neutral was the question in dispute, and that must be judged from a view of the whole of your conduct. I do not mean to put it merely upon the particular transaction relative to the Alabama. I insist upon it in that case undoubtedly; but I contend that, from beginning to end, you had an undue preference and predilection for the Confederate States; that you were therefore not loyal in your neutrality; and I appeal to the precipitancy with which you issued your Proclamation, thereby involving a recognition of the Confederate States as a belligerent power, as a proof of your insincerity and want of impartial attention.' And now, could we prevent him from using that document for such a purpose? How unreasonable it was to say, when you go into arbitration, you shall not use a particular document, even as an argument upon the question whether there was sincere neutrality or not."[1]

Such is the use which the United States ask this Tribunal to make of the foregoing evidence of the unfriendliness and insincere neutrality of the British Cabinet of that day. When the leading members of that Cabinet are thus found counselling in advance with France to secure a joint action of the two governments, and assenting to the declaration of a state of war between the United States and the insurgents, before they could possibly have received intelligence of the purposes of the Government of the United States; when it is seen that the British Secretary of State for Foreign Affairs advises the representatives of the insurgents as to the course to be pursued to obtain the recognition of their independence, and at the same time refuses to await the arrival of the trusted representative of the United States before deciding to recognize them as belligerents; when he is found opening negotiations through Her Majesty's diplomatic representative at Washington with persons in rebellion against the United States; when various members of the British Cabinet are seen to comment upon the efforts of the Government of the United States to suppress the rebellion in terms that indicate a strong desire that those efforts should not succeed, it is not unreasonable to suppose that, when called upon to do acts which might bring about results in conflict with their wishes and convictions, they would hesitate, discuss, delay, and refrain—in fact, that they would do exactly what in the subsequent pages of this paper it will appear that they did do.

---

[1] Hansard's Parliamentary Debates, 3d series, Vol. CXCI, pages 347—348.

PART III.

THE DUTIES WHICH GREAT BRITAIN, AS A NEUTRAL SHOULD HAVE OBSERVED TOWARD THE UNITED STATES.

The Queen's Proclamation a recognition of obligation under the law of nations.

The second branch of the subject, in the order in which the United States desire to present it to the Tribunal of Arbitration, involves the consideration of the duties which Great Britain, as a neutral, should have observed toward the United States during the contest. However inconsiderately and precipitately issued, the Proclamation of Neutrality recognized the obligation, under the law of nations, to undertake the performance of those duties, and it becomes important to have a correct understanding of their character.

Great Britain has recognised its obligations in various ways.

In attempting to define these duties it is natural, first, to endeavor to ascertain whether Great Britain itself has, by legislative or official acts, recognized any such obligations; and next, to inquire whether the canons of international law, as expounded by publicists of authority, demand of a neutral the observance of any other or broader rules than have been so recognized. The United States will pursue the examination in this order.

Recognised by the Foreign Enlistment Act of 1819.

They find, first, an evidence of Great Britain's conception of its duties as a neutral in the Foreign Enlistment Act which was enacted in 1819, and was in force during the whole of the Southern rebellion.

Municipal laws designed to aid a government in performance of international duties. It must be borne in mind, when considering the municipal laws of Great Britain, that, whether effective or deficient, they are but machinery to enable the Government to perform the international duties which they recognize, or which may be incumbent upon it from its position in the family of nations. The obligation of a neutral state to prevent the violation of the neutrality of its soil is independent of all interior or local law. The municipal law may and ought to recognize that obligation; but it can neither create nor destroy it, for it is an obligation resulting directly from International Law, which forbids the use of neutral territory for hostile purpose.[1]

The local law, indeed, may justly be regarded as evidence, as far as it goes, of the nation's estimate of its international duties, but it is not to be taken as the limit of those obligations in the eye of the law of nations.

History of Foreign Enlistment Act of 1819. It is said by Lord Tenterden, the distinguished Secretary of the British High Commissioners, in his memorandum attached to the report[2] of Her Majesty's Commissioners upon the neutrality law,[3] that the neutrality law of the United States formed the foundation of the neutrality law of England.[4] "The act for the amendment of the neutrality laws," he says, "was introduced by Mr. Canning on the 10th of June, 1819, in an eloquent speech, in the course of which he said, 'It surely could not be forgotten that in 1793 this country complained of various breaches of neutrality (though much inferior in degree to those now under consideration) committed on the part of subjects of the United States of America. What was the conduct of that nation in consequence? Did it resent the complaint as an infringement of its independence? Did it refuse to take such steps as would insure the immediate

---

[1] Ortolan, Diplomatie de la mer, Vol. 2, page 215.
[2] Vol. IV, page 79.
[3] Vol. IV, page 93, Appendix No. 3, by Mr. Abbott, now Lord Tenterden.
[4] Vol. IV, page 124.

observance of neutrality? Neither. In 1794, immediately after the application from the British Government, the Legislature of the United States passed an act prohibiting, under heavy penalties, the engagement of American citizens in the armies of any belligerent Power. Was that the only instance of the kind? It was but last year that the United States passed an act by which the act of 1794 was confirmed in every respect, again prohibiting the engagement of their citizens in the service of any foreign Power, and pointing distinctly to the service of Spain or the South American Provinces."[1] It appears from the whole tenor of the debate which preceded the passage of the act that its sole purpose was *to enable the Executive to perform with fidelity the duties toward neutrals which were recognized as imposed upon the Government by the Law of Nations.*

Great Britain bound to perform the duties recognised by that act. The United States assume that it will be conceded that Great Britain was bound to perform all the duties of a neutral toward the United States which are indicated in this statute. If this obligation should be denied, the United States beg to refer the Tribunal of Arbitration to the declaration of Earl Russell in his communication to Mr. Adams of August 30, 1865, where he [2] "lays down with confidence the following proposition;" "That the Foreign Enlistment Act is intended in aid of the *duties* * * of a neutral nation."[3] They also refer to Lord Palmerston's speech in the House of Commons, July 28, 1863,[4] in which he says: "The American Government have a distinct right to expect that a neutral will enforce its municipal law, if it be in their favor."

Indeed, Great Britain is fully committed to this principle in its dealings with other Powers. Thus, during the Crimean war, Her Majesty's Government, feeling aggrieved at the acts of the Prussian Government in tolerating the furnishing of arms and other contraband of war to Russia, were advised by the Law Officers of the Crown that they might justly remonstrate against violations of Prussian law.[5]

---

[1] Vol. IV, pages 123—124. [2] Vol. III, page 549.
[3] Vol. III, page 550. [4] Vol. V, page 695.
[5] Earl Granville to Count Bernstorff, September 15, 1870.

After these declarations by British authorities, it will scarcely be contended that the United States had not the right to expect, and to demand of Great Britain the performance of the measure of duty recognized by existing municipal laws, however inadequate those laws might be as an expression of international obligations.

Duties recognized by Foreign Enlistment Act of 1819. The British Foreign Enlistment Act of 1819 consisted of twelve sections, written in the verbiage which the customs of England make necessary in the laws providing for the punishment of crimes. These sections relate to four distinct subjects. First, they repeal all former statutes; secondly, they define the acts which the British legislators regarded as acts which a neutral ought not to permit to be done within its jurisdiction; thirdly, they provide modes for prosecuting persons found guilty of committing the acts which are prohibited by the statute, and they indicate the punishments which may be inflicted upon them when convicted; fourthly, they exempt certain parts of the Empire from the operation of the statute.[1]

This Tribunal need take no notice of the penal portions of the statute, which affect only the relations between the State and those who owe allegiance to its laws by reason of residence within its territory. The United States will therefore confine themselves to attempting to deduce from the statute the definitions of the principles, and the duties, which are there recognized as obligatory on the nation in its relations with other Powers. The adjudicated cases often disregard the distinction between the duties of a neutral, however defined, and the proceedings in its courts against persons charged as criminals for alleged violations of its laws for the preservation of neutrality. Even some of the best publicists, in referring to this class of decisions, have not always remembered that, while in the former we have only to do with principles of public law, in the latter we are dealing with the evidence necessary for the conviction of an offender. Bearing this distinction in mind, the Tri-

---

[1] Vol. IV, page 86.

bunal of Arbitration may be able to reconcile many apparently conflicting authorities, and arrive at just conclusions.

The acts which, if commited within the territory of the neutral, are to be regarded as violations of its international duties, are enumerated in the second, fifth, sixth, seventh, and eighth sections of the statute.

Translating this statutory language into the expressions commonly employed by publicists and writers on International Law, this statute recognizes the following as acts which ought to be prevented within neutral territory during time of war:

1. The recruitment of subjects or citizens of the neutral, to be employed in the military or naval service of a foreign government or of persons assuming to exercise the powers of government over any part of foreign territory; or the acceptance of a commission, warrant, or appointment for such service by such persons; or the enlisting or agreeing to enlist in such service; the act in each case being done without the leave or license of the Sovereign.

2. The receiving on board a vessel, for the purpose of transporting from a neutral port, persons who may have been so recruited or commissioned; or the transporting such persons from a neutral port. Authority is given to seize the vessels violating these provisions.

3. The equipping, furnishing, fitting out, or arming a vessel, with intent or in order that it may be employed in the service of such foreign government, or of persons assuming to exercise the powers of government over any part of a foreign country, as a transport or store-ship, or to cruise or carry on war against a power with which the neutral is at peace; or the delivering a commission for such vessel, the act in each case being done without the leave or license of the Sovereign.

4. The augmenting the warlike force of such a vessel of war by adding to the number of guns, by changing those on board for other guns, or by the addition of any equipment of war, if such vessel at the time of its arrival in the dominions of the neutral was a vessel of war in the service of such foreign government, or of such persons,

the act being done without the leave or license of the sovereign.¹

---

¹ It may interest the members of the Tribunal of Arbitration to see in this connection an abstract of the acts which are made penal by the United States Neutrality Law of 1818. The law itself will be found in Vol. IV, pages 90—92. The abstract is taken from President Grant's Proclamation of Neutrality in the late Franco-German war, dated October 8, 1870.

"By the act passed on the 20th day of April, A. D. 1818, commonly known as the „Neutrality Law", the following acts are forbidden to be done, under severe penalties, within the territory and jurisdiction of the United States, to wit:

"1. Accepting and exercising a commission to serve either of the said belligerents by land or by sea against the other belligerent.

"2. Enlisting or entering into the service of either of the said belligerents as a soldier, or as a marine or seaman on board of any vessel of war, letter of marque, or privateer.

"3. Hiring or retaining another person to enlist or enter himself in the service of either of the said belligerents as a soldier, or as a marine or seaman on board of any vessel of war, letter of marque, or privateer.

"4. Hiring another person to go beyond the limits or jurisdiction of the United States with intent to be enlisted as aforesaid.

"5. Hiring another person to go beyond the limits of the United States with the intent to be entered into service as aforesaid.

"6. Hiring another person to go beyond the limits of the United States with intent to be enlisted as aforesaid.

"7. Retaining another person to go beyond the limits of the United States with intent to be entered into service as aforesaid. (But the said act is not to be construed to extend to a citizen or subject of either belligerent who, being transiently within the United States, shall, on board of any vessel of war, which, at the time of its arrival within the United States, was fitted and equipped as such vessel of war, enlist, or enter himself, or hire, or retain another subject or citizen of the same belligerent, who is transiently within the United States, to enlist, or enter himself to serve such belligerent on board such vessel of war, if the United States shall then be at peace with such belligerent.)

"8. Fitting out and arming, or attempting to fit out and arm, or procuring to be fitted out and armed, or knowingly being concerned in the furnishing, fitting out, or arming of any

DUTIES OF A NEUTRAL.

Royal Commission to revise Foreign Enlistment Act of 1819. During the insurrection, as will be seen hereafter, this act was, by the construction of the English courts, stripped of its effective power. The United States repeatedly and in vain invited Her Majesty's Government to amend it. Although these calls proved abortive during the contest with the South, the appalling magnitude of the injury which had been inflicted by British-built and British-manned cruisers upon the commerce and industry of a nation with which Great Britain was at peace, appears to have awakened its senses, and to have impelled it to take some steps toward a change. In January, 1867, the Queen's Commission was issued to some of the most eminent of the British lawyers

---

ship or vessel, with intent that such ship or vessel shall be employed in the service of either of the said belligerents.

„9. Issuing or delivering a commission within the territory or jurisdiction of the United States for any ship or vessel to the intent that she may be employed as aforesaid.

"10. Increasing or augmenting, or procuring to be increased or augmented, or knowingly being concerned in increasing or augmenting, the force of any ship of war, cruiser, or other armed vessel, which at the time of her arrival within the United States was a ship of war, cruiser, or armed vessel in the service of either of the said belligerents, or belonging to the subjects or citizens of either, by adding to the number of guns of such vessels, or by changing those on board of her for guns of a larger caliber, or by the addition thereto of any equipment solely applicable to war.

"11. Beginning or setting on foot or providing or preparing the means for any military expedition or enterprise to be carried on from the territory or jurisdiction of the United States against the territories or dominions of either of the said belligerents."

The Tribunal of Arbitration will also observe that the most important part of the American act is omitted in the British act, namely, *the power conferred by the eighth section on the Executive to take possession of and detain a ship without judicial process, and to use the military and naval forces of the Government for that purpose, if necessary.* Earl Russell is understood to have determined that the United States should, in no event, have the benefit of such a summary proceeding, or of any remedy that would take away the trial by jury. — *Speeches and Dispatches of Earl Russell*, Vol. II, page 266.

and judges, authorizing them to inquire into and consider the character, working, and effect of the laws of the Realm, available for the enforcement of neutrality, during the existence of hostilities between other States with whom Great Britain might be at peace, and to inquire and report whether any and what changes ought to be made in such laws for the purpose of giving to them increased efficiency, and bringing them into full conformity with international obligations.[1]

Report of that Commission. That Commission held twenty-four sittings, and finally reported that the old Foreign Enlistment Act of 1819 was capable of improvement, and might be made more efficient by the enactment of several provisions set forth in the report.[2]

Among other things, the Commission recommended that it be made a statutory offense to "fit out, arm, *dispatch or cause to be dispatched, any ship, with intent or knowledge* that the same shall or will be employed in the military or naval service of any foreign Power in any war then being waged by such Power against the subjects or property of any foreign belligerent Power with whom Her Majesty shall not then be at war."[3] It was also proposed to make it a statutory offense to "*build or equip any ship with the intent that the same shall, after being fitted out and armed, either within or beyond Her Majesty's Dominions, be employed as aforesaid;*"[4] and it was proposed that the Executive should be armed with summary powers similar to those conferred upon the President of the United States by the eighth section of the act of 1818. It was further proposed to enact that "in time of war no vessel employed in the military or naval service of any belligerent, which shall have been built, equipped, fitted out, armed, or dispatched contrary to the enactment, should be admitted to any port of Her Majesty's Dominions."[5]

The Tribunal of Arbitration will not fail to observe that these recommendations were made by a board composed of

---

[1] Vol. IV, page 79.
[2] Vol. IV, pages 80, 81.
[3] Vol. IV, page 82.
[4] Vol. IV, page 80.
[5] Vol IV, page 81.

the most eminent judges, jurists, publicists, and statesmen of the Empire, who had been in public life and had participated in the direction of affairs in Great Britain during the whole period of the Southern rebellion; and that they were made under a commission which authorized these distinguished gentlemen to consider and report what changes ought to be made in the laws of the Kingdom, for the purpose of giving to them increased efficiency, *and bringing them into full conformity with the international obligations of England*. The Tribunal of Arbitration will search the whole of that report, and of its various appendices, in vain, to find any indication that that distinguished body imagined, or thought, or believed that the measures which they recommended were not "in full conformity with international obligations." On the contrary, the Commissioners say that, so far as they can see, the adoption of the recommendations will bring the municipal law into full conformity with the international obligations.[1] Viewing their acts in the light of their powers and of their instructions, the United States feel themselves justified in asking the Tribunal to assume that that eminent body regarded the acts which they proposed to prevent by legislation, as forbidden by International Law.

The Foreign Enlistment Act of 1870. The report of the Commissioners was made in 1868, but was not acted upon until after the breaking out of the late war between Germany and France. On the 9th of August, 1870, Parliament passed "An act to regulate the conduct of Her Majesty's subjects during the existence of hostilities between foreign States with which Her Majesty is at peace." This act, which may be found in Volume VII,[2] embodies the recommendations of the commissioners which are cited above, except that which excludes a ship which has been illegally built or armed &c., &c., from Her Majesty's ports.

Soon after the enactment of this statute, a vessel called the "International," was proceeded against for an alleged violation of its provisions. The case came before Sir Robert J. Phillimore,

Judicial construction of that act.

---

[1] Vol. IV, page 82.   [2] Vol. VII, page 1.

one of Her Majesty's Commissioners who signed the report in 1868. In rendering his decision on the 17th January, 1871, he said: "This statute, passed during the last session, under which the authority of this court is now for the first time evoked, is, in my judgment, very important and very valuable; strengthening the hands of Her Majesty's Government, and *enabling them to fulfill more easily than heretofore that particular class of international obligations which may arise out of the conduct of Her Majesty's subjects toward belligerent Foreign States, with whom Her Majesty is at peace*.[1]

These eminent commissioners and this distinguished jurist have chosen their words with the precision which might have been expected of them. They declare that, in the execution of the commission, they have only sought to bring the law of England into harmony with the law of nations. Their functions ceased when they recommended certain charges with that object in view. Parliament then took up the work and adopted their suggestions. Then, as if to prevent all misapprehension, one of the commissioners, acting as a judge, held that the act of 1870 is intended to bring the law of the realm into harmony with the international duties of the Sovereign.

International law is a part of the common law of England. The United States confidently submit that the new provisions, inserted in the act of 1870, were intended, at least as against the British Government, as a reënactment of the law of nations, as understood by the United States to be applicable to the cases of the Alabama, and other ships of war constructed in England for the use of the insurgents.

They conceive that Great Britain is committed to the doctrines therein stated, not merely by the articles of International Law expressed in its statutes, but also by the long-settled Common Law of England confirmed by acts of Parliament.

---

[1] London Times, January 13, 1871. See also Admiralty and Ecclesiastical Reports, Vol. 3, page 332. See also Report of the Debate on the Foreign Enlistment Act in the House of Commons, in the London Times of August 2, 1870.

The act of 7 Anne, ch. 12, enacted in consequence of the violation of the law of nations by the arrest for debt of the Ambassador of the Czar, Peter the Great, in London, is prominent in the history of the legislation of Great Britain.[1]

Lord Mansfield, commenting on this act in the case of Triquet vs. Buth, 3 Burrow's Reports, p. 148, says that this act was but declaratory. All that is new in this act is the clause which gives a summary jurisdiction for the punishment of the infraction of the law. He further remarks that the Ambassador who had been arrested could have been discharged on motion. This act of Parliament was passed as an apology from the nation. It was sent to the Czar, finely illuminated, by an Ambassador Extraordinary, who made the national excuses in an oration. "The act was not occasioned by any doubt whether the law of nations, particularly the part relative to public ministers, was not part of the law of England, and not intended to vary an iota from it." Lord Mansfield further says, in reference to the case of Brevot vs. Barbot, that Lord Talbot declared "that the law of nations, in its full extent, was part of the law of England;" and adds, "I remember, too, Lord Hardwick declared his opinion to the same effect, and denying that Lord Chief Justice Holt ever had any doubt as to the law of nations being part of the law of England, upon the occasion of the arrest of the Russian Ambassador."[2]

To the same effect is the remark of Lord Tenterden, when he says "that the act of Anne is only declaratory of the common law. It must, therefore, be construed according to the common law, of which the law of nations must be deemed a part."[3]

Blackstone states the doctrine in general terms as follows: "The law of nations is a system of rules, deducible by natural reason, and established by universal consent among the civilized inhabitants of the world, in order to decide

---

[1] See Phillimore's International Law, vol. 2, ch. 6, section 194.
[2] See further 1 Black. Com., pp. 43, 354; 1 Woodson's Lectures, p. 31.
[3] Novillo vs. Toogood, 1 Barnwell and Creswell's Reports, 562.

all disputes, to regulate all ceremonies and civilities, and to insure the observance of justice and good faith, in that intercourse which must frequently occur between two or more independent States, and the individuals belonging to each.

* * * * * *

"In arbitrary States this law, wherever it contradicts, or is not provided for by the municipal law of the country, is enforced by the Royal Power; but since in England no Royal Power can introduce a new law or suspend the execution of the old, therefore the law of nations (whenever any question arises which is properly the object of its jurisdiction) is here adopted in its full extent by the common law of the land. And those acts of Parliament which have from time to time been made to enforce this universal law, or to facilitate the execution of its decisions, are not to be considered as introductive of any new rule, but merely as declaratory of the old fundamental constitutions of the Kingdom; *without which it must cease to be a part of the civilized world.*"[1]

In the presence of these authorities it cannot be doubted, that the law of nations enters integrally into the common law of England, and that any enactment by Parliament on this point derives force only from its conformity with the law of nations, having no virtue beyond that, except in so far as such enactment may afford means for the better enforcement of that law within the realm of England.

That eminent judge and jurist, Lord Stowell, even goes so far as to say that, while an act of Parliament can affirm the law of nations, it cannot contradict it or disaffirm it to any effect as respects foreign Governments.[2]

Lord Stowell's position is in perfect accordance with the observation of Lord Mansfield, in another case, *viz*: Heathfield *vs*. Chilton, that, "The privileges of public ministers and their retinue depend upon the law of nations, which

---

[1] Blackstone's Com., vol. 4, ch. 5. See also Lord Lyndhurst's opinion, ante page 61.

[2] The Louis, Dodson's Admiralty Reports, vol. 2, p. 210.

is part of the common law of England. And the act of Parliament of 7 Anne, ch. 12, did not intend to alter, nor can alter the law of nations."[1]

Duties recognized by the Queen's Proclamation of Neutrality. The next act of the British Government to which the United States invite the attention of the Tribunal, as showing to some extent that Government's sense of its duties toward the United States, is the Proclamation of Neutrality of May 13, 1861, already alluded to.

It is not claimed that a belligerent has the right, by the custom of nations, to require a neutral to enforce in its favor an executive Proclamation of the neutral, addressed to its own citizens or subjects; but it is maintained that, as between Great Britain and the United States, there is a binding precedent for such a request to Great Britain. In 1793, during General Washington's administration, the representative of Great Britain in the United States pointed out to Mr. Jefferson, who was then Secretary of State, acts which were deemed by Her Britannic Majesty's Government to be "breaches of neutrality," done "in contravention of the President's Proclamation" of Neutrality, and he invited the United States to take steps for the repression of such acts, and for the restoration of captured prizes. It appears that the United States complied with these requests.[2]

Relying, therefore, upon this precedent, established against Great Britain, rather than upon a right under the laws of nations, which can be asserted or maintained against the United States or against other nations, the United States invite the attention of the Tribunal to the fact that two principles, in addition to those already deduced from the Foreign Enlistment Act of 1819, appear to be conceded by the Proclamation of May 13, 1861:

1. That it is the duty of a neutral to observe strict neutrality as to both belligerents during hostilities.

---

[1] Heathfield vs. Chilton, 4 Burrows, p. 2016. This observation of Lord Mansfield is cited and adopted by Phillimore, vol. 3, p. 541.

[2] Vol. IV, pages 94—102.

Definition of neutrality. Neutrality is defined by Phillimore "to consist in two principal circumstances: 1. Entire abstinence from any participation in the war; 2. Impartiality of conduct toward both belligerents," "This *abstinence* and this *impartiality* must be combined in the character of a *bona-fide* neutral."[1]

Bluntschli defines it thus; "La neutralité est la *non-participation* à la guerre. Lorsque l'état neutre soutient un des belligérents, il prend part à la guerre, en faveur de celui qu'il soutient, et dès lors *il cesse d'être neutre*. L'adversaire est autorisé à voir dans cette participation un acte d'hostilité. Et cela n'est pas seulement vrai quand l'état neutre livre lui-même, des troupes ou des vaisseaux des guerre, mais aussi lorsqu'il prête à un des belligérents un appui médiat en permettant, *tandis qu'il pourrait l'empêcher*, que, de son territoire neutre, on envoie des troupes ou des navires de guerre."[2]

Hautefeuille says: "Cet état nouveau impose aux neutres des devoirs particuliers: ils doivent s'abstenir complètement de tout acte d'immixion aux hostilités et garder une stricte impartialité envers les deux belligérents. * * * L'impartialité consiste à traiter les deux belligérents de la même manière et avec une parfaite égalité dans tout ce qui concerne les relations d'état à état."[3]

Lord Stowell says: "The high privileges of a neutral are forfeited by the abandonment of that perfect indifference between the contending parties, in which the essence of neutrality consists."[4]

Calvo collects or refers to the definitions given by the various writers on International Law, and expresses a preference for Hubner's: "La mas aceptable es la de Hubner, por la claridad y precision con que fija, no solo la situacion de las

---

[1] 3 Phillimore, Ch. IX.
[2] Opinion impartiale sur la question de l'Alabama. Berlin, 1870, page 22.
[3] Nécessité d'une loi maritime pour régler les rapports des neutres et des belligérents. Paris, 1862, page 7.
[4] The Eliza Ann, (1 Dodson's Reports, 244.)

naciones pacificas, sino la extension que tiene sobre ellas el status belli."[1]

2. The proclamation also distinctly recognizes the principle that the duties of a neutral in time of war do not grow out of, and are not dependent upon municipal laws. Offenders against the provisions of the act are therein expressly forewarned that such offenses will be "acts in derogation of their duty as subjects of a neutral sovereign in the said contest, *or in violation or contravention of the law of nations in that behalf.*"

Duties recognized by Instructions to British officials during the Insurrection. The next acts of the British Government, indicating its sense of its duties as a neutral toward the United States, to which the attention of the Tribunal is invited, are the several instructions issued during the contest, for the regulation of the official conduct of its naval officers and of its colonial authorities toward the belligerents.[2]

These various instructions state or recognize the following principles and rules:

1. A belligerent may not use the harbors, ports, coasts, and waters of a neutral in aid of its warlike purposes, or as a station or place of resort for any warlike purpose, or for the purpose of obtaining any facilities of warlike equipment.

2. Vessels of war of the belligerents may be required to depart from a neutral port within twenty-four hours after entrance, except in case of stress of weather, or requiring provisions or things for the crew, or repairs; in which case they should go to sea as soon as possible after the expiration of the twenty-four hours.

3. The furnishing of supplies to a belligerent vessel of war in a neutral port may be prohibited, except such as may be necessary for the subsistence of a crew, and for their immediate use.

4. A belligerent steam-vessel of war ought not to receive in a neutral port more coal than is necessary to take it to

---
[1] Calvo Derecho Internacional, tom 2, page 151, § 608.
[2] Vol. IV, page 175, et seq.

the nearest port of its own country, or to some nearer destination, and should not receive two supplies of coal from ports of the same neutral within less than three months of each other.

Correspondence between the two Governments in 1793–94. The attention of the Tribunal is further invited to the official opinions expressed by the representative of Great Britain in the United States during the administration of President Washington upon the duties of a neutral toward a belligerent; and to the acts of the Government of the United States during that administration, preceding, and accompanying, and subsequent to those expressions of opinion; and to the treaty concluded between the United States and Great Britain in 1794.

The first acts took place in the United States in 1793, a year before the passage of the first American Neutrality Law, when the United States had nothing but the law of nations and the sense of their duties as a neutral to guide them.

The envoy from the new French Republic, M. Genet, arrived at Charleston, in the United States, early in April, 1793, with the purpose of making the ports and waters of the country the base of hostile operations against Great Britain. The steps which he took are fairly referred to by Lord Tenterden in the memorandum already cited.[1]

The Capital was then at Philadelphia, several hundred miles distant from Charleston, with few regular means of communication between the two towns. The Government of the United States was in its early infancy. Four years only had passed since it was originated, and it had not been tested whether the powers confided to it would prove sufficient for an emergency that might arise in its Foreign Relations. It had neither navy, nor force that could be converted into one, and no army on the sea-coast; and it was obliged to rely upon, and did actually call out, the irregular militia of the States to enforce its orders.

Under the directions of M. Genet, privateers were fitted out, manned, and commissioned, from Charleston and other ports,

---

[1] Vol. IV, page 93, et seq.

before he reached Philadelphia, and prizes were brought in by them. On the 22d of April, 1793, M. Genet not having yet reached Philadelphia, President Washington issued his celebrated proclamation, the first of its kind, in which he declared that "the duty and interest of the United States require that they should, with sincerity and good faith, adopt and pursue a conduct friendly and impartial toward the belligerent Powers;" and he warned all persons against "committing, aiding, or abetting hostilities against any of the said Powers." [1]

The news of the coming of M. Genet had preceded his arrival at Philadelphia. On the 17th May, 1793, Mr. Hammond, the then British Minister, made complaint of his acts, and called attention to the fact that privateers were fitting in South Carolina, which he conceived to be "breaches of that neutrality which the United States profess to observe, and direct contraventions of the Proclamation."

He invited the Government to "pursue such measures as to its wisdom may appear the best calculated for repressing such practices in future, and for restoring to their rightful owners any captures which these particular privateers may attempt to bring into any of the ports of the United States." [2]

Two days before the receipt of that representation, Mr. Jefferson had already complained to the French Minister of these proceedings, and M. Genet, on his arrival, claimed to justify himself by the existing treaties between France and the United States.

Other cases subsequently occurred, in which Mr. Hammond intervened; for an account of which the Tribunal of Arbitration is respectfully referred to Lord Tenterden's memorandum.

The subject of Mr. Hammond's complaints and his demand for the restoration of the captured vessels were under consideration until the 5th of June, 1793, when answers were given simultaneously to M. Genet and to Mr. Hammond.

The former was told that the United States could not tolerate these acts of war within their territories. The latter

---

[1] Vol. IV, page 94.   [2] Vol. IV, page 95.

was told that effectual measures would be taken to prevent a repetition of the acts complained of; but as to restoring the prizes, it could not be done for two reasons: first, because if commissions to the privateers were valid and the captures were legal, the Executive of the United States had no control over them; and if they were illegal, the owners had a sufficient remedy in the national courts; secondly, because the act complained of had been done at a remote port, without any privity of the United States, "impossible to have been known, and therefore impossible to have been prevented by the Government."[1]

It is worthy of note that the owners did resort to the courts, and that prizes taken by these privateers were restored by judicial process.[2]

The Government of General Washington determined, however, as it had been informed of these attempts at violating the sovereignty of the nation, that it was the duty of the United States not only to repress them in future, but to restore prizes that might be captured by vessels thus illegally fitted out, manned, equipped, or commissioned within the waters of the United States; or, if unable to restore them, then to make compensation for them.

The reasons for this course are stated in a letter from Mr. Jefferson to Mr. Hammond, dated the 5th of September, 1793.[3]

The United States Government also, on the 4th of August, 1793, issued instructions to collectors of the customs,[4] which were intended to enforce the President's Proclamation of April 22. We have the authority of Lord Tenterden for saying that the result of the publication of those instructions was, that the system of privateering was, generally speaking, suppressed.[5]

---

[1] Vol. IV, page 97.
[2] Dana's Wheaton, section 439, note 215, page 536. This note, which contains an exhaustive review of the American policy, may be found in Vol. VII, page 11.
[3] Vol. IV, page 100. The United States also refer to Mr. Jefferson's letter to Mr. Hammond, of November 14, 1793.
[4] Vol. IV, page 97. [5] Vol. IV, page 101.

From this examination, it appears that a well conceived and extended system of violating the neutrality of the United States, when they were weak and the powers confided to their Executive were untried, was put in operation in April by the representative of one of the powerful nations of Europe, and was suppressed before August without legislation; and also that *the United States undertook to make compensation for the injuries resulting from violations that had taken place where they had failed to exert all the means in their power to prevent them.*

The Treaty of Nov. 19, 1794.
It was subsequently agreed between the two Governments[1] that in cases where restitution of the prizes should be impossible, the amount of the losses should be ascertained by a method similar to that provided by the Treaty of Washington, and that a money payment should be made by the United States to Great Britain in lieu of restitution. The examination of these claims extended over a period of some years, and the amounts of the ascertained losses were eventually paid by the United States to Great Britain.

Construction of that Treaty by the commissioners appointed under it.
In the case of the "Jamaica," before the commission, under the 7th article of the treaty of 1794, the capturing vessel was alleged to have been armed in the United States, but the prize, (the Jamaica,) with her cargo, was burned by the captors, and never brought within the jurisdiction of the United States. Upon this bare case, without any allegation of permission or neglect by the Government of the United States as to the arming of the French cruiser, the advocate for the claimants contended that the law of nations obliged the United States to make compensation. The claim was rejected; "the board [one gentleman only dissenting] were of opinion that the case was not within the stipulation of the article under which the commissioners act."

A rehearing being granted and counsel heard, Mr. Gore delivered the opinion sustaining the original determination.

---

[1] Treaty concluded between the United States and Great Britain, at London, November 19, 1794, commonly known as "Jay's Treaty." See United States Statutes at Large, Vol. VIII, page 116.

After reviewing British precedents cited by the counsel for the claimants, as supporting his view of international law, Mr. Goro says:

"The counsel for the claimant seemed to suppose that the obligation to compensate arose from the circumstance of the privateer's having been originally armed in the United States; but as *there is not the smallest evidence to induce a belief that in this or in any other case the Government permitted, or in any degree connived at, such arming, or failed to use all the means in their power to prevent such equipment,* there is no ground to support a charge on the fact that the armament originated in their ports."[1]

All these steps prior to 1794 were taken by the United States under the general rules of International Law, without the aid of a local statute, in order to perform what Mr. Jefferson called "their duty as a neutral nation to prohibit such acts as would injure one of the warring Powers."[2] In 1794, however, the Congress of the United States, on the application of Great Britain, passed a statute prohibiting such acts, under heavy penalties.[3]

The neutrality laws of the United States enacted at the request of Great Britain. The general provisions of the United States Act of 1818 (which is still in force) are set forth in note 1, on page 114. This act was passed at the request of the Portuguese Government. The act of 1838 was enacted on the suggestion of Great Britain: In the year 1837 a formidable rebellion against Great Britain broke out in Canada. Sympathizers with the insurgents beginning to gather on the northern frontier of the United States, Mr. Fox, the British Minister at Washington, "solemnly appealed to the Supreme Government promptly to interpose its sovereign authority for arresting the disorders," and inquired what means it proposed to employ for that purpose. The President immediately addressed a communication to Congress, calling attention to defects in the existing statute, and asking that the Executive might be clothed with adequate power to restrain all persons within the jurisdiction

---

[1] 2d Vol. Mms. Opinions, Department of State.
[2] Mr. Jefferson to M. Genet, June 5, 1793. Jefferson's Works, Vol. III, page 572.
[3] Mr. Canning's speech, cited *ante*, page 107.

of the United States from the commission of acts of the character complained of. Congress, thereupon, passed the act of 1838. Thus Great Britain once more asked the United States to amend their neutrality laws, in British interest, so as to give more power to the Executive, and the request was complied with.

Case of the bark Maury. In the year 1855, Great Britain being then at war with Russia, it was supposed by the British Consul, at New York, that a vessel called the Maury, which was being innocently fitted out at New York for the China trade, was intended as a Russian privateer. The British Minister at Washington at once called the attention of Mr. Marcy, the then Secretary of State, to this vessel. The affidavits which he inclosed for the consideration of the Secretary of State fell far, very far, short of the evidence which Mr. Adams submitted to Earl Russell in regard to the Liverpool cruisers. The whole foundation which the British Minister furnished for the action of the United States was the "belief" of the Consul, his lawyer, and two police officers, that the vessel was intended for Russian service. This was communicated to the Government of the United States on the 11th of October. Notwithstanding the feebleness of the suspicion, the prosecuting officer of the United States was, on the 12th of October, instructed by telegraph to "prosecute if cause appears," and was at work on the 13th in order to prevent a violation of the sovereignty of the United States to the injury of Great Britain.[1] The proceedings given at length in the accompanying volumes show with what rapidity and zeal the investigation was made, and that the charge was at once proved to be unfounded.

Principles thus recognised by the two Governments. In all this correspondence and these precedents, the following principles appear to have been assumed by the two Governments:

1. That the belligerent may call upon the neutral to enforce its municipal proclamations as well as its municipal laws.

2. That it is the duty of the neutral, when the fact of

---

[1] Vol. IV, pages 53—62.

the intended violation of its sovereignty is disclosed, either through the agency of the representative of the belligerent, or through the vigilance of the neutral, to use all the means in its power to prevent the violation.

3. That when there is a failure to use all the means in the power of a neutral to prevent a breach of the neutrality of its soil or waters, there is an obligation on the part of the neutral to make compensation for the injury resulting therefrom.

Obligation to make compensation for injuries. The United States are aware that some eminent English publicists, writing on the subject of the "Alabama Claims," have maintained that the obligation in such case to make compensation would not necessarily follow the proof of the commission of the wrong; but the United States confidently insist that such a result is entirely inconsistent with the course pursued by Great Britain and the United States, during the administration of General Washington, when Great Britain claimed of the United States compensation for losses sustained from the acts of cruisers that had received warlike additions in the ports of the United States, and the United States admitted the justice of the claim, and paid the compensation demanded. The United States also point to the similar compensation made by them to Spain in the treaty of 1819, for similar injuries inflicted on Spanish commerce during the War of the Independence of the Spanish American Colonies, as showing the sense of Spain on this point.

Correspondence between the United States and Portugal. In the course of the long discussions between the two Governments on the Alabama claims, Great Britain has attempted to justify its course by a reference to the conduct of the United States toward Portugal between 1816 and 1822.[1]

The several replies of Mr. Adams amply defended the course of the United States in that affair. From the replies and from the official documents referred to in them, it would appear that in the year 1850 the United States had brought to the point of settlement a long-standing claim against Por-

---

[1] Vol. III, pages 550—560.

tugal, for the destruction of the American armed brig General Armstrong, in the harbor of Fayal, in the year 1814. They were at the same time pressing some other claims against Portugal, and were conducting a correspondence with the Portuguese Legation at Washington, growing out of the seizure of a Portuguese slaver.[1]

The Portuguese Government, as an offset to these claims of the United States, revived some exploded claims of Portugal against the United States, for alleged violation of neutrality, that had slumbered for nearly thirty years. These are the claims referred to by Earl Russell in his note to Mr. Adams of May 4, 1865,[2] and his note to the same of August 30, 1865,[3] and his note to the same dated November 2, 1865.[4] Lord Russell asserts that the complaints of Portugal were more frequent and extended to a larger amount of property after 1818 than they had done before. Mr. Adams denies this allegation,[5] and his denial is supported by the evidence in possession of the Government of the United States.

The facts appear to be these: On the 20th December, 1816, the Portuguese Minister informed the then Secretary of State (Mr. Monroe) of the fitting out of privateers at Baltimore to act against Portugal, in case it should turn out that that Government was at war with the "self-styled Government of Buenos Ayres." He further stated that he did not make the application in order "to raise altercations or to require satisfaction," but that he solicited "the proposition to Congress of such provisions by law as will prevent such attempts for the future," being "persuaded that my [his] magnanimous Sovereign will receive a more dignified satisfaction, and worthier of his high character, by the enactment of such laws by the United States." Mr. Monroe replied, on the 27th of the same month, "I have communicated your letter to the President, and have now the honor to transmit to you a copy of a message which he has addressed

---

[1] Executive Document No. 53, 32d Congress, 1st session.
[2] Vol. III, page 525. [3] Vol. III, page 584.
[4] Vol. III, page 548. [5] Vol. III, page 621.

to Congress on the subject, with a view to obtain such an extension, by law, of the Executive power as will be necessary to preserve the strict neutrality of the United States, * * * and effectually to guard against the danger in regard to the vessels of your Sovereign which you have anticipated." The act of 1817 was passed and officially communicated to the Portuguese Minister on the 13th of March 1817. On the 13th of May, 1817, the Portuguese Minister informed the Secretary of State that although "the law passed at the last session of Congress obviated a great part of the evils" of which he complained, he feared there would be a lack of vigilance on the part of some of the officials, and he asked for special instructions to them. On the 8th of March, 1818, he complained to Mr. John Quincy Adams, then Secretary of State, of the capture of "three Portuguese ships, captured by privateers fitted in the United States, manned by American crews, and commanded by American captains, though under insurgent colors;" and he asked for satisfaction and indemnification for the injury. The note making this complaint contained neither proof of the allegations in the note as to the fitting out of vessels in the United States, or as to their being manned by Americans, nor indications from which the United States might have discovered those facts for themselves. The Secretary of State, therefore, in reply to such an allegation, very properly stated the fact that the United States had "used all the means in its power to prevent the fitting out and arming of vessels in their ports to cruise against any nation with whom they were at peace," *and* had "faithfully carried into execution the laws to preserve inviolate the neutral and pacific obligations of the Union;" and *therefore* could not consider themselves "bound to indemnify individual foreigners for losses by captures." It will not escape the notice of the Tribunal that Mr. Adams calls attention to the distinction between the national obligations under the law of nations and the duty of the Government to execute the municipal law; and that he grounds his refusal upon the fact that both have been complied with.

The Portuguese Minister next complains (October 15, 1818)

that a privateer is fitting out in Baltimore, and the Secretary of State orders a prosecution and asks for the names of the witnesses, and it appears that before November 13th the Portuguese Minister is informed that the grand jury have found a bill against the accused. On the 14th of November the Portuguese Minister sends to the Secretary of State depositions and the names of witnesses, and informs him that he is alarmed at the "thick crowd of individuals who are engaged in this iniquitous business," and that "great care has been taken to intercept the notice of such facts from the knowledge of the Executive." Mr. Adams, on the 18th of November, informs the Minister that the evidence has been placed in the hands of the prosecuting attorney of the United States. It thus appears that the second complaint was disposed of to the satisfaction of the representative of Portugal.

The third complaint, made on the 11th of December, 1818, states that an armed vessel called the Irresistible, sailing under so-called Artigan colors, was committing depredations on the coast of Brazil, and that the commander and crew of the vessel were all Americans. It will be observed that in this complaint there is no charge made of an illegal use of the soil or waters of the United States in violation of their duties as a neutral. The charge is that citizens of the United States, beyond their jurisdiction, have taken service under a belligerent against Portugal.

The next communication from the Portuguese Minister is made on the 4th of February, 1819. He asks to have the neutrality act of 1817 continued. The Secretary of State answers, on the 9th, that that has already been done by the passage of the act of 1818. This appears to have been regarded as entirely satisfactory.

The next note is dated the 17th March, 1819. Although stating that there were persons in the United States "interested in this iniquitous pursuit of plundering the lawful property of an inoffensive friendly nation," in which statement the Minister undoubtedly supposed that he was correct, he says that he has "abstained from written applications about the new individual offenses," and he makes no particular complaint, furnishes no evidence, and indicates no suspicions. It appears to be the object of the note to induce the Government of the United States to withdraw its recognition of the Artigan flag. "If this," he says, "is once declared illegal, and the prizes made under it acts of piracy, all occasions of bitterness and mistrust are done away." "I can, in the capacity of Minister of my Sovereign, certify you solemnly, and officially too, if necessary, that Artigas and his followers have been *expelled far from the countries that could afford them the least means and power of navigating, and consequently have no right to fight by sea.* What becomes, then, of the rights of privateers under this flag?" When the Tribunal come to consider the case of the Shenandoah at Melbourne they will find this language, which was referred to with approbation, and assumed by Earl Russell,[1] to be exactly in point in disposing of the claims growing out of the acts of that vessel.

On the 22d of April the Secretary of State acknowledges the note of December 11, 1818, and says that he is informed the commander of the Irresistible has returned to Baltimore, and will be prosecuted for a violation of neutrality, and asks the Minister to furnish proof for the trial.

On the 23d of November, 1819, the Minister again complained. He says: "One city alone on this coast has armed twenty-six ships, which prey on our vitals, and a week ago three armed ships of this nature were in that port waiting for a favorable occasion of sailing for a cruise." But he furnishes no facts, and he gives neither proof nor fact indicating the city or the district which he suspected, and nothing to afford the Government any light for inquiry or investigation. On the contrary, he says: "*I shall not tire you with the numerous instances of these facts;*" and he adds, as if attaching little or no real importance to the matter: "Relying confidently on the successful efforts of this Government, *I choose this moment to pay a visit to Brazil.*"

On the 4th of June, 1820, the Minister, not yet having departed, informs the Secretary of State that he desires to

---

[1] Vol. III, page 556.

offer his "thanks for the law that prohibits the entrance of privateers in the most important ports of the Union;" that he "acknowledges the salutary influence of the Executive in obtaining these ameliorations;" and that he is "fully persuaded of the sincere wishes of this Government to put a stop to practices so contrary to friendly intercourse."

On the 8th of June, 1820, he gives information of a formidable privateer, which he says is to be fitted out at Baltimore, and adds that he "has not the least doubt that the supreme Executive has both the power and the will of putting a stop to this hostile armament;" to which the Secretary of State, on the 20th July, replies that "such measures have been and will continue to be taken, under direction of the President, as are within the competency of the Executive, and may serve to maintain inviolate the laws of the United States applicable to the case."

On the 16th of July the Minister "laid before this Government the names and value of nineteen Portuguese ships and their cargoes, taken by private armed ships fitted in the ports of the Union by citizens of these States;" but he did not accompany this allegation with proof of such fitting, or with anything tending in the remotest degree to fix a liability on the United States, or to afford them the means of an independent examination. He also proposed a joint commission for the settlement of these matters, which the Secretary of State, on the 30th September, 1820, declined, saying that "the Government of the United States has neither countenanced nor permitted any violation of neutrality by their citizens. They have, by various and successive acts of legislation, manifested their constant earnestness to fulfill their duties toward all parties to the war. They have repressed every intended violation of them which has been brought before their courts and substantiated by testimony." Other claims were transmitted to the United States Government on the 4th December, 1820, unaccompanied, as had been the invariable case before, by anything tending to show a liability in the United States to make compensation.

The case appears to have been closed by an offer from Portugal, on the 1st of April, 1822, to grant to the United

States exceptional commercial advantages if the United States would recognize the claims, and the refusal of the United States, on the 30th of April, to do so.

It is worthy of remark that in Earl Russell's elaborate statement of this correspondence, in his note of the 30th of August, 1865, he omits, with a completeness which argues design, certain parts of it which showed that the United States were animated with a constant desire to perform their international duties. Thus, nothing is said of the Portuguese note of February 4, 1819, asking that the neutrality act of 1817 may be continued in force, and the American reply, stating that it had been so continued. Nothing is said of the American note of the 22d of April, 1818, stating that the commander of the Irresistible, the vessel referred to in the Portuguese note of December 11, 1818, had returned to Baltimore and would be prosecuted. The American note of the 20th of July, 1820, is also omitted, in which, in answer to the Portuguese note of the 8th of June, 1820, it is stated that measures have been, and will continue to be, taken to maintain inviolate the laws of the United States.

The Tribunal of Arbitration cannot fail to observe that these suppressed notes had an important bearing in forming a judgment upon the correctness of the conduct of the Government of the United States in this case—a case which has received the official approval of Earl Russell, as Her Majesty's Principal Secretary of State for Foreign Affairs. From a candid review of the whole correspondence, it appears that the United States admitted or asserted the following propositions, to which Her Majesty's Government, through Earl Russell, has given its assent:

Principles recognized in that correspondence. 1. That a neutral government is bound to use all the means in its power to prevent the equipping, fitting out, or arming, within its jurisdiction, of vessels intended to cruise against a Power with which it is at peace.

2. If the means within its power are, in the opinion of either belligerent, inadequate for the purpose, it is bound to receive suggestions of changes from the belligerent, and if it be true that the means are inadequate, it should so amend

its laws, either in accordance with such suggestions or otherwise, as to put new and more effective means in the hands of its Executive.

3. That it is bound to institute proceedings under its laws against all vessels as to which reasonable grounds for suspicion are made to appear, even if the grounds for suspicion fall short of legal proof.

The Government of Portugal, during the whole correspondence, offered no evidence to prove that captures had been made by armed vessels illegally fitted out, equipped, or armed in the United States, nor even statements of facts tending to lead to the discovery of such evidence, which were not at once used for the purpose of detaining such vessels, or of punishing the guilty parties; nor did they contest by proof the allegation of Mr. John Quincy Adams that the Government of the United States had done everything in its power to perform its duties as a neutral, and to execute its laws. The correspondence shows conclusively that in every case in which the United States was furnished either with positive legal proof, or with such an intimation of the facts as would enable them to pursue the investigation themselves, they acted with the vigor which was required of them by International Law, and which Great Britain failed to show in similar cases during the rebellion.

The claims lay buried until they were exhumed by Mr. Figaniere, in 1850, as an offset to the "General Armstrong" case; and would have been forgotten if Earl Russell had not rescued them from oblivion.

Rules in the Treaty of Washington. The latest official act of Her Majesty's Government, indicating the views of Great Britain as to the duties of a neutral in time of war, is to be found in the Rules contained in Article VI of the Treaty of Washington. It is true that it was thought essential by the British negotiators to insert in that instrument a declaration on the part of Her Majesty's Government that they could not consent to those Rules as a statement of principles of International Law which were in force at the time when the claims now under discussion arose. But the United States were then, and are still, of the opinion, and they confidently think that the Tribunal of Arbitration will agree with them, not only that those rules were then in force, but that there were also other rules of International Law then in force, not inconsistent with them, defining, with still greater strictness, the duties of a neutral in time of war.

Article VI of the Treaty of Washington contains the following rules:

"A neutral government is bound—

"First, to use due diligence to prevent the fitting out, arming, or equipping, within its jurisdiction, of any vessel which it has reasonable ground to believe is intended to cruise or to carry on war against a Power with which it is at peace; and also to use like diligence to prevent the departure from its jurisdiction of any vessel intended to cruise or carry on war as above, such vessel having been specially adapted, in whole or in part, within such jurisdiction, to warlike use.

"Secondly, not to permit or suffer either belligerent to make use of its ports or waters as the base of naval operations against the other, or for the purpose of the renewal or augmentation of military supplies or arms, or the recruitment of men.

"Thirdly, to exercise due diligence in its own ports and waters, and, as to all persons within its jurisdiction, to prevent any violation of the foregoing obligations and duties."

Article VII contains the following provision as to compensation: "In case the Tribunal finds that Great Britain has failed to fulfill any duty or duties as aforesaid, it may, if it think proper, proceed to award a sum in gross, to be paid by Great Britain to the United States, for all the claims referred to it;" and Article X provides that, "in case the Tribunal find that Great Britain has failed to fulfill any duty or duties as aforesaid, and does not award a sum in gross, the High Contracting Parties agree that a Board of Assessors shall be appointed to ascertain and determine what claims are valid and what amount or amounts shall be paid by Great Britain to the United States on account of the liability arising from such failure."

The obligation to prevent vessels of war from being fitted out, armed, or equipped, within the jurisdiction of a neutral, when such vessels are intended to cruise or to carry on war against a Power with which the neutral is at peace, is recognized almost in the identical terms in which it was stated in the original United States act of 1794, which Mr. Canning said was passed at the request of the British Government, and in the British act of 1819, passed to aid Great Britain in the performance of its duties as a neutral.

What is "due diligence." The Rules impose upon the neutral the obligation to use *due diligence* to prevent such fitting out, arming, or equipping. These words are not regarded by the United States as changing in any respect the obligations of a neutral regarding the matters referred to in the Rules, as those obligations were imposed by the principles of International Law existing before the conclusion of the Treaty.

The phrases "negligence" and "diligence", though opposite, are correlative expressions: the presence of the one implies the absence of the other. It happens that in the ordinary course of judicial proceedings the term "negligence" is the one most frequently employed, and is therefore the one most often commented on and explained by writers on law. "Negligence," which is only the absence of the diligence which the nature and merits of any particular subject and the exigencies of any particular case demand as "due" from the nature of its inherent circumstances, implies blamable fault, called in the Roman law *culpa*, with responsibility for consequences. The idea of obligation, either legal or moral, and of responsibility for its non-performance, is found in all the forms and applications of the question, either of diligence or of negligence.

Legal writers in England, in America, and on the Continent of Europe, have treated this matter in reference to numerous subjects of controversy, public and private. It has come under the consideration of courts in questions relating to the custody of property, to the performance of contracts, to the transportation of persons or property, to the collision of ships and railway-trains, to the discharge of private trusts, to the execution of public duties, and in many other ways.

In most of these cases, with the Roman, Continental, and Scottish jurists, and to a certain extent with English and American courts, the question has generally been put as one of negligence or *culpa*, rather than as an absence of diligence. But, nevertheless, the phrase "due diligence," *exacta diligentia*, is of received use in the civil law.[1]

The extent of the diligence required to escape responsibility is, by all authorities, gauged by the character and magnitude of the matter which it may affect, by the relative condition of the parties, by the ability of the party incurring the liability to exercise the diligence required by the exigencies of the case, and by the extent of the injury which may follow negligence.

One of the earliest and one of the best of the English expositors of the Roman law is Ayliffe, (New Pandects of Roman Civil Law as anciently established in that Empire and practiced in most European Nations, London, 1734.) He says: "A fault is blamable through want of taking proper care; and it obliges the person who does the injury, because by an application of due diligence it might have been foreseen and prevented."[2]

---

[1] Vinnius, Comment. ad Inst., lib. 3, tit. 15.

[2] Ayliffe, in his Pandects, (D. 2, tit. 13, pp. 108, 109, 110,) has given an elaborate view of the different sorts of fault or negligence, and fraud and deceit. The passage is long, but as it contains a very ample view of the opinions of the Civilians it may be useful to place a part of it in a note.

"The word fault, in Latin called *culpa*, is a general term; and according to the definition of it, it denotes an offense or injury done unto another by imprudence, which might otherwise be avoided by human care. For a fault, says Donatus, has a respect unto him who hurts another not knowingly nor willingly. Here we use the word offense or injury by way of a genus, which comprehends deceit, malice, and all other misdemeanors, as well as a fault; for deceit and malice are plainly intended for the injury of another, but a fault is not so designed. And therefore we have added the word imprudence in this definition, to point out and distinguish a fault from deceit, malice, and an evil purpose of mind, which accompanies all trespasses and misdemeanors. A fault arises from simplicity, a dullness of mind, and a barrenness of thought, which is

Mr. Justice Story has elaborately discussed the meaning of these terms, and the extent of diligence required to avoid responsibility. He says, as the result of a comparative ex-

always attended with imprudence; but deceit, called *dolus*, has its rise from a malicious purpose of mind, which acts in contempt of all honesty and prudence, with a full intent of doing mischief, or an injury. And by these last words in the definition, namely, which might otherwise be avoided by human care, we distinguish a fault from a fortuitous case. For a fault is blamable through want of taking proper care; and it throws an obligation upon the person that does the injury, because by an application of due diligence it might have been foreseen and prevented. But fortuitous cases often cannot be foreseen, or (at least) prevented by the providence of man; as death, fires, great floods, shipwrecks, tumults, piracies &c. These things are superior to the prudence of any man, and rather happen by fate, therefore are not blamable. But if fraud or some previous fault be the occasion of these nocuments, they are not then deemed to be fortuitous cases. A fault is a deviation from that which is good; and, according to Bartolus, erring from the ordinance and disposition of a law. It is sometimes difficult to judge what is the difference betwixt a fault and a *dolus*, since these words very often stand for one and the same thing. There is no one in this life lives without a fault; but he that would speak distinctly and properly, must impute a *dolus* to some wickedness or knavery, and a fault to imprudence. The first consists chiefly in acting, and the other in not acting or doing something which a man ought to do. According to Bartolus, a fault is divided into five species, *viz. culpa latissima, latior, lata, levis,* and *levissima*. The first he makes to be equal to manifest deceit, and the second to be equivalent unto presumptive malice or deceit. The first and second of these distinctions (he says) approach unto fraud, and are sometimes called by the name of fraud. But a *lata culpa*, which is occasioned by gross sloth, rashness, improvidence, and want of advice, is never compared unto deceit or malice. For he that understands not that which all other men know and understand may be styled (says Bartolus) a supine and unthinking man, but not a malicious and deceitful person. But, I think, none of those distinctions of his have any foundation in law; for such things as admit of any degree of comparison, in respect of being more or less so, do not admit of any specific difference; as *majus et minus diversas species non constituunt.* For that which the law says *de latiore culpâ* sometimes is to be understood *de lata culpâ,* after the manner

amination of the authorities of different nations, "What is usually done by prudent men in a particular country in respect to things of a like nature, whether it be more or

---

that a word of the comparative degree is sometimes put for a word of the positive, as in Virgil: *Tristior et lacrymis oculos suffusa nitentes.* Wherefore I shall here distinguish a fault into two species only, to wit, into *lata* and *levis*, though others mention a *culpa levissima* too. The first denotes a negligence extremely blamable; that is to say, such a negligence as is not tempered with any kind of diligence. The other imports such a kind of negligence, whereby a person does not employ that care in men's affairs which other men are wont to do, though he be not more diligent in his own business. But as often as the word *culpa* is simply used in the law, it is taken for that which we style *culpa levis*, a light fault, because words are ever understood in the more favorable sense. A *culpa levissima*, or simple negligence, is that which proceeds from an unaffected ignorance and unskilfulness, (say they,) and it is like unto such a fault, which we easily excuse, either on the account of age, sex, rusticity, &c. Or, to set the matter in a clearer light, a *lata culpa* is a diligence in a man's own affairs, and a negligence in the concerns of other men. And a *levis culpa* is, when a man employs the same care or diligence in other men's affairs as he does in his own, but yet does not use all care and fidelity which more diligent and circumspect men are wont to make use of; and this may be called an accustomed negligence as well in a man's own affairs as in the business of other men. A *lata culpa*, I mean a great fault, is equivalent or next unto deceit or malice. And it may be said to be next unto deceit or malice two ways, namely, either because it contains in it a presumptive deceit, as when a man does not use the same diligence in another's concerns as in his own; or else because the fault is so gross and inexcusable, that, though fraud be not presumed, yet it differs but little from it. As when a person becomes negligent in favor of a friend; for though favor, or too great a facility of temper, excuses a man from malicious or knavish purpose, yet it is next of kin thereunto. And it is a rule laid down in law, that when the law commands any act of deceit to be made good, it is also always understood of a *lata culpa*, or a gross fault. Wherefore, since a great fault is equivalent or next unto deceit, it follows, that in every disposition of law where it is said that an intent or *dolus* ought only to be repaired, it is to be understood also of a *lata culpa*; which is true, I think, unless it be in the Cornelian law de Sicariis. For he

less, in point of diligence, than what is exacted in another country, becomes in fact the general measure of diligence."[1]

Following the example of Sir William Jones, and other writers on the civil law, Mr. Justice Story favors the idea that there may be three degrees of diligence, and three degrees of negligence, which are capable of being accurately defined and applied to the various circumstances of life. But while asserting, as the authorities supported him in doing, that not only the Roman law, but the jurists of Continental Europe and of Scotland all recognize this division, he candidly concedes the difficulty of applying such a fictitious system, and he is obliged to admit the general and only sound principle, that "diligence is usually proportioned to the degree of danger of loss, and that danger is, in different states of society, compounded of very different elements."[2]

The highest court of the United States has doubted the

---

who commits the crime of murder *ex latâ culpâ*, shall be punished according to the severity of that law, but in a more gentle manner; and thus herein a *lata culpa* is distinguished from malice, or an evil design, called *dolus malus*; for a murderer is liable on the score of his wicked purpose, and not on the account of gross negligence. Some say, that generally speaking, whenever the law or an action is touching a pecuniary penalty, and the law expressly mentions a *dolus*, a *lata culpa* is insufficient, and is excluded."

Numerous authorities to the same effect might be cited; but it will suffice at this stage to refer to such as are most familiar to jurists in Great Britain and the United States.

Wood's Institutes, p. 106.
Hallifax's Civil Law, p. 78.
Bell's Commentaries, § 232 et seq.
Browne's Civil and Admiralty Law, vol. 1, p. 354.
Erskine's Institutes, bk. 3, tit. 1.
Bowyer's Civil Law, p. 174.
Mackenzie's Roman Law, p. 186.
Domat's Civil Law by Strahan, vol. 1, p. 317.
Heineccius, Elementa Juris Civilis, lib. 3, tit. 14, Opera, tom. V.

[1] Story on Bailments, § 14.
[2] Story on Bailments, § 14.

philosophy of grading the degrees of diligence and negligence into fixed classes.¹

The Scottish courts have laid down a rule which is perhaps more philosophical,—that where an injury has been suffered through the act or omission of another, it must be shown, in order to avoid liability, that the accident was caused without any fault of the party doing or suffering the act or omission, and through some latent cause, which could not be discerned, obviated, controlled, or averted.²

In the discussion upon the Treaty of Washington in the House of Lords, Lord Granville, the Minister for Foreign Affairs, is represented as saying: "The obligation to use due diligence implies that the Government will do all in its power to prevent certain things, and to detain vessels which it has reasonable ground for believing are designed for warlike purposes."³ Lord Cairns, in the same debate, is represented as saying: "The point turns upon the words 'due diligence.' Now, the moment you introduce those words you give rise to another question, for which I do not find any solution in this rule. What is the standard by which you can measure due diligence? Due diligence by itself means nothing. What is due diligence with one man, with one Power, is not due diligence with another man, with a greater Power." Sir Roundell Palmer, in a subsequent debate in the House of Commons, said that he supposed that due diligence "meant that a neutral should use, within a reasonable sense, all the means legitimately in its power."

It is needless to say that the United States do not agree in these official definitions by Lord Granville and Sir Roundell Palmer, in the sense in which they are probably made. The definition to which Lord Cairns has given the

---

¹ Steamboat New World *vs.* King, 17 Howard Reports page 475. See also the authorities there cited.
² Hay on Liabilities, ch. 8.
³ London Times, June 13, 1871.
⁴ A speech delivered in the House of Commons, on Friday, August 4, 1871, by Sir Roundell Palmer, M. P. for Richmond. London and New York, Macmillan & Co., 1871—page 28.

weight of his authority appears to be nearer to the opinions as to these words, entertained by the United States.

The United States understand that the diligence which is called for by the Rules of the Treaty of Washington is a *due* diligence; that is, a diligence proportioned to the magnitude of the subject and to the dignity and strength of the Power which is to exercise it:—a diligence which shall, by the use of active vigilance, and of all the other means in the power of the neutral, through all stages of the transaction, prevent its soil from being violated;—a diligence that shall in like manner deter designing men from committing acts of war upon the soil of the neutral against its will, and thus possibly dragging it into a war which it would avoid:—a diligence which prompts the neutral to the most energetic measures to discover any purpose of doing the acts forbidden by its good faith as a neutral, and imposes upon it the obligation, when it receives the knowledge of an intention to commit such acts, to use all the means in its power to prevent it.

No diligence short of this would be "due;" that is, *commensurate with the emergency, or with the magnitude of the results of negligence.* Understanding the words in this sense, the United States find them identical with the measure of duty which Great Britain had previously admitted.

Fitting out, arming, or equipping, each an offense. It wil also be observed that fitting out, or arming, or equipping, each constitutes in itself a complete offense. Therefore a vessel which is fitted out within the neutral's jurisdiction, with intent to cruise against one of the belligerents, although not equipped or armed therein, (and *vice versa*,) commits the offense against International Law, provided the neutral government had reasonable ground to believe that she was intended to cruise or carry on war against such belligerent, and did not use due diligence to prevent it.

The second clause of the first Rule. The neutral is required by the second clause of the first Rule of the Treaty to prevent the departure from its jurisdiction of any vessel intended so to cruise or carry on war, such vessel having been *specially adapted, in whole or in part, within such jurisdiction, to warlike use.*

Reasons for change of language. The Tribunal of Arbitration probably will not have failed to observe that a new term is employed here. In the first clause of the first Rule the obligation of the neutral is limited to the prevention of the "fitting out, arming, and equipping" the vessel. In the second clause, the language is much broader: a vessel which has been "specially adapted, in whole or in part, to warlike use," may not be permitted to depart. The reasons for this change may probably be found in the different interpretations which have been put by the Executive and Judicial Departments of the two Governments upon the words "fitting out" and "equipping," and in the desire of the negotiators of the Treaty to avoid the use of any words that could be deemed equivocal. The United States will endeavor to explain to the Tribunal what these differences of interpretation were.

The eighth section of the United States law of 1818 empowers the President to take possession of and detain vessels which have been "*fitted out and armed*" contrary to the provisions of the act. In the year 1869, while there was a state of recognized war between Spain and Peru (although there had been no active hostilities for several years), the Spanish Government made contracts for the construction of thirty steam gun-boats in the port of New York. After some of these boats were launched, but while most of them were on the stocks, and before any had received machinery or had been armed, the Peruvian Minister, on behalf of his Government, represented to the Government of the United States that this was being done in violation of the neutrality of the United States. The President, proceeding under the section of the statute above referred to, took possession of the vessels, and they remained in the custody of the naval forces of the United States until they were released, with the consent of the Peruvian Minister at Washington. This was done under the assumption that the construction of a vessel in neutral territory during time of war, which there is reasonable ground to believe may be used to carry on war against a power with which the neutral is at peace, is an act which ought to be prevented; and that the constructing or building such a vessel was included in the offense of fitting it out. The same interpretation (in substance) has been given to this language by the judicial authorities of the United States.[1] The British tribunals have given a different opinion upon the meaning of these words. In the case of the Alexandra,[2] against which proceedings were had in London, in 1863, for an alleged violation of the provisions of the act of 1819, it was held that the proof of the construction of a vessel for the purpose of hostile use against the United States did not establish such an equipment, or fitting out, or furnishing, as would bring the vessel within the terms of the Foreign Enlistment Act[3] and enable the Government to hold it by proceedings under that statute. When the Joint High Commissioners met at Washington, and had to consider what words they would use in the Treaty, they found the Executive of the United States and the Judiciary of Great Britain differing as to the meaning of these important words.[4] The Tribunal of Arbitration may therefore reasonably presume that the framers of that Treaty, after the experience of the American insurrection, sought for language which would, beyond any question, indicate the duty of the neutral to prevent the departure from its ports, of any vessel that had been specially adapted for the hostile use of a belligerent, *whether that adaptation*

---

[1] United States *vs.* Quincy, 6 Peters's Reports, 445.

[2] Vol. V, pages 3—470.

[3] This opinion was on the Act of 1819. The Act of 1870 provides that "equipping shall include the furnishing a ship with any tackle, apparel, furniture, provisions, arms, munitions, or stores, or any other thing which is used in or about a ship for the purpose of fitting or adapting her for the sea or for naval service."

[4] "It is perfectly true that Lord Chief Baron Pollock and Baron Bramwell, as well as other great legal authorities, thought that such words as these did not convey the true meaning of our then Foreign Enlistment Act; which, in their opinion, was intended to apply only to those vessels which might be armed within our jurisdiction, either completely or at least so far as to leave our waters in a condition immediately to commence hostilities."—Sir R. Palmer's Speech, August 4, 1871, page 32.

began when the keel was laid to a vessel intended for such hostile use, or whether it was made in later stages of construction, or in fitting out, or in furnishing, or in equipping, or in arming, or in any other way.

The undoubted duty of the neutral to *detain* such a vessel, although it had not been formulated by Great Britain in any of the acts prior to 1861 which have been passed in review, is understood to have been included in the obligation to prevent her construction. The United States regard this duty as one that existed by the law of nations prior to the Treaty of Washington; but as that Treaty provides that, for the purpose of the present discussion, the rule is to be taken as having the force of public law during the Southern Rebellion, it is needless to discuss that point.

Continuing force of this rule. The United States invite the particular attention of the Tribunal to the continuing character of the second clause of this rule. The violation of the first clause takes place once for all when the offending vessel is fitted out, armed, or equipped within the jurisdiction of the neutral; but the offense under the second clause may be committed as often as a vessel, which has at any time been specially adapted, in whole or in part, to warlike use, within the jurisdiction of the neutral, enters and departs unmolested from one of its ports. Every time that the Alabama, or the Georgia, or the Florida, or the Shenandoah came within British jurisdiction, and was suffered to depart, there was a renewed offense against the sovereignty of Great Britain, and a renewed liability to the United States.

Duty to detain offending vessels admitted by Great Britain. The British Government, certainly once, if not oftener, during the rebellion, admitted its duty to detain these cruisers. Mr. Cobden stated it forcibly in a speech in the House of Commons.[1] "The Government admit, through their legal adviser, that they have the power, if they choose to exercise it, to prevent these vessels from entering our harbors; but the honorable and learned gentleman doubts the expediency of exercising it, and his reason is that he thinks we have not clear proof

---

[1] Vol. V, page 590.

of guilt. This brings me to a striking piece of inconsistency on the part of the honorable and learned gentleman. He begins with administering a solemn exhortation, and something like a solemn reproof to English ship-builders, for infringing our neutrality laws and disregarding the Queen's Proclamation by building these ships. Well, but if they are violating our neutrality and disregarding the Queen's Proclamation, it must have been because they built these vessels for a belligerent to be employed against some Power with which we are at peace. The honorable and learned gentleman assumes that these individuals are guilty of these acts. He knows they have been guilty of these acts; he knows that these three vessels in particular, and the *Alabama* more especially, have been built for the Confederate Government, and employed solely for that Government, and yet he doubts the expediency of stopping them from entering our ports. He speaks as though we were asking that he should send out ships of war to order away these vessels without trial. He says there must be legal proof; but it does not require legal proof to warrant you in telling a Government, 'You have got these vessels clandestinely; you got them by the infringement of our neutrality code, or, at least we suspect you upon fair grounds of doing so; and unless you prove that they came legitimately into your hands we must refuse them the hospitality of our ports.' Why, how do you act in private life? You hear charges and reports compromising the honor of your acquaintance or friend. You may have a moral conviction in your mind that that individual's honor is compromised, but you may not have legal proof of it, and still you may be quite justified in saying to him, "Until you clear up these charges, which on the face of them criminate you, I must refuse you the hospitality of my house.' I hold that you have the right to say the same thing in regard to these cruisers. But what was the course of the Government in the case of the Alabama? *They told Mr. Adams, the American Minister, that they should give orders to stop the Alabama, either at Queenstown or Nassau. Therefore the principle was recognized in the case of that vessel that you had a right to stop her when she reached your jurisdiction.* I say, therefore, in the same way, prevent their entering your harbors until they give an account of themselves, to show how they became possessed of that vessel. This has a most important bearing, and one so apparent that it must be plain to the apprehensions of every honorable gentleman who hears it."

<small>Also recognized by France.</small> The French Government, during the insurrection, practically asserted the same power in the neutral to protect its violated sovereignty. The British Government in 1864 sold a screw gun-boat to persons who proved to be agents of the insurgents. This was done at a time when it was a matter of public notoriety that those agents were in England making great efforts to fit out a navy. The purchasers took the vessel to Calais to complete the equipment. On the way from the Thames to Calais the name of the vessel was changed to the "Rappahannock," the insurgent flag was hoisted, an insurgent officer, holding an insurgent commission, took the command, and the crew were mustered into the service of the insurgents. On arrival at Calais, attempts were made to complete the equipment. The French Government stopped this by placing a man-of-war across the bows, and holding the vessel as a prisoner, and the Rappahannock was thus prevented from destroying vessels and commerce, sailing under the flag of a nation with which France was at peace.

<small>The second Rule of the Treaty.</small> The second Rule provides that a neutral government is bound not to permit or suffer either belligerent to make use of its ports or waters as the base of naval operations against the other, or for the purpose of the renewal or augmentation of military supplies or arms, or the recruitment of men.

A question has been raised whether this rule is understood to apply to the sale of military supplies or arms in the ordinary course of commerce. The United States do not understand that it is intended to apply to such a traffic. They understand it to apply to the use of a neutral port by a belligerent for the *renewal* or *augmentation* of such military supplies or arms for the *naval operations* referred to in the rule. Taken in this sense, the United States maintain that the same obligations are to be found, (expressed in other words,) first, in the Foreign Enlistment Act of 1819; and, secondly, in the instructions to the naval forces of Great Britain during the rebellion.

The Tribunal of Arbitration will not fail to observe the breadth of this rule.

The ports or waters of the neutral are not to be made the base of naval operations by a belligerent. Vessels of war may come and go under such rules and regulations as the neutral may prescribe; food and the ordinary stores and supplies of a ship not of a warlike character may be furnished without question, in quantities necessary for immediate wants; the moderate hospitalities which do not infringe upon impartiality may be extended; but no act shall be done to make the neutral port a base of naval operations. Ammunition and military stores for cruisers cannot be obtained there; coal cannot be stored there for successive supplies to the same vessel, nor can it be furnished or obtained in such supplies; prizes cannot be brought there for condemnation. The repairs that humanity demand can be given, but no repairs should add to the strength or efficiency of a vessel, beyond what is absolutely necessary to gain the nearest of its own ports.

In the same sense are to be taken the clauses relating to the renewal or augmentation of military supplies or arms and the recruitment of men. As the vessel enters the port, so is she to leave it, without addition to her effective power of doing injury to the other belligerent. If her magazine is supplied with powder, shot, or shells; if new guns are added to her armament; if pistols or muskets or cutlasses, or other implements of destruction, are put on board; if men are recruited; even if, in these days when steam is a power, an excessive supply of coal is put into her bunkers, the neutral will have failed in the performance of its duty.

The third Rule of the Treaty. The third Rule binds the neutral to exercise the same measure of diligence as required by the first Rule, in order to prevent, in its own ports and waters, and as to all persons within its jurisdiction, any violation of the obligations and duties prescribed by the first and second Rules. The same wakefulness and watchfulness, proportioned to the exegencies of the case and the magnitude of the interests involved, that was required by the first Rule, is likewise required in the performance of the duties prescribed by the second Rule, without which the neutral will have failed in the performance of his duty.

Duty to make compensation for injuries. The express recognition in the Treaty of an obligation (in case the Tribunal finds that Great Britain has failed to fulfill any of her duties in these respects) to pay to the United States the amount or amounts that may be found due, "*on account of the liability arising from such failure,*" makes it unnecessary, in this connection, to do more than to refer to what has already been said on that subject.

Foregoing views in harmony with opinions of European publicists. The doctrines of International Law which have thus been deduced from the practice of Great Britain are in harmony with the views of the best publicists. The discussions between the two Governments growing out of the acts herein complained of, and unfortunately made necessary by the unwillingness of Great Britain to apply to the United States the same measure of justice which was applied to Spain in 1819, to Portugal in 1827, and which was received by Great Britain from the United States in 1793, have evoked the comments of many writers in England, in America, and on the continent of Europe. For obvious reasons the opinions of the English or American writers favorable to their respective countries —(as for instance Professor Bernard in Great Britain or President Woolsey in America)—will not be regarded.

On the 20th of May, 1865,[1] Mr. Adams had occasion to quote to Lord Russell the opinion of Hautefeuille: "What the obligation of Her Majesty's Government really was, in this instance," he said, "is so clearly laid down by a distinguished writer, notoriously disposed never to exaggerate the duties nor to undervalue the privileges of neutrals, that I will ask the liberty to lay before you his very words: 'Le fait de construire un bâtiment de guerre pour le compte

---

[1] Vol. III, page 538.

d'un belligérant, ou de l'armer dans les états neutres, est une violation du territoire. Toutes les prises faites par un bâtiment de cette nature sont illégitimes, en quelque lieu qu'elles ont été faites. Le souverain offensé a le droit de s'en emparer, même de force, si elles sont amenées dans ses ports, et d'en réclamer la restitution lorsqu'elles sont, comme cela arrive en général, conduites dans les ports hors de sa juridiction. Il peut également réclamer le désarmement du bâtiment illégalement armé sur son territoire, et même le détenir, s'il entre dans quelque lieu soumis à sa souveraineté jusqu'à ce qu'il ait été désarmé.'"[1]

Bluntschli. The distinguished Dr. Bluntschli, professor at the University of Heidelberg, in his pamphlet, entitled "Opinion impartiale sur la question de l'Alabama et sur la manière de la résoudre," reprinted at Berlin, in 1870, from the *Revue de Droit International*, says as follows:

"La violation des devoirs d'un état ami, dont l'Angleterre se rendit coupable lors de l'équipement de l'Alabama, fut la circonstance la plus éclatante, mais non la seule dans laquelle se révélèrent les dispositions hostiles du gouvernement anglais. Il y eut encore d'autres croiseurs sudistes du même genre. Les nombreux coureurs de blocus qui transportaient en même temps de la contrebande de guerre, avaient tous également leur origine et leurs propriétaires en Angleterre. Partout où les troupes de l'union finirent par l'emporter et s'emparèrent des places ennemies, elles trouvèrent des armes anglaises et des canons anglais.

"Tous les faits ainsi allégués n'ont pas la même importance. Mais plusieurs d'entre eux, si tant est qu'il faille les tenir pour avoués ou prouvés,—ce dont nous n'avons pas à juger ici,—doivent certainement être considérés comme constituant une infraction aux devoirs d'un état neutre.

"L'état neutre qui veut garantir sa neutralité, doit s'abstenir d'aider aucune des parties belligérantes dans ses opérations de guerre. Il ne peut prêter son territoire pour permettre

---

[1] Hautefeuille. Des droits et des devoirs des nations neutres, Paris, 1849,) tome II, pages 79–80.

à l'une des parties d'organiser en lieu sûr des entreprises militaires. Il est obligé de veiller fidèlement à ce que des particuliers n'arment point sur son territoire des vaisseaux de guerre, destinés à être livrés à une des parties belligérantes. (BLUNTSCHLI, *Modernes Völkerrecht*, § 768.)

"Ce devoir est proclamé par la science, et il dérive tant de l'idée de neutralité que des égards auxquels tout état est nécessairement tenu envers les autres états, avec lesquels il vit en paix et amitié.

"La neutralité est la *non-participation* à la guerre. Lorsque l'état neutre soutient un des belligérants, il prend part à la guerre en faveur de celui qu'il soutient, et dès lors *il cesse d'être neutre*. L'adversaire est autorisé à voir dans cette participation un acte d'hostilité: Et cela n'est pas seulement vrai quand l'état neutre livre lui-même des troupes ou des vaisseaux de guerre, mais aussi lors qu'il prête à un des belligérants un appui médiat en permettant, *tandis qu'il pourrait l'empêcher*, que, de son territoire neutre, on envoie des troupes ou des navires de guerre.

"Partout où le droit de neutralité étend le cercle de son application, il restreint les limites de la guerre et de ses désastreuses conséquences, et il garantit les bienfaits de la paix. Les devoirs de l'état *neutre* envers les *belligérants* sont en substance *les mêmes* que ceux de l'état *ami*, *en temps de paix*, vis-à-vis des autres états. Aucun état ne peut non plus, en *temps de paix*, permettre que l'on organise sur son territoire des aggressions contre un état ami. Tous sont obligés de veiller à ce que leur sol ne devienne pas le point de départ d'entreprises militaires, dirigées contre des états avec lesquels ils sont en paix.

"Ces devoirs internationaux universels sont aussi consacrés, dans le droit public interne, par les législations anglaise et américaine. La loi anglaise du 3 juillet 1819 contient à ce sujet (art. 7) la disposition suivante:

"'*And be it further enacted*, That if any person within any part of the United Kingdom, or in any part of His Majesty's Dominions beyond the seas, shall, without the leave and license of His Majesty for that purpose first had and obtained as aforesaid, equip, furnish, fit out, or arm, or attempt or endeavor to equip, furnish, fit out, or arm, or procure to be equipped, furnished, fitted out, or armed, or shall knowingly aid, assist, or be concerned in the equipping, furnishing, fitting out, or arming of any ship or vessel, with intent or in order that such ship or vessel shall be employed in the service of any foreign prince, state, or potentate, or of any foreign colony, province, or part of province, or people, as a transport or store-ship, or with intent to cruise or commit hostilities against any prince, state, or potentate, or against the persons exercising, or assuming to exercise, the powers of government in any colony, province, or part of any province or country, or against the inhabitants of any foreign colony, province, or part of any province or country with whom His Majesty shall not then be at war . . .'

"Cette loi défend incontestablement tout appui prêté en cas de guerre, peu importe que les parties belligérantes soient des états étrangers reconnus, ou des usurpateurs du pouvoir, ou des colonies ou des provinces révoltées. Donc le gouvernement anglais, en permettant intentionnellement ou par une négligence évidente,—alors qu'il aurait pu et dû l'empêcher,—l'équipement de l'Alabama, a méconnu du même coup un devoir international à l'égard de l'union américaine et les prescriptions d'une loi nationale. Par ces motifs il est aussi, d'après les règles du droit des gens, responsable envers l'état lésé.

"Il est notoire que la loi anglaise est une imitation de la loi américaine de 1818, sur la neutralité, laquelle ne faisait elle-même que reviser et rétablir la loi antérieure de 1794. C'est même précisément la question de l'équipement de corsaires sur un territoire neutre, au profit d'une partie belligérante, qui donna la première impulsion à cette législation. En 1793 l'Angleterre, qui était à cette époque en guerre avec la France, se plaignit de ce qu'à New-York on équipât des corsaires français, pour nuire au commerce maritime anglais. Le Président Washington sévit avec une grande énergie contre cette violation de la neutralité et, malgré la sympathie de la population américaine pour les Français, malgré les démarches de l'ambassadeur français Genet, il fit saisir les corsaires. Il empêcha de la même manière la construction, en Géorgie, d'un corsaire destiné à entraver la navigation française. Des deux côtés, il observa consciencieusement et raisonnablement les devoirs d'un état neutre, et détermina ensuite le Congrès à régler ces devoirs par voie législative.¹

"Le ministre libéral Canning invoqua dans le Parlement anglais, en 1823, cette honorable attitude de Washington, pour défendre de son côté la loi anglaise sur la neutralité contre les attaques d'hommes politiques passionés ou de particuliers égoïstes.²

"L'opinion du monde savant et du monde politique éclairé est presque unanime à reconnaître ces principes, que le peuple américain et son premier Président ont l'honneur d'avoir proclamés avant tous les autres, dans des textes de lois clairs et formels."

Rolin-Jacquemyns. Mr. Rolin-Jacquemyns, in a notice of the able treatise of Mr. Mountague Bernard, published in the same review in 1871, says:

"Dans le cas spécial de l'Alabama, M. M. Bernard insiste sur le fait que ce vaisseau, en sortant du port de Liverpool, n'avait ni un canon, ni un mousquet. Il reçut dans la baie de Moëlfra environ quarante hommes d'équipage qui lui furent amenés de Liverpool, mais sans aucun matériel de guerre. C'est seulement à Terceira, une des îles Açores, par conséquent dans les eaux portugaises, qu'il fut rejoint par la barque *Agrippine*, de Londres, et un peu plus tard par le steamer *Bahama*, de Liverpool, qui lui amenèrent ses officiers, son armement, les habits de l'équipage et un supplément de charbons.³ Un fait analogue s'est présenté pour les corsaires *Shenandoah* et *Géorgie*, qui, également construits en Angleterre, en étaient également partis sans armes ni équipement. 'Il est vrai,' dit M. M. Bernard, (p. 382,) 'que l'armement fourni à ces vaisseaux leur fut expédié de différents ports anglais, chaque

---

¹ (*Note by M. Bluntschli.*)—"Bemis, *American Neutrality*, Boston, 1866, p. 17, seq.

² (*Note by M. Bluntschli.*)—"Phillimore, *Intern. Law*, III, 217.

³ (*Note by Mr. Rolin-Jacquemyns.*)—"Ce point n'était pas nettement indiqué dans la version donnée par M. Sumner, V. t. 1, p. 452, de la *Revue*, ainsi que l'article de M. Bluntschli. V. aussi les publications citées plus haut de MM. Esperson et Pierantoni.

fois évidemment en vertu d'un concert préalable, mais c'est ce que le gouvernement anglais ne savait ni ne pouvait savoir,' et plus loin il essaie d'établir la thèse qu'un gouvernement neutre n'est pas obligé, en droit international, d'empêcher la sortie de ses ports de bâtiments ayant l'apparence de vaisseaux de guerre, mais désarmés, alors même que l'on a des raisons de les croire construits pour le service d'un des belligérants. (V. p. 385 et pp. 390 et ss.)

"Il nous semble que l'adoption d'une pareille proposition équivaudrait à l'indication d'un moyen facile d'éluder la règle, qui déclare incompatible avec la neutralité d'un pays l'organisation, sur son territoire, d'expéditions militaires au service d'un des belligérants. Il suffira, s'il s'agit d'une entreprise maritime, de faire partir en deux ou trois fois les éléments qui la constituent; d'abord le vaisseau, puis les hommes, puis les armes, et si tous ces éléments ne se rejoignent que hors des eaux de la puissance neutre qui les a laissés partir, la neutralité sera intacte. Nous pensons que cette interprétation de la loi internationale n'est ni raisonnable, ni équitable. Sans doute il ne faut pas demander l'impossible, et puisque le droit international actuel n'empêche pas les neutres de permettre à leurs sujets l'exportation d'armes et de munitions de guerre à l'usage des belligérants, on ne peut exiger que l'on arrête les armes dans le cas dont il s'agit. Mais cette tolérance n'est qu'une raison de plus pour se montrer scrupuleux à l'égard des vaisseaux et des hommes. La considération que la fraude, même confinée dans ces limites, sera encore praticable, que les hommes pourront être nominalement engagés pour une destination pacifique, que la différence entre les vaisseaux de guerre et ceux de commerce ne se reconnaît pas toujours à des caractères certains, peut servir, dans les cas particuliers, à excuser ou à justifier la conduite du gouvernement neutre qui se laisse tromper aux apparences. Mais dans l'espèce ces motifs de justification ou d'excuse n'existent certainement pas. Bien que l'Alabama n'ait été armée ni dans la Mersey, ni dans la baie de Moëlfra, il est certain que, dès le 24 juin, (plus d'un mois avant son départ,) M. Adams avait informé officiellement Lord Russell qu'un nouveau et puissant *steamer* était prêt à quitter Liverpool, dans le dessein manifeste de servir à la guerre maritime, et que les parties intéressées dans l'entreprise étaient des personnes bien connues à Liverpool comme agents et officiers des insurgés sudistes.[1] Il est certain que, le 21 juillet, comme le collecteur et les autorités des douanes avaient prétendu ne pouvoir agir sur des renseignements vagues, le consul des États-Unis leur remit six affidavits, et que le 23 juillet il leur en remit deux autres; que trois de ces documents étaient les dépositions de marins engagés à bord de l'Alabama, et attestant comme chose notoire 'que le vaisseau était un vaisseau de combat, (a *fighting vessel*,) construit et aménagé tel, avec de grandes quantités de poudre, de charbons et de provisions; que les déposants avaient été enrôlés par des personnes bien connues comme agents des États-Confédérés; qu'ils n'avaient pas encore d'articles formels d'engagement, mais qu'il était généralement su à bord que le vaisseau était un corsaire du gouvernement fédéral, destiné à combattre les États-Unis en vertu d'une commission de M. Jefferson Davis.[2] Un des marins ajoutait cette déclaration caractéristique, qu'il avait été déjà capturé comme coureur de blocus, et que son idée fixe était de retourner dans le sud 'pour se venger sur les gens du nord de ce qu'ils lui avaient pris ses habits.' On lui avait promis que cette occasion ne tarderait pas à se présenter.[3]

"A ces affidavits était jointe une consultation émanée d'un des premiers avocats d'Angleterre, M. Collier, lequel, sur le vu des pièces, émettait l'opinion qu'une violation du '*Foreign Enlistment Act*' était établie, et que le collecteur des douanes avait le droit et le devoir d'arrêter le vaisseau.

"Six jours encore s'écoulèrent avant le rapport des juris-

---

[1] "M. BERNARD, p. 339.

[2] (*Note by Mr. Rolin-Jacquemyns*.)—"'It is well known by the hands on board that the vessel is a privateer for the confederate government to act against the United States under a commission from Mr. Jefferson Davis.' Affid. No. 1, BERNARD, p. 360.

[3] (*Note by Mr. Rolin-Jacquemyns*.)—"Affid. No. 8, p. 369. 'I wanted to get South in order to have retaliation of the Northerners for robbing me of my clothes. He [l'agent des états du sud] said that if I went with him in his vessel I should very shortly have that opportunity.'

consultés Officiels, (Law Officers.) Ce fut le 29 juillet seulement qu'ils conclurent également à ce que le vaisseau fût arrêté. Mais le 28, le corsaire, averti qu'on allait l'empêcher de partir, se hâtait de quitter, *quatre jours plus tôt qu'il ne se l'était proposé*, le bassin où il se trouvait, et le 29 il prenait la mer.[1] Cependant, il ne quitta les eaux anglaises que le 31.

"M. Bernard ne croit pas que la sortie de l'Alabama, effectuée dans ces circonstances, suffise pour justifier l'imputation de *faute grave*, de *coupable négligence*, à la charge du gouvernement anglais. Il convient toutefois que ni un Anglais, ni un Américain n'a peut-être le droit d'avoir sur cette question une confiance implicite dans son propre jugement. Mais il ne voit pas ce qui l'empêcherait de dire que l'accusation lui paraît *légère et déraisonnable*. Quant à nous, nous ne voyons pas comment il serait possible à quelqu'un qui n'est ni Anglais, ni Américain, de partager cette patriotique indulgence."

Ortolan.

Mr. Theodore Ortolan, of the French navy, from his practical experience, as well as from his theoretical knowledge and his high reputation as a publicist, is recognized as a writer of authority on these subjects. In a late edition of his *Diplomatie de la mer*[2] he discusses the subject of neutral obligations with special reference to the differences between Great Britain and the United States. He says:

"Si l'on suppose un navire construit sur le territoire neutre, non pas sur commande d'un belligérant ou par suite d'un traité ostensible ou dissimulé avec ce belligérant, mais en vue d'un dessein quelconque, soit de navigation commerciale, soit tout autre, et que ce navire, déjà par lui-même propre à la guerre ou de nature à être converti à cet usage, une fois sorti des ports de la nation neutre, soit vendu, dans le cours de sa navigation, occasionellement, à l'un des belligérants, et se mette à naviguer en destination directe pour ce belligérant: un tel navire dans de telles circonstances tombe uniquement

---

[1] (*Note by Mr. Rolin-Jacquemyns.*) "Affidavit de Clarence Yonge, cité par M. BERNARD, p. 345, en note.
[2] Diplomatie de la mer, tome 2, page 208.

sous le coup des règles relatives à la contrebande de guerre. Il est sujet à être arrêté et confisqué par l'ennemi qui pourra s'en emparer, mais sans qu'aucun grief de violation des devoirs de la neutralité puisse sortir de ce fait contre l'état neutre pour n'avoir pas défendu à ses nationaux de telles ventes ou ne les avoir pas réprimées. C'est une opération de trafic qui a eu lieu, trafic de contrebande de guerre, dont aucune circonstance particulière n'est venue changer le caractère.

"Tel fut, en l'année 1800, le cas du navire américain le Brutus, capturé par les Anglais et jugé de bonne prise par la cour d'amirauté d'Halifax.

* * * * * * *

"Mais la situation change, la contrebande de guerre n'est plus la question principale, d'autres règles du droit des gens interviennent et modifient profondément la solution, si l'on suppose qu'il s'agisse de bâtiments de guerre construits, armés ou équipés sur un territoire neutre pour le compte d'un belligérant, par suite d'arrangement pris à l'avance avec lui, sous la forme d'un contrat commercial quelconque: vente, commission, louage d'industrie ou de travail; que les arrangements aient été pris ostensiblement ou qu'ils le soient d'une manière secrète ou déguisée; car la loyauté est une condition essentielle dans la solution des difficultés internationales, et sous le couvert de fausses apparences, il faut toujours aller au fond des choses. Il y a ici, incontestablement, une seconde hypothèse qu'il importe de distinguer soigneusement de la précédente.

"Nous nous rattacherons, pour résoudre en droit des gens les difficultés que présente cette nouvelle situation, à un principe universellement établi, qui se formule en ce peu de mots: 'Inviolabilité du territoire neutre.' Cette inviolabilité est un droit pour l'état neutre, dont le territoire ne doit pas être atteint par les faits de guerre, mais elle impose aussi à ce même état neutre une étroite obligation, celle de ne pas permettre, celle d'empêcher, activement au besoin, l'emploi de ce territoire par l'une des parties ou au profit de l'une des parties belligérantes, dans un but hostile à l'autre partie.

"Les publicistes en crédit ne font aucun doute pour ce qui

concerne l'armement et l'équipement dans un port neutre de bâtiments de guerre destinés à accroître les forces des belligérants. Ils s'accordent pour reconnaître l'illégalité de ces armements ou équipements, comme une infraction de la part de l'état neutre qui les tolérerait aux devoirs de la neutralité.

"N'est-il pas évident qu'il en doit être de même *a fortiori* de la construction de pareils bâtiments, lorsque cette construction a lieu dans les conditions prévues en notre seconde hypothèse?"

The attention of Italian jurists and publicists has also been attracted to the discussion. A learned and exhaustive pamphlet appeared at Florence in 1870 from the pen of Professor Pierantoni. Without claiming the extreme rights which this learned gentleman concedes to them, the United States invite the attention of the Tribunal of Arbitration to the following expression of opinion:

Pierantoni.
"Dopo che nella sez. XXII, il professor di Pavia sostiene che nè il governo inglese nè gli altri governi debbano assumere la giuridica responsabilità delle depredazioni commesse dai corsari separatisti, nella seguente sez. XXIII, passa ad esaminare il secondo suo assunto: se la neutralità fu violata dalla Gran Bretagna per la costruzione dell' Alabama, legno corsaro, o pel consentito armamento nei cantieri inglesi. Egli in brevi termini chiama l'Inghilterra responsabile dei soli danni cagionati dalle depredazioni del detto legno, scrivendo: 'Di queste perdite soltanto deve rispondere il governo britannico, per essere le medesime una conseguenza immediata di un fatto illegittimo, che ebbe luogo da sua parte, violando apertamente le leggi della neutralità.'

"Io non posso acconsentire a questa mite conchiusione, anzi me ne discosto per considerazioni di fatto e di diritto. In linea di fatto, io non intendo come il chiarissimo autore escluda le altre specie di offese, che il Sumner ed il suo governo adducono di aver patite dalla nazione americana. (*sic.*) Nella esposizione dell' argomento ho citato i tre capi, nei quali riassume il Sumner la serie delle offese patite. Il caso del vascello costrutto a Liverpool è il più grave; ma gli Americani sostengono che avvennero altri simiglianti casi, e sino a prova contraria non è lecito circoscrivere il numero dei fatti addotti come offensivi.

"In diritto, io non so, chè in questa seconda parte lo scrittore non ricorre ad alcuna dimostrazione dottrinale, perchè egli limiti le conseguenze della violata neutralità al semplice rifacimento de' danni cagionati dal legno corsaro.

"I principii della neutralità soltanto accennati dimostrano più grave la responsabilità del governo che la violò."[1]

Lord Westbury. Lastly, the United States cite, for the consideration of the Tribunal, the authority of Lord Westbury, Lord High Chancellor of England during the rebellion, who, on the 7th day of March, 1868, in a discussion in the House of Lords on these questions, said: "There was one rule of conduct which undoubtedly civilized nations had agreed to observe, and it was that the territory of a neutral should not be the base of military operations by one of two belligerents against the other. In speaking of the base of operations, he must, to a certain degree, differ from the noble earl, (Earl Russell.) *It was not a question whether armed ships had actually left our shores; but it was a question whether ships with a view to war had been built in our ports by one of two belligerents. They need not have been armed; but if they had been laid down and built with a view to warlike operations by one of two belligerents, and this was knowingly permitted to be done by a neutral Power, it was unquestionably a breach of neutrality.*"[2]

The public and official acts of other European Governments have also been in harmony with the principles which are claimed in this paper to have been violated by Great Britain.

Case of Swedish vessels. During the war between Spain and the Spanish-American Colonies, the Government of Sweden sold, in the ordinary course of commerce, to some private individuals, some vessels of war, after first dismantling them of their armament, and reducing them to a much less formidable condition than the Alabama was in when she left

---

[1] La Questione Anglo-Americana dell' Alabama, per l'Avv. A. Pierantoni, Firenze 1870, pages 46—7.
[2] Hansard, 3d series, Vol. CXCI, pages 346—347.

Liverpool. Some of the correspondence which took place between the Spanish Minister at Stockholm, the Russian Minister, and the Swedish Government may be found in *De Marten's Causes Célèbres*, Vol. 5, page 229, *et seq*. A good *résumé* of the whole case may be found in De Cussy,[1] to which the United States invite the attention of the Tribunal of Arbitration in full, as follows:

"Dans l'année 1820, le roi de Suède prit la résolution de faire vendre, quand l'occasion s'en présenterait, quelques bâtiments de guerre dont la construction remontait à plus de vingt-cinq ans, ordonnant d'ailleurs de les remplacer immédiatement par des bâtiments nouveaux, en appliquant aux frais de construction de ceux-ci le produit de la vente des premiers: le but et les intentions du roi, en cette circonstance, étaient de rendre, au sein de la paix, quelque activité aux chantiers de la marine royale, par la construction de cinq ou six vaisseaux de guerre.

"La Suède fit proposer à l'Espagne d'acheter ces bâtiments, tant par l'intermédiaire de M. de Moreno, envoyé de la cour de Madrid à Stockholm, que par celui de M. de Lorichs, chargé d'affaires de Sa Majesté suédoise auprès du gouvernement de S. M. catholique. Le ministère fit également proposer, en même temps, à la cour d'Espagne de lui céder, à des prix modérés, de la poudre et des projectiles, et de mettre les chantiers de la marine royale de Suède à la disposition de S. M. catholique.

"La cour de Madrid déclina ces propositions diverses: l'Espagne possédait, répondit M. de Moreno, tous les éléments nécessaires pour la fabrication de la poudre, et un nombre suffisant de vaisseaux de guerre; l'argent seul manquait pour mettre en activité les moulins à poudre et pour ravitailler les bâtiments.

"Le ministre de la marine de S. M. suédoise avisa donc aux moyens nécessaires pour trouver des acquéreurs. Six vaisseaux, fort bons encore, bien que leur construction remontât à 25 et 30 ans, furent déclarés réformés, et leur vente fut annoncée; c'étaient le vaisseau *Försigtigheten* (la

---

[1] De Cussy, Droit maritime, tome 2, page 402.

Prévoyance) et les frégates *l'Eurydice, la Camille, la Manligheten, le Chapman, et la Tapperheten.*

"Avant de procéder à la vente, qui eut lieu au commencement de l'année 1825, le ministre suédois fit renouveler la proposition d'achat des dits bâtiments au chargé d'affaires d'Espagne qui se trouvait encore, à cette époque, à Stockholm, ainsi qu'à son successeur M. d'Alvarado.

"Sur le refus de la légation espagnole d'entrer en négociation pour l'acquisition des bâtiments désignés, le gouvernement suédois accepta les offres que lui fit la maison de commerce, établie à Stockholm, Michaelson et Benedicks; celle-ci peu après céda les bâtiments dont elle avait fait l'acquisition à la maison anglaise Barclay, Herring, Richardson et Cie, de Londres.

"Or, cette dernière maison ayant, ainsi que la maison Goldsmith, de Londres, fourni les fonds de l'emprunt contracté, peu de temps avant, par le Mexique, l'Espagne crut reconnaître, dans la circonstance de l'achat des bâtiments réformés fait par la maison Barclay, Herring, Richardson et Cie, des mains de la maison de Stockholm, une intention de *simulation* ayant pour but d'éloigner la pensée que le gouvernement suédois était informé (quand il accepta les offres de la maison Michaelson et Benedicks, de Stockholm) de la destination qui serait prochainement donnée aux vaisseaux de guerre vendus par le ministre de la marine.

"Pour M. d'Alvarado, chargé d'affaires d'Espagne, il ne semblait pas douteux que les bâtiments achetés, dans le principe, par la maison Michaelson et Benedicks, pour passer, peu de temps après, entre les mains de la maison Barclay, Herring, Richardson et Compagnie qui se trouvait en relations d'affaires d'argent avec *la colonie révoltée*, étaient destinés à renforcer les armements maritimes des insurgés de l'Amérique espagnole.

"C'est dans cette conviction, fondée, disait-il, sur la notoriété publique à Stockholm, à Carlscrona, à Gothenbourg, et à Londres, que M. d'Alvarado, dans la note qu'il addressa, le 1er juillet 1825, à M. le comte de Wetterstedt, ministre des affaires étrangères de Suède, et par laquelle il faisait appel à la loyauté de S. M. suédoise, dont la religion avait sans doute été surprise, conjura le gouvernement du roi de résilier les contracts de vente, et avant tout de retinir dans ses ports quatre des bâtiments vendus qui s'y trouvaient encore.

"Dans sa réponse au chargé d'affaires d'Espagne, le ministre suédois déclara que si le gouvernement de S. M. suédoise avait vendu, à des négociations, quelques vaisseaux de guerre, qu'on avait jugé à-propos de réformer, en se réservant d'ailleurs la moitié de l'armement, il n'avait fait qu'exercer son droit que personne ne pouvait lui contester. 'Son action,' continuait le ministre, 's'arrête là; et si M. d'Alvarado peut, ou croit pouvoir, prouver que les acquéreurs ont l'intention de faire de ces bâtiments un usage qui pourrait devenir nuisible à l'Espagne, c'est auprès du gouvernement britannique que sa cour doit agir, lui seul pouvant exercer sur ses sujets la surveillance qui lui conviendra. Mais vouloir, sur de simples présomptions, arrêter une vente dans *la crainte d'un danger à venir, qui pourrait en résulter*, ce serait anéantir l'activité et le développement de toutes les transactions commerciales.

"À la suite de diverses notes échangées entre le ministre suédois et M. d'Alvarado, qui obtint des envoyés des puissances amies et alliées de l'Espagne, résidant à Stockholm, d'appuyer ses réclamations, le gouvernement de S. M. le roi de Suède, voulant donner un témoignage de la bonne foi qui l'avait guidé dans toute cette affaire, consentit à résilier les contracts de vente qui avaient été passés, en dernier lieu, à l'occasion de la *Prévoyance*, de *l'Eurydice*, et de *la Camille*.

"Cette résiliation entraîna, pour le gouvernement suédois, une perte d'argent assez considérable, que l'on a évaluée à plus de 60,000 francs.

"Les membres de l'opposition, dans la diète tenue en 1828, cherchèrent à établir que le gouvernement du roi *avait violé la constitution*, (éternel et banal argument de toutes les *oppositions* dans tous les pays!) non-seulement pour avoir vendu des bâtiments de la marine de l'état sans avoir obtenu préalablement l'assentiment des états; mais aussi pour avoir depuis permis la résiliation des marchés, et s'être soumis, de cette sorte, à une perte en argent d'un chiffre élevé. Une commission fut nommée pour examiner la conduite du gouvernement, laquelle, après leur examen, fut trouvée irrépréhensible.

"Les états sollicitèrent, il est vrai, du roi que S. M. voulût bien prendre les mesures nécessaires pour faire rentrer au trésor les sommes que le gouvernement avait cru devoir sacrifier, quand il se vit mieux éclairé sur les inconvénients résultant de la vente effectuée et lorsqu'il céda aux représentations diplomatiques dont cette vente était devenue l'objet; mais la mort du Comte de Cederström, chef de l'administration de la marine, *contre lequel la demande paraissait dirigée*, mit fin à cette affaire; elle ne fut pas reprise, en effet, dans le cours des séances de la diète suivante.

"Le gouvernement suédois en résiliant les contrats de vente, et en s'imposant un sacrifice d'argent en cette circonstance, agit dignement et loyalement; aussi longtemps qu'il ne vit dans la vente des bâtiments de guerre réformés et d'une partie de leur armement, qu'une opération purement commerciale, dont les résultats devaient profiter uniquement, tant au commerce d'aucun acquéreur, qu'au trésor de l'état, au moment où de nouvelles constructions navales allaient être entreprises, le gouvernement suédois était parfaitement dans son droit: mais du jour où il put croire que les bâtiments achetés par la maison de Stockholm et revendus à la maison de Londres, étaient destinés effectivement à renforcer les armements maritimes d'une colonie *que l'Espagne considérait encore comme insurgée contre son autorité* et dont l'indépendance politique n'avait encore été reconnue par aucun des grands états européens, la Suède, alliée ou amie de l'Espagne, ne pouvait se prêter, sans porter atteinte au principe de la neutralité, à ce que ses vaisseaux de guerre réformés concourussent à accroître les forces navales du Mexique.

"Ce ne fut que le 26 décembre 1826 que la Grande-Bretagne signa, à Londres, un traité public avec les états mexicains; dans l'année 1827, la France, les Pays-Bas, le Hanovre, le Danemark suivirent cet exemple, en signant, avec le gouvernement mexicain, des traités de commerce et de navigation; le 28 décembre 1836, enfin, l'Espagne, comprenant l'inutilité de continuer la lutte contre des colonies qui s'étaient séparées d'elle sans retour, conclut avec le Mexique un traité de paix et d'amitié.

"En agissant autrement qu'elle le fit, c'est-à-dire en persistant à repousser les réclamations du chargé d'affaires d'Espagne, la Suède, nous le répétons, aurait manqué aux devoirs et aux obligations de la neutralité. C'eût été se prêter à favoriser l'un des deux belligérants, (et, dans le cas actuel, en 1825, le belligérant favorisé était un peuple dont la condition politique était encore indéterminée,) que de ne pas prendre les mesures nécessaires pour que les bâtiments de guerre réformés, vendus avec un demi-armement, n'allassent pas accroître les forces navales d'une colonie de l'Espagne, insurgée contre l'autorité du roi catholique."

Offending vessels not simply contraband of war. It may possibly be asserted that the construction, or the fitting out, or the arming, or the equipment by neutrals of vessels of war intended for the service of a belligerent were, before the Treaty of Washington, to be regarded as standing upon the same footing with the dealings in articles ordinarily esteemed contraband of war. Should this be the case, the United States might content themselves with a reference to the history of the legislation of the two countries, as a complete answer to such an assertion. While the subjects or citizens of either country have been left by law free to manufacture, or sell muskets or gunpowder, or to export them at their own risk, even if known to be for the use of a belligerent, the legislatures, the executives, and the judiciaries of both Great Britain and the United States, have joined the civilized world in saying that a vessel of war, intended for the use of a belligerent, is not an article in which the individual subject or citizen of a neutral State may deal, subject to the liability to capture as contraband by the other belligerent. Such a vessel has been and is regarded as organized war—more clearly organized war than was that unarmed expedition which left Plymouth in 1828 for Portugal,[1] and was arrested by the British navy

---

[1] During the contest in Portugal between Don Miguel and Donna Maria II, an unarmed expedition of the adherents of

at the same Terceira to which the Alabama fled to receive the arms and ammunition that she failed to take on board at Liverpool, either because the purposes of the Foreign Office were surreptitiously revealed, or because the insurgent agents had reason to believe that they could evade the law by the construction of the vessel on one side of the river Mersey, the collection of the armament on the other side of it, and the putting them together more than three miles out at sea.

It is not, however, necessary for the United States to rely in this respect upon the action of the several branches of the Governments of the two countries. The question has been considered by several of the leading publicists of the Continent. Ortolan, in his "Diplomatie de la mer,"[1] says; in addition to what has already been cited:

Opinion of Ortolan. "A part toute prohibition faite législativement par telle ou telle nation, il faut, en droit international, considérer comme des actes décidément contraires à la neutralité, l'équipement et l'armement et, à plus forte raison, la construction dans les ports neutres de bâtiments de guerre appartenant aux belligérants, ou destinés, par concert ostensible ou dissimulé avec les belligérants à être remis en leur pouvoir. Nous croyons fermement qu'il est impossible d'assimiler de pareils actes à la contrebande de guerre proprement dite, et que l'obligation pour un état neutre de s'opposer à ce qu'ils aient lieu sur son territoire est indépendante de toute loi intérieure ou particulière à

Donna Maria left Portsmouth, ostensibly for Brazil, but really for the Azores. The British Government of that day pursued it to Terceira, fired into it and broke it up; and they were sustained in the House of Lords by a vote of 126 to 31, and in the House of Commons by a vote of 191 to 78. (Hansard for 1830, Vol. XXIII. See also Annual Register for 1829, and Phillimore's International Law, Vol. I, page 229, et seq.) The Tribunal of Arbitration will not fail to observe how differently the powers and duties of the Government were construed by the British Government when it was a question of the disintegration and disruption of the commerce of the United States.

[1] Diplomatie de la mer, Ortolan, tome 2, page 214.

cet état; que la loi intérieure peut et doit sanctionner cette obligation, mais qu'elle ne saurait ni la créer ni la détruire, parceque c'est une obligation qui résulte uniquement de la loi internationale, laquelle défend d'user, dans un but hostile, du territoire neutre."

And of Heffter. Heffter,[1] the distinguished German publicist, says to the same effect:

"C'est un devoir général pour les peuples restés spectateurs tranquilles de la lutte, de n'y prendre aucune part active, ni de participer directement aux actes de la guerre. Les gouvernements, les sujets étrangers qui fournissent à l'un des belligérants des secours directs, commettent une violation du devoir de la neutralité, un acte d'immixion dans les hostilités auquel l'adversaire est en droit de s'opposer par tous les moyens. Dans la pratique on regarde comme de tels actes d'hostilité:

"1°, le transport volontaire des soldats, matelots et autres hommes de guerre;

"2°, la construction dans les ports neutres de vaisseaux de guerre ou de commerce pour le compte de l'ennemi dès leur sortie;

"3°, le transport volontaire de dépêches de l'un des belligérants.

"Ces diverses contraventions, lorsqu'elles sont régulièrement constatées, entraînent la saisie et la confiscation du navire employé au transport. La confiscation s'étend également à la cargaison, s'il est établi que les propriétaires avaient connaissance du but illicite du voyage. Toutefois cette pénalité n'est pas toujours exécutée à leur égard avec la même sévérité. En réalité elle constitue un acte de légitime défense auquel le neutre qui se rend complice de l'un des belligérants, ne saurait échapper du côté de l'adversaire.

"En dehors des cas qui viennent d'être énumérés, il existe encore un certain nombre d'objets dont le commerce est regardé d'une manière plus ou moins générale dans la pratique des états comme prohibé. Il constitue la contrebande de guerre proprement dite."

---

[1] Heffter, *Droit international*, (French translation by Jules Bergson, Paris,) page 296.

Case of the Santisima Trinidad.

Without wearying the patience of the Tribunal in the further discussion of this question, it will be assumed that a vessel of war is not to be confounded with ordinary contraband of war. Indeed, the only respectable authority which has been cited even apparently to the contrary, is an observation which Mr. Justice Story thrust into the opinion of the Supreme Court of the United States, upon the case of the Santisima Trinidad.[1] If that eminent jurist had said that a vessel of war was to be regarded in public law as an article which might be legitimately constructed, fitted out, armed, equipped, or dealt in by a person in the territory of a neutral, with the intent that it should enter the service of a belligerent, subject only to a liability to capture as contraband of war by the other belligerent, the United States would have been forced, with great regret, to ask this Tribunal to disregard an opinion so at variance with common sense, and with the whole current of the action of nations. Happily they are under no necessity of casting an imputation on the memory of one of their brightest juridical ornaments.

During the last war between the United States and Great Britain a privateer, called the Monmouth, was constructed at Baltimore, and cruised against the enemy. After the peace she was stripped of her armament, and converted into a brig. She was subsequently loaded with munitions of war, armed with a portion of her original armament, and sent to Buenos Ayres, (which was then a revolted colony of Spain recognized as a belligerent, but not recognized as an independent government), to find a market for her munitions of war. The supercargo was also authorized "to sell the vessel to the Government of Buenos Ayres *if he could obtain a suitable price.*" He did sell her, and she went into the service of that Government as a man-of-war. She subsequently put into a port of the United States, and while there enlisted thirty new men, and took with her, when she put to sea, the newly-enlisted men, and a tender, which carried some mounted guns and twenty-five men. After this

---

[1] 7 Wheaton's Reports, page 283.

addition to her effective power for injury, assisted by the tender, she captured the Spanish vessel Santisima Trinidad, and carried her cargo into Norfolk, one of the ports of the United States. On the instigation of the Spanish authorities, proceedings were taken for the restitution of this property, on the ground, first, that the Independencia had been originally illegally fitted out, armed, or equipped in the United States; secondly, that she had, after entering the service of Buenos Ayres, illegally recruited men and augmented her force within the United States. The court decreed a restitution of the property on the second ground. Any remarks, therefore, upon the first point were outside of the requirements of the case, and, under the American practice, would be regarded as without authority; but inasmuch as they were made by one of the most eminent writers on public law, they deserve the consideration which they have received. Taking them in connection with the facts as shown in evidence, it is clear that the distinguished judge intended to confine his statement to the case of a vessel of war equipped and dispatched as a commercial venture, without previous arrangement or understanding with the belligerent, and at the sole risk of the owner. "It is apparent," he says, "that she was sent to Buenos Ayres on a commercial venture." The whole of his subsequent remarks turned upon the absence of an intent, in Baltimore, in the mind of the owner, before she sailed, that she should, in any and at all events, whether sold or not, go into the service of the belligerent.

The judges who were brought in contact with the witnesses in that case, and had access to all the original papers, and knew personally both the men and the facts, and who, therefore, had opportunities which are denied to us of judging of the merits of the case, seem to have reached the conclusion that this particular transaction was a purely commercial venture; and they placed the decree of restitution of the captured property upon later violations of law. It may, however, be said that the ordinary experiences of human life show that such deeds border upon the debatable ground between good faith and fraud. The court which decided that case evidently did so on the impressions which the judges received from the particular evidence before them; for, on the very next day, the most illustrious of American judges, John Marshall, then Chief Justice of the United States in the parallel case of the Irresistible, a vessel built at Baltimore, sent to Buenos Ayres, and there commissioned as a privateer, pronouncing the opinion of the same court, declared that the facts as to the Irresistible showed a violation of the laws of the United States in the original construction, equipment, and arming of the vessel; and that, should the court decide otherwise, *the laws for the preservation of the neutrality of the country would be completely eluded.*[1] In justice to the highest court of the United States, these two cases should be read together by all persons wishing to know its views upon the duties of a neutral nation in time of war, since if there be any difference in the principles involved in the two cases, then the true construction of the law is to be found in the carefully considered language of the court in the case of the Gran Para. The cases were both argued in February, 1822: the Gran Para upon the 20th, and the Santisima Trinidad on the 28th. The opinions were delivered in March: that of the Santisima Trinidad on the 12th; that of the Gran Para on the 13th. There can be no doubt that they were considered together in the consultation-room. Therefore any apparently broad or ill considered expressions in the opinion rendered on the 12th of March are to be regarded as limited and corrected by the carefully considered expressions of the Chief Justice on the following day.

<small>Controlled by the case of the Gran Para.</small>

<small>Effect of a commission of the offender as a vessel of war.</small>

Having thus demonstrated that the principles for which the United States contend have been recognized by the statesmen, the jurists, the publicists, and the legislators of Great Britain; that they have the approbation of the most eminent authorities upon the continent of Europe; and that they have been regarded by the other Powers of Europe in their dealing with each other, it only remains to show how the

---

[1] The Grand Para, 7 Wheaton's Reports, 471.

liability of the neutral for the acts of cruisers illegally built, or equipped, or fitted out, or armed within its ports, may be terminated.

It has been intimated, in the course of the discussions upon these questions between the two Governments, that it may be said, on the part of Great Britain, that its power to interfere with, to arrest, or to detain either of the belligerent cruisers whose acts are complained of ceased when it was commissioned as a man-of-war; and that, consequently, its liability for their actions ceased.

The United States might well content themselves with calling the attention of the Tribunal of Arbitration to the utter uselessness of discussing these questions, if the liability to make compensation for the wrong can be escaped in such a frivolous way. It is well known how the several British-built and British-manned cruisers got into the service of the insurgents. Few of them ever saw the line of the coast of the Southern insurgent States. The Florida, indeed, entered the harbor of Mobile, but she passed the blockading squadron as a British man-of-war. In most cases the commissions went out from England — from a branch office of the insurgent Navy Department, established and maintained in Liverpool at the cost and expense of the insurgent so-called Government. From this office the sailing orders of the vessels were issued; here their commanders received their instructions; and hence they departed to assume their commands and to begin the work of destruction. They played the comedy of completing on the high seas what had been carried to the verge of completion in England. The parallel is complete between these commissions and those issued by Genet in 1793, which were disregarded by the United States at the instance of Great Britain. If a piece of paper, emanating through an English office, from men who had no nationality recognized by Great Britain, and who had no open port into which a vessel could go unmolested, was potent not only to legalize the depredations of British built and manned cruisers upon the commerce of the United States, but also to release the responsibility of Great Britain therefor, then this arbitration is indeed a farce. Such, however, cannot be the case.

Opinion of Sir Roundell Palmer. Sir Roundell Palmer, the Attorney General of Lord Palmerston's Cabinet, as well as of the present Government, well said, in the House of Commons, in 1864, when defending the course of Great Britain as to the Tuscaloosa, a tender of the Alabama, "Can it be said that a neutral Sovereign has not the right to make orders for the preservation of his own neutrality, or that any foreign Power whatever violating these orders, provided it be done willfully or fraudulently, is protected to any extent, by International Law, within the neutral territory, or has the right to complain, on the ground of International Law, of any means which the neutral Sovereign may see fit to adopt for the assertion of his territorial rights?" * * "It is a mere question of practical discretion, judgment, and moderation what is the proper way of vindicating the offended dignity of the neutral Sovereign."[1]

Opinion of Chief Justice Marshall. The United States do not deny the force of the commission of a man-of-war issuing from a recognized Power. On the contrary, they point with a pardonable pride to the exhaustive language of Chief Justice Marshall on this subject[2] as evidence of what they understand to be the practice of nations. Nor do they deny that since Great Britain had, however precipitately and unjustly, recognized the existence of a civil war between the United States and the insurgents, and avowed a determination to remain neutral between the parties, she might, without a violation of the law of nations, commit the further injustice of allowing to such vessels of war of the insurgents as had not been built, armed, equipped, furnished, fitted out, supplied, or manned within her territory, in violation of her duty to the United States, the same rights of asylum, hospitality, and intercourse which she conceded to the vessels of war of the United States. They do, however, most confidently deny that the receipt of a commission by a vessel like the Alabama, or the Florida, or the Georgia, or the

---

[1] Hansard, 3d series, vol. 174, page 1595.
[2] The Schooner Exchange against McFadden et als., 7 Cranch's Reports, 116.

Shenandoah, exempted Great Britain from the liability growing out of the violation of her neutrality. To this point they are fortunately able to cite two from the many pertinent cases adjudicated in the Supreme Court of the United States, which show directly what the public law in this respect is understood to be, not only by the United States, but also by Spain and by Portugal.

<small>Decision of the Supreme Court of the United States in the cases of the Santisima Trinidad and the Gran Para.</small> The first is the case of the Santisima Trinidad,[1] the facts of which have already been given. The property for which restitution was claimed in this case was Spanish. The libel was filed by the Spanish Consul at Norfolk on behalf of the owners. The capture was shown to have been made after a commission to the vessel, expressly recognized by the court rendering the decision. Nevertheless, restitution was decreed on the ground of an illegal increase of armament in the neutral territory *after the commission*.

The second case is that of the Gran Para,[2] also already alluded to. The libel was filed by the Consul General of Portugal. The opinion of the court was given by Chief Justice Marshall. The facts are set forth so clearly in the opinion that no other statement is necessary. The Chief Justice, in announcing the judgment of the court, said:

"The principle is now firmly settled that prizes made by vessels which have violated the acts of Congress that have been enacted for the preservation of the neutrality of the United States, if brought within their territory, shall be restored. The only question, therefore, is, Does this case come within the principle?

"That the Irresistible was purchased, and that she sailed out of the port of Baltimore, armed and manned as a vessel of war, for the purpose of being employed as a cruiser against a nation with whom the United States were at peace, is too clear for controversy. That the arms and ammunition were cleared out as cargo cannot vary the case. Nor is it thought to be material that the men were enlisted in form as for a common mercantile voyage. There is nothing re-

---

[1] 7 Wheaton, 283.   [2] 7 Wheaton, 471.

sembling a commercial adventure in any part of the transaction.
The vessel was constructed for war and not for commerce.
There was no cargo on board but what was adapted to the
purposes of war. The crew was too numerous for a merchantman, and was sufficient for a privateer. These circumstances
demonstrate the intent with which the Irresistible sailed out
of the port of Baltimore. But she was not commissioned
as a privateer, nor did she attempt to act as one until she
reached the river La Plata, when a commission was obtained,
and the crew reënlisted. This court has never decided that
the offense adheres to the vessel, whatever changes may have
taken place, and cannot be deposited at the termination of
the cruise in preparing for which it was committed; and as
the Irresistible made no prize on her passage from Baltimore
to the river of La Plata, it is contended that her offense
was deposited there, and that the court cannot connect her
subsequent cruise with the transactions at Baltimore.

"If this were to be admitted in such a case as this, the
laws for the preservation of our neutrality would be completely eluded, so far as this enforcement depends on the
restitution of prizes made in violation of them. Vessels
completely fitted in our ports for military operations need
only sail to a belligerent port, and there, after obtaining a
commission, go through the ceremony of discharging and
reënlisting their crew, to become perfectly legitimate, cruisers,
purified from every taint contracted at the place where all
their real force and capacity for annoyance was acquired.
This would, indeed, be a fraudulent neutrality, disgraceful to
our own Government, and of which no nation would be the
dupe. It is impossible for a moment to disguise the facts
that the arms and ammunition taken on board the Irresistible
at Baltimore were taken for the purpose of being used on
a cruise, and that the men there enlisted, though engaged
in form as for a commercial voyage, were not so engaged
in fact. There was no commercial voyage, and no individual
of the crew could believe there was one. Although there
might be no express stipulation to serve on board the Irresistible after her reaching the La Plata and obtaining a
commission, it must be completely understood that such was

to be the fact. For what other purpose could they have
undertaken this voyage? Everything they saw, everything that
was done, spoke a language too plain to be misunderstood.

* * * * *

"It is, therefore, very clear that the Irresistible was armed
and manned in Baltimore, in violation of the laws and of
the neutral obligations of the United States. We do not
think that any circumstances took place in the river La Plata,
by force of which this taint was removed."

The principle recognized by France, Great Britain, Spain, Portugal, and the United States. The course of the French Government during the insurrection in the case of the Rappahannock, already referred to, practically asserted the power of the neutral to protect its violated sovereignty, even against a commissioned vessel of war. The British Government itself recognized this principle when it ordered the Alabama to be seized at Nassau, and when it found fault with the Governor of the Cape of Good Hope for not detaining the Tuscaloosa at Cape Town. The principle for which the United States contend has therefore been recognized by Great Britain, Spain, Portugal, France, and the United States.

Deposit of the offense. It is not deemed necessary to add to the forcible views of Chief Justice Marshall in the case of the Gran Para, as to the deposit of the offense of the cruiser. The United States only ask that the same just rules which they, through their highest judicial officer and most eminent jurist, have established for offenses committed on their own soil, may be applied to the offenses against British neutrality from which they have suffered. The Alabama, the Georgia, the Florida, the Shenandoah, and the other insurgent vessels of war made no cruise that was not planned on British soil. Their respective cruises were to last till the independence of the Confederacy should be established. The career of the Florida terminated at Bahia—that of the Alabama off Cherbourg. The Shenandoah and the Georgia came eventually into the possession of the United States. The principal injuries, which will be hereinafter set forth, came from the acts of these vessels. There were, however, other vessels, whose careers and crimes, as well as those of the above-named four, will now be given in detail.

Résumé of principles. Before proceeding to do so, it will be well to note the points which have been thus far made.

The United States trust that they have established to the satisfaction of the Tribunal of Arbitration as against Great Britain—

1. That it is the duty of a neutral to preserve strict and impartial neutrality as to both belligerents during hostilities. (*See the Queen's Proclamation; also extracts from various writers on International Law above cited.*)

2. That this obligation is independent of municipal law. (*See as above.*)

3. That a neutral is bound to enforce its municipal laws and its executive proclamation; and that a belligerent has the right to ask it to do so; and also the right to ask to have the powers conferred upon the neutral by law increased if found insufficient. (*See the precedents in General Washington's administrations; Lord Palmerston's speech of July 23, 1863; the opinion of the British Attorney General during the Crimean war; and the United States Special Law of March 10, 1838.*)

4. That a neutral is bound to use due diligence to prevent the fitting out, arming, or equipping, within its jurisdiction, of any vessel which it has reasonable ground to believe is intended to cruise or to carry on war against a Power with which it is at peace. (*See 1st Rule of the Treaty; also the Foreign Enlistment Acts of 1819 and 1870; also the precedents in General Washington's administration; also the writers on International Law who have been cited.*)

5. That a neutral is bound to use like diligence to prevent the construction of such a vessel. (*See Foreign Enlistment Act of 1870; also the action of the United States Government in 1869; also the writers on International Law above cited.*)

6. That a neutral is bound to use like diligence to prevent the departure from its jurisdiction of any vessel intended to cruise or carry on war against any Power with which it is at peace; such vessel having been specially adapted, in whole or in part, within its jurisdiction, to warlike use. (*See 1st Rule of the Treaty; also the Foreign Enlistment Act of 1870.*)

7. That a neutral may not permit or suffer either belligerent to make use of its ports or waters as the base of naval operations against the other. (*See 2d Rule of the Treaty, the Foreign Enlistment Act of* 1870, *and the writers on International Law above cited; also the instructions to the British naval forces during the Southern insurrection.*)

8. That a neutral is bound to use due diligence in its ports or waters, to prevent either belligerent from obtaining there a renewal or augmentation of military supplies, or arms for belligerent vessels, or the recruitment of men. (*See 2d Rule of the Treaty; also the precedents of General Washington's administration; also the Foreign Enlistment Acts of* 1819 *and* 1870; *also the Queen's Proclamation*).

9. That when a neutral fails to use all the means in its power to prevent a breach of the neutrality of its soil or waters, in any of the foregoing respects, the neutral should make compensation for the injury resulting therefrom. (*See precedents of General Washington's administration between Great Britain and the United States; treaty of* 1794 *between Great Britain and the United States; treaty of* 1819 *between the United States and Spain; correspondence between Portugal and the United States,* 1817—22, *and Articles VII and X of the Treaty of Washington.*)

10. That this obligation is not discharged or arrested by the change of the offending vessel into a public man-of-war. (*See the cases of the Santisima Trinidad and the Gran Para, above cited.*)

11. That this obligation is not discharged by a fraudulent attempt of the offending vessel to evade the provisions of a local municipal law. (*See the Gran Para, as above; also Bluntschli and other writers on International Law.*)

12. That the offense will not be deposited so as to release the liability of the neutral even by the entry of the offending vessel in a port of the belligerent, and there becoming a man-of-war, if any part of the original fraud continues to hang about the vessel. (*See the Gran Para, as above.*)

PART IV.

WHEREIN GREAT BRITAIN FAILED TO PERFORM ITS DUTIES AS A NEUTRAL.

Admissions of British Cabinet Ministers.
"There is no doubt that Jefferson **Davis** and other leaders of the South have made an army; they are making, it appears, a navy."—*Speech of Mr. Gladstone, Chancellor of the Exchequer, October 7, 1862.*

"It has been usual for a power carrying on war upon the seas to possess ports of its own in which vessels are built, equipped, and fitted, and from which they issue, to which they bring their prizes, and in which those prizes when brought before a court are either condemned or restored. But it so happens that in this conflict the Confederate States have no ports except those of the Mersey and the Clyde, from which they fit out ships to cruise against the Federals; and having no ports to which to bring their prizes, they are obliged to burn them on the high seas."—*Speech of Earl Russell, Principal Secretary of State for Forein Affairs, April 26, 1864.*

"Her Britannic Majesty has authorized her High Commissioners and Plenipotentiaries to express in a friendly spirit the regret felt by Her Majesty's Government for the escape, under whatever circumstances, of the Alabama and other vessels from British ports, and for the depredations committed by those vessels."—*Treaty of Washington, Article I.*

The extracts which are placed at the head of this division of the Case of the United States are at once evidence of the facts which will now be set forth, and a condensation of the line of argument which those facts logically suggest. The United States summon no less illustrious a person than the present Prime Minister of England, to prove, not only that the insurgents were engaged in the year 1862 in making a navy, but that the fact was known to the gentlemen who then constituted Her Majesty's Government. They place on the stand as their next witness Her Majesty's Principal Secretary of State for Foreign Affairs during the whole period of the rebellion, to prove where the insurgents were constructing that navy, and why they were constructing it in the Mersey and the Clyde; and further, to prove that these facts, also, were known at the time to the gentlemen who then constituted Her Majesty's Government. And lastly, they lay before the Tribunal of Arbitration the graceful and kindly testimony of the regret of Her Majesty's Government that the escape[1] of the cruisers, which were built in Great Britain, with the knowledge of the Government, and which constituted that navy, should have resulted in the subsequent destruction of the property of citizens of the United States.

In discussing this question, except so far as may be absolutely necessary for the protection of the interests which they are bound to guard, the United States will not attempt to disinter from the grave of the past the unhappy passions and prejudices, and to revive the memory of the injuries, often great and sometimes petty, which caused such poignant regret, such wide-spread irritation, and such deep-seated sense of wrong in the United States. Over much of this feeling the kindly expression of regret in the Treaty of Washington has forever cast the mantle of oblivion.

The reports of the diplomatic and consular officers of the

---

[1] I wish the word 'escape' had not been found in the apology, as it is termed in describing the exit from our ports of the Alabama and other ships of that kind. I cannot help thinking that was an unguarded expression, which may affect the course of the future arbitration. I can easily imagine that in some minds the word 'escape' would be construed unfavorably to this country, for it means that something has got away which might have been retained. We speak of the escape of a prisoner; and the meaning of the term is that there was power to prevent the escape, and that the escape happened in spite of it."—*Lord Cairn's (ex-Chancellor) speech in the House of Lords, June 12, 1871. See London Times, June 13, 1871.*

United States, made from the British dominions to their Government during the war, which are printed in the volumes which will accompany this case, are full of proof of a constant state of irritating hostility to the United States, and of friendship to the insurgents in the several communities from which they are written. These dispatches are interesting, as showing the facilities which the complicity of the community often, if not always, gave to the schemes of the insurgents for violating the sovereignty of Great Britain. The reports from Liverpool, Nassau, Bermuda, and Melbourne are especially interesting in this respect, and tend to throw much light on the causes of the differences which are, it is to be hoped, to be forever set at rest by the decision of this Tribunal.

British ports the base of insurgent operations; a partial hospitality shown to the insurgents; a branch of their Government established in Liverpool; their Government vessels officially aided in evading the blockade and in furnishing them with arms, munitions, and means for carrying on the struggle.

As soon as the authorities who were directing at Richmond the fortunes of the insurgents were sure that their right to carry on a maritime war would be recognized by Great Britain, their Secretary of the Navy recommended to Mr. Jefferson Davis to send an agent to Great Britain for the purpose of contracting for and superintending the construction of men-of-war; and Mr. James Dunwoody Bullock, who had been an officer in the Navy of the United States, was, in accordance with that recommendation, sent there in the summer of 1861, and entered upon his duties before the autumn of that year. Mr. North, also formerly of the United States Navy, was empowered "to purchase vessels"[1] for the insurgents; and Mr. Caleb Huse, formerly of the Ordnance Department of the Army of the United States, was sent to London for "the purchase of arms and munitions of war."[1] Mr. Bullock, Mr. North, and Mr. Huse continued to discharge their duties during most of the struggle, and served the purposes of those who sent them there, with intelligence and activity.

The means for carrying on these extensive operations were

---

[1] Walker to Green, 1st July, 1861, Vol. VI, page 30.

to be derived from the proceeds of the cotton crop of the South. It will probably be within the personal recollection of the several gentlemen, members of the Tribunal, that in the year 1860 the world was dependent upon the fields of the insurgent States for a large portion of its supply of cotton, and that, when the blockade was established by the United States, a large part of the crop of 1860 was still unexported.[1] This, and all subsequent crops that might be produced during the struggle, would yield their value in gold as soon as landed in Liverpool.

The insurgent agents took advantage of this fact. They secured, through their assumed authority as a Government, the control of so much as might be necessary for their purposes, and they early made arrangements for a credit in Liverpool upon the faith of it.

The firm of Fraser, Trenholm & Co. It so happened that there was at Charleston, at that time, a well-established commercial house, doing business under the name of John Fraser & Co. The head of this firm was George A. Trenholm, of Charleston. Another prominent member was Charles K. Prioleau, also a citizen of the United States. Before or about the time the insurrection broke out, and, as the United States believe, in anticipation of it, this house established a branch in Liverpool, under the name of Fraser, Trenholm & Co. Prioleau was dispatched thither to take charge of the Liverpool business, and became, for purposes that may easily be imagined, a naturalized British subject. George A. Trenholm remained in Charleston, and, in due course of

---

[1] "It was estimated that only about 750,000 bales at most of the crop of 1860 remained on hand in the South when the blockade began. The crop of 1861 was about 2,750,000 bales—a little more than half the total quantity consumed in 1860—and this supply, or so much of it as could be properly picked, cleaned, and baled, would, together with what remained from the previous year, have been available for exportation in the winter and spring of 1861—'62. The quantity actually sent abroad, however, up to July or August, 1862, was reckoned not to exceed 50,000 bales, the great bulk of which, but not the whole, went to England."—*Bernard's Neutrality of Great Britain, page 286.*

time, became the Secretary of the insurgent Treasury, and a member of the so-called Government at Richmond. An arrangement was made by which the cotton of the insurgent authorities was to be sent to Fraser, Trenholm & Co., to be drawn against by the purchasing agents of the insurgents.[1]

The first amount (five hundred thousand dollars) was placed to their credit in Liverpool, somewhere about the month of May, or early in June, 1861; and, under the name of "depositories," Fraser, Trenholm & Co. remained a branch of the Treasury of the insurgent Government.

Thus there was early established in Great Britain a branch of the War Department of the insurgents, a branch of their Navy Department, and a branch of their Treasury, each with almost plenary powers. These things were done openly and notoriously. The persons and places of business of these several agents were well known to the communities in which they lived, and must have been familiar to the British officials. If there was any pretence of concealment in the outset, it was soon abandoned.

On the 22d of July, 1861, Huse writes to the officer in charge of the insurgent Ordnance Department, complaining of the activity of the agents of the United States in watching and thwarting his movements. "It is difficult," he says, "for a stranger to keep his actions secret when spies are on his path." He says that he shall have ready, by the 1st of August, some of the goods that had been ordered on the 17th of the previous April, and more by the 1st of October,

---

[1] "Of twenty steamers, which were said to have been kept plying in 1863 between Nassau and two of the blockaded ports, seven belonged to a mercantile firm at Charleston, who had a branch-house at Liverpool, and through whom the Confederate Government transacted its business in England." "The name of the Charleston firm was John Fraser & Co.; that of the Liverpool house, Fraser, Trenholm & Co. Of the five members of the house, four, I believe, were South Carolinians, and one a British subject."—*Bernard's Neutrality of Great Britain*, page 289 *and note*. The British subject referred to by Mr. Bernard was Prioleau, naturalized for the purpose.

and that "the shipping of the articles will be left in the hands of the Navy Department."[1]

On the 18th of September, the steamer "Bermuda" ran the blockade, and arrived at Savannah with "arms and munitions on board."[2] She came from Fraser, Trenholm & Co., consigned to John Fraser & Co. Information of the character and purposes of this steamer, and of the nature of her freight had been given to Lord Russell by Mr. Adams on the 15th of the previous August,[3] and he had declined to "interfere with the clearance or sailing of the vessel."[4] On the fourth day after her arrival at Savannah, her consignees offered to charter her to the insurgents, and the offer was accepted."[5]

The experience of the "Bermuda," or the difficulties which she encountered in running the blockade, seem to have induced the insurgent authorities to think that it would be well, to have some surer way for receiving the purchases made by their agents in Liverpool. The stringency of the blockade established by the United States, and the nature of the coast that was blockaded, made it necessary to have a set of agents in the West Indies also.

Character of the blockaded coast. The coast of the United States, from Chesapeake Bay to the Mexican frontier, is low, with shoaly water extending out for some distance to sea. A range of islands lies off the coast, from Florida to Charleston, and islands also lie off Wilmington and the coast to the north of it. The waters within these islands are shallow, affording an inland navigation for vessels of light draught. The passages to the sea between the islands are generally of the same character. This outlying frontier of islands, or of shallow waters, is broken at Wilmington, at Charleston, and at Savannah. At these three points large steamers can approach and leave the coast; but these points were at that time

---

[1] Huse to Gorgas, Vol. VI, page 33.
[2] Lawton to Cooper, 20th September, 1861, Vol. VI, page 36.
[3] Adams to Russell, Vol. I, page 760.
[4] Russell to Adams, Vol. I, page 762.
[5] Benjamin to John Fraser & Co., 27th September, 1861, Vol. VI, page 37.

guarded by the blockading vessels of the United States, so as to make the approach difficult. Vessels not of light draught and great speed were almost certain of capture; while vessels of such draught and speed could not carry both coal and a cargo across the Atlantic.

To avoid this risk it was resolved to send the purchases which might be made in England to Nassau in British bottoms, and there transship them into steamers of light draught and great speed, to be constructed for the purpose,[1] which could carry coal enough for the short passage into the waters that connected with either Charleston, Savannah, or Wilmington. The first order from Richmond that is known to have been given for such a shipment is dated the 22d of July, 1861.[2]

Geographical situation of Nassau and Bermuda. The attention of the Tribunal of Arbitration is invited to the accompanying map, showing how admirably the British ports of Nassau and Bermuda were adapted for the illegal purposes for which it was proposed to use them. Nassau was surrounded by a cluster of British islands, so that even a slow-sailing blockade-runner, pressed by a pursuing man-of-war, could in a short time reach the protection of British waters. Bermuda had the advantage of being more directly off the ports of Wilmington and Charleston. Neither Nassau nor Bermuda, however, was more than two days distant from the blockaded ports for the swift steamers that were employed in the service.[3]

On the 4th of October, 1861, Mr. Benjamin, writing from Richmond and signing himself as "Acting Secretary of War,"

---

[1] Huse to Gorgas, 15th March, 1862, Vol. VI, page 69.
[2] Walker to Huse and Anderson, Vol. VI, page 31.
[3] "The British Island of New Providence, in the Bahamas, became the favorite resort of ships employed in these enterprises. Situated in close neighborhood to the coast of Florida, and within three days' sail of Charleston, it offered singular facilities to the blockade-runners. The harbor of Nassau, usually quiet and almost empty, was soon thronged with shipping of all kinds; and its wharves and warehouses became an entrepot for cargoes brought thither from different quarters. Agents of the Confederate Government resided there, and were busily employed in assisting and developing the traffic."—*Bernard's Neutrality of Great Britain, page* 299.

addressed Mr. Mallory as "Secretary of the Navy," and asked if he could "spare an officer from his department to proceed to Havana and take charge of funds there, to be used by agents of this department in the purchase of small-arms and ammunition."[1]

Mr. Lewis Heyliger, of New Orleans, was apparently designated for this purpose. On the 30th of November, 1861, he takes a letter from Mr. Benjamin to Mr. Helm, the agent of the insurgents at Cardenas, in Cuba, saying that he is "an active and accomplished business man;" that he is to aid Helm, "whether in the disposal of the cotton or the arrangements for the shipments;" and that "the articles first in importance, and to be sent in preference to everything else, are small-arms and *cannon* powder."[2]

Heyliger went to Cuba, and in a few days after was transferred to Nassau to take charge of "the British Steamer Gladiator, Commander G. G. Bird, with a cargo for the Confederate States."[3] He remained there as the agent, treasury depositary, and representative of the insurgents during the rebellion.

What was done at Nassau. The Gladiator was a steamer bought and fitted out in England under an agreement made at London, October 24, 1861, between Mr. T. O. Stock, a subject of Her Majesty, and Mr. Caleb Huse.[4] The evident object of this agreement was to enable her to sail under the British flag, although owned by the insurgents. She was to take out five hundred tons of goods, and was "to proceed to a port in the Confederate States or an intermediate port." No concealment of her object or destination was made in England.[5] She arrived at Nassau from London on the 9th of December, 1861.[6]

The day after she arrived there a United States vessel of war came into the port. Heyliger, finding that this vessel

---

[1] Benjamin to Mallory, Vol. VI, page 39.
[2] Benjamin to Helm, Vol. VI, page 43.
[3] Helm to Heyliger, 20th December, 1861, Vol. VI, page 51.
[4] See the agreement, Vol. VI, page 42.
[5] Adams to Seward, Vol. I, page 769.
[6] Whiting to Seward, Dec. 10, 1861, Vol. VI, page 44.

would not leave, and that therefore the Gladiator, which was slower than the man-of-war, could not leave with safety, represented to the British authorities that such a course "would tend to cut off the trade" which the insurgents desired to divert to Nassau, and that he thought "some steps should be adopted to remind him [the commander] that he is infringing on the laws of hospitality." He reported this to Richmond and added, "I have reason to know that these arguments have not been without their effect, inasmuch as the matter was incidentally discussed at a meeting of the Council the other day; and I really believe that in the course of a week or two some action will be taken to impress the captain of the enemy's vessel with the conviction that his absence will be preferable to his company." "We have succeeded," he continued, "in obtaining a very important modification of the existing laws, viz.: *the privilege of breaking bulk and transshipment.*"[1] That modification was all that the insurgents wanted. That privilege converted the port of Nassau into an insurgent port, which could not be blockaded by the naval forces of the United States. Further stay of the United States vessels of war was therefore useless. The United States ask the Tribunal to find that this act, being a permission from the British authorities at Nassau, enabled a vessel chartered by the insurgents, and freighted with articles contraband of war, to diverge from its voyage, and to tranship its cargo in a British port, when not made necessary by distress, was a violation of the duties of a neutral.

On the 27th of January, 1862, Maffitt, an officer in the service of the insurgents, (the same who afterward commanded the Florida,) was sent to take command of the Gladiator as an insurgent vessel,[2] (although under British colors,) and on the 30th of January, 1862, a portion of the Gladiator's valuable cargo was transshipped to the "Kate," a small steamer sailing under British colors, and eventually all went in the same way. In the dispatch announcing the transfer

---

[1] Heyliger to Benjamin, 27th December, 1861, Vol. VI, page 55.
[2] Benjamin to Maffit, 27th January, 1862, Vol. VI, page 57.

to the "Kate," Heyliger said: "You may readily imagine how intensely disgusted the Yankees are at this partiality, as they style it. It is called another flagrant violation of neutral rights. * * My relations with the authorities here are of the most friendly character. I receive many marked attentions, which I value as going to show the increased cordiality of feeling toward the Confederate Government."[1]

The United States are not able to say what "effect" the colonial authorities of Nassau induced Heyliger to think would come from his "arguments." They point out, however, to the Tribunal of Arbitration the fact, that in about one month after that time, *viz.*, on the 31st day of January, 1862, Earl Russell informed the Lords Commissioners of the Admiralty that "during the continuance of the present hostilities * * * * no ship of war or privateer belonging to either of the belligerents shall be permitted to enter or remain in the port of Nassau, or in any other port, roadstead, or water of the Bahama Islands, except by special leave of the Lieutenant Governor of the Bahama Islands, or in case of stress of weather."[2]

An order more unfriendly to the United States, more directly in the interest of the insurgents, could not have been made, even if founded upon Heyliger's friendly intimations to the Colonial Authorities. Under the construction practically put upon it, the vessels of war of the United States were excluded from this harbor for any purpose, while it was open for free ingress and egress to vessels of the insurgents, purchased, or built, and owned by the authorities at Richmond, bringing their cotton to be transshipped in British bottoms to Fraser, Trenholm & Co., in Liverpool, and taking on board the cargoes of arms and munitions of war which had been dispatched thither from Liverpool. The Tribunal of Arbitration will not fail to observe that this was no British commerce which had existed before the war, and which the neutral might claim the right to continue. It was to a large extent the commerce of the authorities at

---

[1] Heyliger to Benjamin, January 30, 1862, Vol. VI, page 58.
[2] Vol. IV, page 175.

Richmond—carried on in their own vessels, and for their own benefit—and consisted of the export of cotton from the South on account of the so-called Government, and the returns of arms, munitions of war, and quartermaster stores from Great Britain, for the purpose of destroying the United States—a nation with which Great Britain was at peace. The United States confidently insist that Great Britain, by shielding and encouraging such a commerce, violated its duties as a neutral toward the United States.

The United States denied permission to deposit coal at Nassau. It is a most unpleasant duty of the United States to call the attention of the Tribunal of Arbitration to the fact that, at the very time of this affair of the Gladiator, another matter was going on in the same port, which furnished a commentary on the ideas of neutrality entertained by the Colonial Authorities.

The day after the arrival of that vessel, the United States Consul at Nassau wrote to his Government thus: "The coal which is being landed here for Government has caused great excitement among the Nassau masses, and a deputation visited Governor Nesbitt yesterday to remonstrate against its being landed."[1] The remonstrances were successful. On the same day the Colonial Secretary wrote to the Consul that the coal could be admitted only "on the express condition and understanding that such coal should not afterward be reshipped or otherwise used in any manner which may, in the opinion of the law authorities of the Colony, involve a breach of Her Majesty's Proclamation of the 13th of May last, *and particularly that such coal shall not be used for the purpose of coaling, or affording facilities for coaling, at this port, the vessels of war of the United States Navy, during the continuance of the hostilities.*"[2]

The sincerity of the desire of the Colonial Authorities to obey Her Majesty's Proclamation may be estimated from the following facts: 1. That that Proclamation inhibited Her Majesty's subjects from "breaking, or endeavoring to break,

---

[1] Whiting to Seward, Vol. VI, page 44; Vol. I, page 696.
[2] Thompson to Whiting, Vol. VI, page 45.

any blockade lawfully or actually established by or on behalf of either of the said contending parties;"[1] yet the Colonial Authorities finding that the Gladiator, which had been chartered to break a blockade established by the United States, would probably be intercepted by the vessels of the United States, permitted the cargo to be transshipped into smaller steamers, with the avowed purpose of breaking that blockade; 2. That Her Majesty's Proclamation also inhibited British subjects from "carrying military stores or materials, or any article or articles considered and deemed to be contraband of war, according to the law or modern usage of nations, for the use or service of either of the said contending parties;" yet the Colonial Authorities welcomed the Gladiator, sailing under the British flag with contraband of war in violation of the Proclamation, and permitted her to shift her illegal cargo into other vessels, in like manner using the British flag for the purpose of transporting it to and on account of a belligerent. 3. That Her Majesty's Proclamation made no mention of coal, and that coal is not regarded by Her Majesty's Government as an article necessarily contraband of war;[2] yet the Government of the United States was forbidden by the same authorities, in the same week, to deposit its coal at Nassau, except upon the condition that it would not use it.

The United States have no reason to suppose that either of these partial decisions met with the disapproval of Her Majesty's Government.

Complaints to Earl Russell and his reply. On the contrary, Earl Russell, on the 8th of January, 1862, in reply to a complaint from Mr. Adams that the port of Nassau was used as a depot of supplies by the insurgents, officially informed that gentleman that he had received "a report from the receiver general of the port of Nassau *stating that no warlike stores have been received at that port*, either from Great Britain or elsewhere, and that no munitions of war have been shipped from thence to the Confederate States."[3] The

---

[1] Vol. I, page 44.
[2] Lord Granville to Count Bernstorff, 15th September, 1870.
[3] Russell to Adams, Vol. VI, page 57.

United States with confidence assert, in view of what has been already shown, that, had Earl Russell seriously inquired into the complaints of Mr. Adams, a state of facts would have been disclosed entirely at variance with this report—one which should have impelled Her Majesty's Government to suppress what was going on at Nassau. The foregoing facts were all within the reach of Her Majesty's Government, although at that time not within the reach of the Government of the United States. The failure to discover them, after Mr. Adams had called attention to them, was a neglect of the diligence in the preservation of its neutrality, which was "due" from Great Britain to the United States; and it taints all the subsequent conduct of Great Britain toward the United States during the struggle.

On the 31st day of the same month, instructions issued from the Foreign Office, prescribing the amount of hospitalities to be extended to the belligerents.

Instructions as to hospitalities to the belligerents. These instructions have already been referred to. They provided that: 1. No ship of war or privateer of either belligerent was to be permitted to enter any port, roadstead, or water in the Bahamas except by special leave of the Lieutenant Governor, or in case of stress of weather; and in case such permission should be given, the vessel was nevertheless to be required to go to sea as soon as possible, and with no supplies except such as might be necessary for immediate use. 2. No ship of war or privateer of either belligerent was to be permitted to use British ports or waters as a station or place of resort for any warlike purpose, or for the purpose of obtaining any facilities of warlike equipment. 3. Such ships or privateers entering British waters were to be required to depart within twenty-four hours after entrance, except in case of stress of weather, or requiring provisions or things for the crew or repairs; in which cases they were to go to sea as soon as possible after the expiration of the twenty-four hours, taking only the supplies necessary for immediate use; they were not to remain in port more than twenty-four hours after the completion of necessary repairs. 4. Supplies to such ships or privateers were to be limited to what might be necessary for the subsistence of the crew, and to enough coal to take the vessel to the nearest port of its own country or to some nearer destination; and a vessel that had been supplied with coal in British waters could not be again supplied with it within British jurisdiction, until after the expiration of three months from the date of the last supply taken from a British port.[1]

Lord Palmerston's threats. Almost simultaneously with the announcement by Earl Russell of an imaginary condition of affairs at Nassau, Lord Palmerston stated to Mr. Adams that "it would no do for the United States ships of war to harass British commerce on the high seas, under pretense of preventing the Confederates from receiving things that are contraband of war."[2] Thus, Great Britain, in the month of January, 1862 through Earl Russell and Lord Palmerston, and the instructions to the Admiralty excluding United States vessels of war from the port of Nassau, except by permission of the Governor, virtually said to the United States: "You complain that the insurgents make illegal use of Nassau, to your injury, in violation of the Queen's Proclamation, and of our duties as a neutral. We deny the fact; at the same time we exclude your vessels from that port, the place where you can best establish the truth of your allegations, and we warn you not to attempt to prove them by examining too closely, on the high seas, the vessels which sail under the British flag."

Having now shown how the operations of the insurgents began at Nassau, and how they were facilitated by the coöperation and complicity of the local authorities, it will not be necessary to trespass on the patience of the Tribunal of Arbitration by a similarly minute examination of the doings at that port for the rest of the year 1862. Other vessels, freighted with contraband of war, followed the Gladiator. The Economist and the Southwick came closely upon her track, and Heyliger was directed to do with their cargoes as he had done with the Gladiator's.[3] Huse was also instructed to continue his purchases, and to send to the West

---

[1] Vol. IV, page 175.
[2] Earl Russell to Lord Lyons, Vol. II, page 591.
[3] Benjamin to Heyliger, 22d March, 1862, Vol. VI, page 71.

India Islands, where the steamers could break bulk.[1] Huse called the attention of his principals to the efficiency of the blockade; said that the vessels which brought the cargoes across the Atlantic could not enter the blockaded ports; urged them to continue the system of transshipment; and complained of the activity of the United States officials.[2] It was considered important to have a naval officer in charge of the transshipments, and Maffitt was detailed for the purpose.[3] He arrived there on or about the 21st of May, and reported that he had assumed command of the Manassas, [Florida;] which had arrived there from Liverpool on the 28th day of April: said that his "ambition was great;" and promised to give "annoyance to the enemy."[4] In May the supply of coal for the insurgent vessels fell short, and Heyliger went to Bermuda to buy some.[5] The steps taken about this time for the detention of the Florida will be alluded to later.

Contraband of war fraudulently cleared at Nassau for British ports. The cargoes of contraband of war that were thus transshipped were entered on the manifests as for St. John's, New Brunswick. It could not but have been well known at the custom-house that this was a fraud; yet the customs authorities winked at the fraud, and gave the vessels clearances as British vessels sailing for British ports.[6]

Heyliger continued to report the transshipment and forwarding of these arms and military supplies. He noticed the arrival and departure of the "Kate," and other vessels, on account of the insurgent authorities, and on the 26th of July, 1862, he reported that the "Steamer Scotia, a private venture,"[7] was about to leave with a large supply of rifles, powder, and other ammunition. He did not report any other "private venture," so far as known to the United States.

---

[1] Benjamin to Huse, 10th March, 1862, Vol. VI, page 68.
[2] Huse to Gorgas, 15th March, Vol. VI, page 69.
[3] Randolph to Heyliger, 11th April, 1862, Vol. VI, page 72.
[4] Maffitt to Randolph, 21st May, 1862, Vol. VI, page 83.
[5] Heyliger to Randolph, 28th June, 1862, Vol. VI, page 87.
[6] Hawley to Seward, 27th June, 1863, Vol. VI, page 127.
[7] Heyliger to Randolph, Vol. VI, page 92.

Résumé for the year 1862. The operations of Huse during this year, and his shipments through Heyliger, are detailed as follows in a letter from Colonel Gorgas, insurgent Chief of Ordnance, to the insurgent Secretary of War, dated December 3, 1862.[1] "The purchase of ordnance and ordnance stores in foreign markets on Government account are made by Major Caleb Huse, C. S. Artillery, who resides in London, and whose address is No. 38, Clarendon Road, Notting Hill, London, West. Major Huse was detailed for this duty in April, 1861. * * * He has purchased arms to the amount of 157,000, [stands?] and large quantities of gunpowder, some artillery, infantry equipments, harness, swords, percussion caps, saltpeter, lead, &c. In addition to ordnance stores, using a rare forecast, he has purchased and shipped large supplies of clothing, blankets, cloth, and shoes for the quartermaster's department, without specific orders to do so. * * To pay for these purchases, funds have been from time to time sent to him by the Treasury Department, on requisition from the War Department, amounting in the aggregate to $3,095,139 18. These have been wholly inadequate to his wants, and have fallen far short of our requisitions. He was consequently in debt at latest advices to the amount of £444,850, a sum equivalent, when the value of exchange is considered, to $5,925,402 of our currency. " * An agent, Mr. Norman S. Walker, was lately dispatched with $2,000,000 in bonds of the Confederate States. The instructions to Mr. Walker direct him to return to Bermuda, after the disposition of the bonds in England, and after conference with Major Huse. He is to remain there as a resident disbursing agent, and is, in conjunction with Mr. S. G. Porter, charged with the transfers of the cargo of the 'Harriet Pinkney,' now there, and other ships hereafter to arrive, to the ports of the Confederate States. * * * A large part of the cargoes have been landed at Nassau, and thence transmitted to the ports of the Confederate States in fast steamers. Their destination has lately been changed to Bermuda, where several most valuable car-

---

[1] Gorgas to Seddon, Vol. VI, page 104.

goes are now awaiting transportation. It appears to me to be the appropriate duty of the Navy Department to assist in the running in of these cargoes; but if the burden of it is to be borne entirely by the War Department, it is highly important that light-draught steamers should be purchased, and used solely for the transportation of cargoes from Bermuda."

Base changed to Bermuda. This change to Bermuda had been recommended by Huse in the previous August.[1] The reason given was that "the port of Nassau had become dangerous;" and he had appointed as agent there "Mr. S. G. Porter, a gentleman highly recommended by Commander J. D. Bullock." Gorgas inquired of the insurgent Secretary of War whether Huse's appointment of Porter should be approved,[2] and the reply is to be found in the above extract. Walker went there before January 1, 1863,[3] and on the 9th day of February, 1863, it was reported that Bermuda was a good depot for the purpose, and that the insurgent authorities "had then three steamers running there."[4]

Having thus shown that the branch of the insurgent War Department, established in Great Britain had, during the years 1861 and 1862, purchased arms, ammunition, and supplies to the amount of about nine millions of dollars, and that the branch of their Treasury established at Liverpool, had during the same time, paid on account of these purchases over three millions of dollars, and that vessels either belonging to or chartered by the insurgent authorities were occupied as transports, (in violation of the Foreign Enlistment Act of 1819,) in carrying this large quantity of war material from British ports to the insurgents, and in bringing back cotton, the property of the insurgent authorities, to be used in making payments therefor, it is now necessary to see what the branch of their Navy Department, under the direction of Bullock, was engaged in during the same period.

---

[1] Huse to Gorgas, 4th August, 1862, Vol. VI, page 93.
[2] Gorgas to Randolph, 1st November, 1862, Vol. VI, page 103.
[3] Gorgas to Huse, 1st January, 1863, Vol. VI, page 107.
[4] Gorgas to Huse, 9th February, 1863, Vol. VI, page 111.

The United States are not able to trace these transactions with the minuteness with which they have been able to narrate the doings of Huse and Heyliger. The correspondence of those who assumed to direct the naval affairs of the insurgents has not come into the possession of the United States, as did the confidential correspondence of other agents heretofore cited. Bullock's operations, however, were on so large a scale that it will not be difficult to follow him. In doing this the United States will confine themselves to general statements, reserving the particulars for the remarks that will be made upon the career of each cruiser.

What was done at Liverpool by Bullock.

Bullock, as has been said, established himself in Liverpool in the summer of 1861. The United States Consul reports him on the 20th of September as "residing in private lodgings in Liverpool," and as being "chiefly in communication with Fraser, Trenholm & Co., whose office he visits daily." Prioleau, one of the firm of Fraser, Trenholm & Co., says that he occupied for a year after his arrival a room in their office.[1]

It is probable that as early as October, 1861, he had made the contracts for the two gun-boats which were afterward known as the Florida and the Alabama. The drawings of the Alabama were signed by the Lairds, who built her, on the 9th of October, 1861. The United States have no means for determining the date when the contract was made with Fawcett, Preston & Co., for the Florida. Their Consul at Liverpool has stated that on his arrival at the consulate in November, 1861, his attention was called by the acting consul to this vessel, then called the Oreto, and to the Alabama. It is clear, therefore, that the work was advanced at that time.[2] Prioleau also testifies that he introduced Bullock to Fawcett, Preston & Co., for the purpose of making the contract for the Florida.[3]

The Florida.

By the 4th of February, 1862, the Florida was so nearly completed that the Consul at

---

[1] Vol. VI, page 185.
[2] Dudley to Edwards, Vol. III, page 17.
[3] Dudley to Seward, Vol. VI, page 186.

Liverpool wrote, "She is now taking in her coal, and appearances indicate that she will leave here the latter part of the week without her armament." Her gun-carriages were soon taken on board, in pieces, some in a rough state, and were put in the hold,[1] and a day or two later she received her provisions, and the crew was shipped. The steamer Bahama preceded her by a few days with her armament, but reached Nassau after her.

When the Florida sailed she took a crew of fifty-two men and some guns,[2] and was in every respect a man-of-war except that her armament was not in place. It was conclusively shown at Nassau that she might have been fitted for battle in twenty-four hours after leaving the dock in the Mersey.[3]

The vessel in that condition was consigned by Bullock to Heyliger.[4] The condition of Bullock with the vessel from the beginning is established by this act, as well as by the evidence of Prioleau. The connection of Fraser, Trenholm & Co. is shown by the admission of Prioleau, and by the fact that a member of that firm accompanied her on her trial trip and on her departure.[5]

Mr. Adams called the attention of Earl Russell to the character and destination of this vessel on the 29th of February, and again on the 25th of March, 1861. Her Majesty's Government had ample time to ascertain her character and to detain her. They did go through the form of an examination which, seen in the light of subsequent events, reads like a farce.[6]

The Alabama.   The work on the Alabama progressed more slowly that that on the Florida, possibly because it was a larger vessel. She was launched on the 15th of May, and made her trial trip on the 12th of June.[7]

---

[1] Dudley to Seward, Vol. II, page 593.
[2] Report of Board of Customs, Vol. II, page 605.
[3] Captain Hickley's affidavit, Vol. VI, page 263.
[4] Heyliger to Randolph, 2d May, 1862, Vol. VI, page 76.
[5] Dudley to Edwards, Vol. III, page 17.
[6] Vol. II, pages 595 and 604.
[7] Dudley to Seward, Vol. III, page 1.

"The money for her was advanced by Fraser, Trenholm & Co."[1] Captain Bullock was "all the time in communication with Fawcett, Preston & Co., who fitted out the Oreto, and with the Lairds, who were fitting out this vessel," and went "almost daily on board the gun-boat, and seemed to be recognized as in authority." It was even said in Liverpool that he was to command her.[2] Mr. Adams, on the 23d of June, invited Earl Russell's attention to this vessel, and an examination was ordered. The examiners reported to the Lords Commissioners of Her Majesty's Treasury that it was "most apparent that she is intended for a ship of war," and that "the description of her in the communication of the United States Consul is most correct, with the exception that her engines are not constructed on the oscillatory principle."[3]

The evidence of the criminal character of the vessel became so overwhelming that Her Majesty's Government was at length induced to give an order for her detention. Before the order reached Liverpool she had escaped. She ran down to Moelfra Bay, on the coast of the Isle of Anglesey, and there took on board twenty or thirty men from the tug Hercules, with the knowledge of the British officials at Liverpool. She then sailed to the Azores, where she was met by the Agrippina from London and the Bahama from Liverpool. These vessels brought her officers, her armaments, and her coal. The transshipments were made, and then the British ensign was hauled down, and the insurgent flag hoisted.

It is not deemed necessary to examine further, in this connection, the evidence showing the palpable character of this vessel, especially as Lord Russell, in the course of the discussion which ensued, admitted that "*it is undoubtedly true that the Alabama was partly fitted out in a British port.*"[4] That evidence will be discussed more at length in its appropriate place. For the present, the United States

---

[1] Dudley to Edwards, Vol. III, page 16.
[2] Dudley to Adams, Vol. III, page 6.
[3] Report of Board of Customs, Vol. III, page 7.
[4] Earl Russell to Mr. Adams, 26th September, 1864, Vol. III, page 299.

only aim to satisfy the Tribunal that, flagrant as was the violation of neutrality in the case of the Alabama, it was but a part of the great scheme which was set on foot when Huse, Bullock, and Fraser, Trenholm & Co., combined together in Liverpool.

The Sumter at Gibraltar. The operations of Captain Bullock were manifest about this time in quite another quarter of the globe. The insurgent steamer Sumter put into Gibraltar in January, 1862, out of coal, and not being able immediately to obtain any was obliged to remain there until United States men-of-war arrived in those waters. Deeming it impossible to escape she was then offered for sale, and when the sellers came to make title, the officer in charge produced "a power of attorney from a certain Bullock, who styles himself senior naval officer in Europe."[1] Great Britain, in spite of the protests of the United States officials,[2] permitted a sale to take place,[3] and it is not improbable that, if the sale was *bona fide*, the money went to the insurgent agents to swell the fund for the payment of the Alabama and the Florida, then in the Mersey.

The Florida at Nassau. When the Florida reached Nassau, it was again found necessary to depend upon the Liverpool combination for funds.

The insurgent Secretary of the Navy making application to their Secretary of the Treasury for fifty thousand dollars, to fit out and equip the C. S. Steamer "Manassas," [Florida,] "now at Nassau,"[4] was answered that "the department had funds in England," and that he could have "a bill of exchange on England for the amount required."[5] Mallory accepted the suggestion, and requested Memminger to "transmit to Nassau, through Messrs. J. Fraser & Co., of Charleston, a bill of exchange in favor of Lieutenant John N. Maffitt,

---

[1] Sprague to Adams, 9th December, 1862, Vol. II, page 507.
[2] Sprague to Freeling, Vol. II, page 511.
[3] Sprague to Adams, Vol. II, page 515.
[4] Mallory to Memminger, 26th May, 1862, Vol. VI, page 84.
[5] Memminger to Mallory, 27th May, 1862, Vol. VI, page 85.

for fifty thousand dollars, ($50,000,) or its equivalent in pounds,"[1] which was done.

Contracts for constructing six iron-clads. The construction and dispatch of these vessels were by no means all that was planned in Liverpool during that year. On the 21st day of August, 1862, Mallory, the insurgent Secretary of the Navy, wrote Mr. Jefferson Davis: "A contract has been made *for the construction abroad* and delivery of six iron-clad steam-vessels of war, upon plans and specifications prepared by this department, which, with the outfits to be furnished, together with six complete extra engines and boilers, are estimated to cost about $3,500,000."[2] The estimates annexed to this letter are to the same amount. Thus it appears that, before the 1st of January, 1863, Bullock had dispatched from Great Britain two formidable cruisers, the Alabama and the Florida, to prey upon the commerce of the United States, had sold another cruiser at Gibraltar, and had possibly turned the proceeds into the Treasury of the insurgents, at the office of Fraser, Trenholm & Co., and had, by himself or through another agent, made some sort of a contract for the construction of six iron-clads; and that Fraser, Trenholm & Co. had provided the funds for these vessels, and also for what was necessary in order to complete the fitting of the Florida at Nassau.

The Sumter at Trinidad. Before proceeding further in this history, it is better to pause to take note of two other acts of the Colonial Authorities, which, so far as known, were not censured by Great Britain. The first of these was the hospitality extended to the Sumter in Trinidad, in August, 1861. She was allowed to remain five days in port, and to "supply herself with coals and other necessary outfits."[3] The second case was the reception of the Florida at Nassau, in 1863. The Florida steamed into Nassau on the morning of the 26th of January, in that year. What took place is

---

[1] Mallory to Memminger, 27th May, 1862, Vol. VI, page 85.
[2] Vol. VI, page 96. See also, on the same point, Mallory to Mason, 30th October, 1862, Vol. I, page 573.
[3] Bernard to Seward, Vol. II, page 485.

The Florida at Nassau. thus described by an insurgent writer: "This seems to be our principal port of entry, and the amount of money we throw into the hands of the Nassauites *probably* influences their sentiments in our favor. *We took on board coal and provisions to last us for several months.*"[1]

Mr. Adams represents the foregoing facts to Earl Russell. This history has now arrived at the time when the United States were in a position to confirm to Great Britain all, and more than all, that Mr. Adams had represented to Earl Russell as to the course of the insurgents in Liverpool, and to place in the hands of Her Majesty's Government the thread for the discovery of all the violations of British sovereignty, and of all the injuries to the United States perpetrated on British soil, which have been set forth in this paper. On the 19th of January, 1863, Mr. Seward transmitted to Mr. Adams "a copy of some treasonable correspondence of the insurgents at Richmond, with their agents abroad, which throws a flood of light upon the naval preparations they are making in Great Britain."[2] On the 9th day of February, 1863, Mr. Adams inclosed this correspondence to Earl Russell, with a note in which he said—what could be said without the least exaggeration—"These papers go to show a deliberate attempt to establish within the limits of this Kingdom a system of action in direct hostility to the Government of the United States. This plan embraces not only the building and fitting out of several ships of war under the direction of agents especially commissioned for the purpose, but the preparation of a series of measures under the same auspices for the obtaining from Her Majesty's subjects the pecuniary means essential to the execution of those hostile projects. * * * Taken as a whole, these papers serve most conclusively to show that no respect whatever has been paid in her own realm by these parties to the neutrality declared by Her Majesty at the outset of these hostilities; and that, so far as may be in their power, they are bent on making her

---

[1] Journal of Confederate Steamer Florida, Vol. VI, page 335.
[2] Seward to Adams, Vol. I, page 546.

Kingdom subservient to their purpose of conducting hostilities against 'a nation with which she is at peace."[1]

Earl Russell declines to act. Lord Russell delayed his answer to this communication exactly one month. On the 9th day of March, 1863, he made a reply, the substance of which was that Her Majesty's Government would not examine into the truth of Mr. Seward's and Mr. Adam's allegations, because, even if they were true, the papers which had been submitted by Mr. Adams went "merely to show that the agents of the so-called Confederate States resident in this country [Great Britain] have received instructions from their own Government to endeavor to raise money on securities of that Government in England, and to enter into contracts for the purchase of munitions of war, and for the building of iron-clad vessels; but there is no *proof* in these papers that the agents referred to have as yet brought themselves within the reach of any criminal law of the United Kingdom."[2]

Inefficiency of the Foreign Enlistment Act. In order fully to comprehend the force of this answer, it is necessary to ask the Tribunal to pause, for the purpose of inquiring into what had taken place between the two Governments as to alleged defects in the Foreign Enlistment Act, and as to the necessity of amending it so as to give the Government greater powers.

It was found when the Foreign Enlistment Act of 1819 came to be put into operation, under the direction of a Government inspired by unfriendly feelings toward the United States, that there were practical and multiplying difficulties in the way of using it so as to prevent the departure of the cruisers. Earl Russell, as early as March, 1862, in reply to an earnest representation[3] made by Mr. Adams under instructions, said that *"the duty of nations in amity with each other is not to suffer their good faith to be violated by evil-disposed persons within their borders, merely from the inefficiency of their prohibitory policy."*[4]

---

[1] Adams to Russell, Vol. I, page 562.
[2] Vol. I, page 578.   [3] Adams to Russell, Vol. I, page 30.
[4] Russell to Adams, Vol. I, page 633.

Within a few months after this the Alabama escaped from the port of Liverpool, and never returned. The openness and the audacity with which this was done seemed at one time to induce the British Cabinet to entertain the idea of amending the Foreign Enlistment Act.

Propositions to amend the Foreign Enlistment Act. On the 19th day of December, 1862,[1] Lord Russell, in reply to what he called Mr. Adams's "demand for a more effective prevention for the future of the fitting out of such vessels from British ports," informed him that Her Majesty's Government were "of opinion that certain amendments might be Introduced into the Foreign Enlistment Act, which, if sanctioned by Parliament, would have the effect of giving greater power to the Executive *to prevent the construction in British ports of ships destined for the use of belligerents.*" He also said that he was ready at any time to confer with Mr. Adams, and to listen to any suggestions which he might have to make by which the British Foreign Enlistment Act and the corresponding Statute of the United States might be made more efficient for their purpose.

Propositions declined by Great Britain. Mr. Adams communicated with his Government, and, having obtained instructions, informed Lord Russell that his "suggestion of possible amendments to the enlistment laws in order to make them more effective had been favorably received. Although the law of the United States was considered as of very sufficient vigor, the Government were not unwilling to consider propositions to improve upon it." Lord Russell replied that, since his note was written, the subject had been considered in Cabinet, and the Lord Chancellor had expressed the opinion that the British law was sufficiently effective, and that under these circumstances he did not see that he could have any change to propose.[2]

The United States are unable to state what amendments to the Foreign Enlistment Acts of the two countries the British Government might have proposed had they not changed

---

[1] Russell to Adams, Vol. I, page 667.
[2] Adams to Seward, Vol. I, page 668.

their minds between December, 1862, and March, 1863. It is to be presumed, from the use of the word "*construction*" in Lord Russell's note, that it was in contemplation to make some proposition to remedy a supposed defect in the British statute as to the *construction* of a vessel intended to carry on war, as distinguished from the "*equipping, furnishing, fitting out, or arming*" such a vessel. It was understood to be the opinion of the British lawyers that the construction of such a vessel was not an offense under the act of 1819. It is also possible that Her Majesty's Government may have desired to give to the Executive in Great Britain some power similar to that possessed by the Executive of the United States for the arrest of vessels so constructed. As the proposal for negotiations on the subject was withdrawn, it is impossible to do more than conjecture what was contemplated.

From the hour when Lord Russell informed Mr. Adams that the Lord Chancellor was satisfied that the British laws were sufficiently effective, the British Government resisted every attempt to change the laws and give them more vigor.

Propositions renewed and declined.

Mr. Adams again, on the 26th of March, 1863, sought an interview with Lord Russell on the subject of the rebel hostile operations in British territory. What took place there is described by Lord Russell in a letter written on the following day to Lord Lyons.[1] "With respect to the law itself, Mr. Adams said either it was sufficient for the purposes of neutrality, and then let the British Government enforce it; *or it was insufficient, and then let the British Government apply to Parliament to amend it*. I said that the Cabinet were of opinion that the law was sufficient, but that legal evidence could not always be procured; that the British Government had done everything in its power to execute the law, *but I admitted that the cases of the Alabama and Oreto*

---

[1] Vol. 1, page 585. See also Mr. Hammond's letter to Messrs. Lamport and Holt and others, Vol. 1, page 602; also Lord Palmerston's speech already cited, Vol. IV, page 530.

were a scandal, and, in some degree, a reproach to our laws."

The Tribunal of Arbitration will thus see that about three weeks before Earl Russell made his extraordinary official reply to the representations of Mr. Adams, he had informed Mr. Adams "that the Lord Chancellor had expressed the opinion that the British [neutrality] law was sufficiently effective, and that, under these circumstances, he did not see that he could have any change to propose"[1] in it. It will also now be observed that when that declaration was made, Mr. Adams's note of February 9, 1863, with the proof of the complicity of the insurgent agents in England, had been in Earl Russell's portfolio four days. It will also be observed that that proof established, or afforded to Earl Russell the clew by which he could, and, as the United States say, should have satisfied himself — 1. "That contracts were already made for the constructions of iron-clad 'fighting-ships' in England."[2] 2. That Fraser, Trenholm & Co. were the "depositaries" of the insurgents in Liverpool, and that the money in their hands was "to be applied to the contracts."[3] 3. That they (F., T. & Co.) were to pay purchases made by Mr. Huse and other agents.[4] 4. That other contracts for the construction of vessels besides those for the six iron-clads had been taken by parties in Great Britain.[5] 5. That parties in England were arranging for an insurgent cotton loan, the proceeds of which were to be deposited with Fraser, Trenholm & Co. for the purpose of carrying out all these contracts.[6]

When the United States found that the proof of such aggravated wrong was not deemed worthy of investigation

---

[1] Vol. I, page 668.
[2] Mallory to Mason, Vol. I, page 573.
[3] Memminger to Spence, Vol. I, page 574.
[4] Memminger to Fraser, Trenholm & Co., Vol. I, page 574; and same to same, Vol. I, page 575.
[5] Memorandum No. 11, in Vol. I, page 572.
[6] Benjamin to Mason, Vol. I, page 564. Memminger to Mason, Vol. I, page 565. Memminger to Spence, Vol. I, page 574. Memminger to Fraser, Trenholm & Co., Vol. I, page 574.

by Her Majesty's Government, because it contained no statements which could be used as evidence to convict a criminal before an English jury,[1] they were most reluctantly forced from that time forward, throughout the struggle, to believe, that no complaints would be listened to by Her Majesty's Government which were not accompanied by proof that the persons complained of had brought themselves "within reach of the criminal law of the United Kingdom;" that the penal provisions of the Foreign Enlistment Act of 1819 were to be taken by Great Britain as the measure of its duty as a neutral; and that no amendment or change in that act was to be made with the assent of the existing Government.

These proceedings were an abandonment, in advance, of "due diligence." They earnestly and confidently insist before this tribunal, that this decision of Her Majesty's Government was in violation of its obligations toward the United States; that it was an abandonment, in advance, not only of that "due diligence" which is defined in the Treaty of Washington as one of the duties of a neutral, but of any measure of diligence, to restrain the insurgents from using its territory for purposes hostile to the United States.

Encouraged by the immunity afforded by these several decisions of Her Majesty's Government, the insurgent agents in Great Britain began to extend their operations.

The Georgia. Early in April, 1863, a steamer, called the "Japan," which was afterward known as the "Georgia," left the Clyde, "with intent to depredate on the commerce of the United States."[2] This vessel had been publicly launched on the 10th of the previous January as an insurgent steamer, at which time "a Miss North, daughter of a Captain North, of one of the Confederate States, offi-

---

[1] It is supposed to be a principle of English law that a person accused of crime has the right to have the witnesses against him subjected to a personal cross-examination. The absurdity of Earl Russell's position is shown by the fact that every witness whose correspondence was inclosed in Mr. Adams's note of February 9, 1863, was then in Richmond, behind the bayonets of General Lee's army.

[2] Mr. Adams to Earl Russell, Vol. II, page 666.

ciated as priestess, and christened the craft "Virginia."[1] "Some seventy or eighty men, twice, the number that would be required for any legitimate voyage, were shipped at Liverpool for this vessel, and sent to Greenoch."[2] A small steamer called the "Alar," belonging to a British subject was loaded with a large supply of guns, shells, shot, powder, &c.,"[3] and dispatched to meet her. The two vessels met off the French coast; the "Alar" was made fast alongside the "Japan," and in twenty-four hours the whole of the guns and ammunition were transferred.[4] The "Japan" then dropped her Oriental name, hoisted the flag of the insurgents, and steamed away; one day's work after leaving the Clyde having converted her into an armed cruiser. It was not, however, until the 23d of the following June that her British register was canceled and the transfer made to foreign owners.[5]

The Alexandra. Early in March, 1863, Miller & Son, the builders of the Florida, launched, at their yard in Liverpool, a new gun boat, to be called the Alexandra.[6] The evidence of the hostile uses for which this vessel was intended was so overwhelming that proceedings were instituted against her for a violation of the Foreign Enlistment Act.[7] In the trial of this case it was clearly proved that the Alexandra was a man-of-war, and that she was constructed for the purpose of carrying on hostilities against the United States.[8]

---

[1] Underwood to Seward, January 16, 1863, Vol. VI, page 503.
[2] Dudley to Mr. Seward, Vol. II, page 685.
[3] Vol. II, page 666.
[4] Mahon's affidavit, Vol. II, page 673.
[5] Mr. Adams to Earl Russell, July 7, 1863, Vol. II, page 677.
[6] Dudley to Seward, March 11, 1863, Vol. II, page 258.
[7] See Vol. V, pages 1 to 470.
[8] "The evidence as to the build and fittings of the ship proved that she was strongly built, principally of teak-wood; her beams and hatches, in strength and distance apart, were greater than those in merchant vessels; the length and breadth of her hatches were less than the length and breadth of hatches in merchant vessels; her bulwarks were strong and low, and her upper works were of pitch-pine. At the time of her seizure workmen were employed in fitting her with stanchions for hammock nettings; iron stanchions were fitted in the hold; her

But the judge instructed the jury that a neutral might "make a vessel and arm it, and then offer it for sale"[1] to a belligerent; and that, *a fortiori*, "if any man may build a vessel for the purpose of offering it to either of the belligerent Powers who is minded to have it, may he not execute an order for it?" He also instructed them that "to 'equip' is 'to furnish with arms;'" "in the case of a ship, especially, it is to furnish and complete with arms;"[2] that "'equip,' 'furnish,' 'fit out,' or 'arm,' all mean precisely the same thing;" and he closed that branch of the instructions by saying, "the question is whether you think that this vessel was fitted. Armed she certainly was not, but was there an intention that she should be finished, fitted, or equipped, in Liverpool? Because, gentlemen, I must say, it seems to me that the Alabama sailed away from Liverpool without any arms at all; merely a ship in ballast, unfurnished, unequipped, unprepared; and her arms were put in at Terceira, not a port in Her Majesty's Dominions. The Foreign Enlistment Act is no more violated by that than by any other indifferent matter that might happen about a boat of any kind whatever." The jury gave a verdict without delay for the gun-boat. An appeal on this construction of the statute was taken to a higher court. The rulings of the judge on the trial were not reversed, and the decision stood as the law of England until and after the close of the rebellion, and still stands as the judicial construction of the act of 1819.

---

three masts were up, and had lightning conductors on each of them; she was provided with a cooking apparatus for 150 or 200 people; she had complete accommodation for men and officers; she had only stowage room sufficient for her crew, supposing them to be 32 men; and she was apparently built for a gun-boat, with low bulwarks, over which pivot guns could play. The commander of Her Majesty's ship Majestic, stationed at Liverpool, said that she was not intended for mercantile purposes." (*Neutrality of Great Britain during the American Civil War*, by *Mountague Bernard, M. A.*, page 353, note 1.)

[1] Vol. V, page 128.
[2] Vol. V, page 129.

The rulings in the Alexandra case related the Foreign Enlistment Act. Thus, after the political branch of Her Majesty's Government had announced its purpose of limiting its duties to the enforcement of the Foreign Enlistment Acts, and had practically stripped that act of all features except those relating to the prosecution of offenders as criminals, the judicial branch of that Government emasculated it by a ruling which openly authorized the construction of new Alabamas and of new Floridas.

Contracts were also made, some time in the year 1862 for the construction, at Glasgow, of a formidable vessel, known as the Pampero. Mr. Dudley reported that the cost of the construction was to be something over £300,000.[1] This vessel was seized at Glasgow for an alleged violation of the Foreign Enlistment Act. On the trial, which took place in 1864, it appeared that the Scottish courts were not disposed to follow the English courts in depriving the Foreign Enlistment Act of all force. The insurgents, therefore, abandoned the attempt to use the Pampero as a cruiser, and ceased to contract for the construction or fitting out of vessels within the Scottish Kingdom. A similar course in the English courts might have produced similar results in England.

Lairds' iron-clad rams. About the same time the arrangements were made with the Lairds for the construction, at Birkenhead, opposite Liverpool, of the two iron-clads which were afterwards known as "Lairds' iron-clads," or "Lairds' rams." The keel of one of them, as has been already said, was laid in the same stocks from which the Alabama was launched.[2] These vessels were most formidable, and were "pushed forward with all possible dispatch. The men were at work night and day upon them." The machinery and guns were made simultaneously with the hull, and it was reported that "by the time she is launched they will be ready to be placed in her."[3]

Their construction was originally ordered from Richmond,

---

[1] Dudley to Seward, Vol. II, page 201.
[2] Dudley to Seward, Vol. II, page 315.
[3] Dudley to Seward, Vol. II, page 316.

and they were superintended by Captain Bullock,[1] who was at that time in frequent correspondence with Mr. Mallory "about building the two above-named and other war vessels in England," "and about the money to pay for the same."[2] "The drawings for them were in the office of Fraser, Trenholm & Co., as early as June, 1862, in Captain Bullock's hands."[2] By the early part of April, 1863, "the hulls were complete, and the sides were covered with slabs of teak-wood about twelve inches thick." Early in June, 1863, one of the vessels had begun to receive her iron armor plates, "about four inches thick." "The deck of each vessel was prepared to receive two turrets."[3] "Each ram had a stem, made of wrought iron, about eight inches thick, projecting about five feet under the water-line, and obviously intended for the purpose of penetrating and destroying other vessels."[4] These facts, and others, were communicated by Mr. Adams to Earl Russell in a note dated July 11, 1863.[5] Commenting upon them, Mr. Adams said: "A war has thus been practically conducted by a portion of her people against a Government with which Her Majesty is under the most solemn of all national engagements to preserve a lasting and durable peace." On the 16th of July, Mr. Adams sent to Lord Russell further evidence of the character of these vessels.[6] On the 25th of July he again wrote him on the subject, with fresh proof of their purposes.[7] On the 14th of August he again wrote to Earl Russell with "further information;" said that he regretted to see "that the preparation * * * is not intermitted;" and added: "It is difficult for me to give to your Lordship an adequate idea of the uneasiness and anxiety created in the different ports of the United States by the idea that instruments of injury, of so formidable a character, continue to threaten their safety, as issuing from

---

[1] Younge's deposition, Vol. II, page 330.
[2] Younge's deposition, Vol. II, page 331.
[3] Chapman's affidavit, Vol. II, page 333.
[4] Chapman's affidavit, Vol. II, page 333.
[5] Adams to Russell, Vol. II, page 325.
[6] Adams to Russell, Vol. II, page 336.
[7] Adams to Russell, Vol. II, page 341.

the ports of Great Britain, a country with which the people of the United States are at peace."[1] On the 3d of September Mr. Adams again earnestly returned to the subject. He wrote to Earl Russell, inclosing "copies of further depositions relating to the launching and other preparation of the second of the two vessels of war from the yard of Messrs. Laird, at Birkenhead."[2] He said that he believed there was "not any reasonable ground for doubt that these vessels, if permitted to leave the port of Liverpool, will be at once devoted to the object of carrying on war against the United States of America," and he closed by saying that he had been directed "to describe the grave nature of the situation in which both countries must be placed, in the event of an act of aggression committed against the Government and the people of the United States by either of these formidable vessels." The new evidence inclosed in this letter related only to the fact that the second ram was launched, and cannot be said to have strengthened the case as previously presented. Again, on the 4th of September, Mr. Adams sent to the Foreign Office evidence to show the preparation for immediate departure of one of these vessels.[3] Late in the afternoon of the 4th, after the note had been dispatched to Earl Russell and a copy of it sent to Mr. Seward, Mr. Adams received from Earl Russell a note, dated the 1st of September, saying that "Her Majesty's Government are advised that they cannot interfere in any way with these vessels."[4] On the 5th Mr. Adams replied, expressing his "profound regret at the conclusion to which Her Majesty's Government have arrived;" and added: "It would be superfluous in me to point out to your Lordship that this is war."[5] On the 6th of September Mr. Adams received a short note, written in the third person, in which it was said "instructions have been issued which will prevent the departure of the two iron-clad

---

[1] Vol. II, page 346—7.
[2] Adams to Russell, Vol. II, page 353.
[3] Adams to Russell, September 4, 1863, Vol. II, p. 358.
[4] Russell to Adams, Vol. II, page 360.
[5] Adams to Russell, Vol. II, page 365.

vessels from Liverpool."[1] It would appear from the British Blue Book that the instructions for their detention "had scarcely been sent" when Mr. Adams's note of the 3d September was received at the Foreign Office.[2]

Their detention not an abandonment of the lax construction of the duties of a neutral. There was little in all this transaction to lead the United States to hope for a returning and better sense of justice in the British Government. For they could not but observe, when comparing the dates of the receipt of the several notes which passed between Lord Russell and Mr. Adams, that when Her Majesty's Government, after a delay of six weeks, answered that it could not interfere with these vessels, it was in possession of convincing evidence of their character and destination, which was not materially, if at all, strengthened by the evidence contained in Mr. Adams's letter of the 3d of September. They were therefore forced to conclude that, in detaining the vessels, Her Majesty's Government was influenced, not by a change in their opinion as to the force or effect of the Foreign Enlistment Act, or as to the duty of Great Britain toward the United States, but solely by a desire to avoid, in the interest of peace, what Mr. Adams called "the grave nature of the situation in which both countries must be placed, in the event of an act of aggression committed against the Government and people of the United States by either of these formidable vessels." The United States fully and earnestly shared this desire with Great Britain, and they were relieved from a state of painful suspense when the dangers which Mr. Adams pointed out were averted. But they would have felt a still greater relief, could they have received at that time the assurance, or could they have seen in the transaction any evidence from which they could assume, that the Executive Branch of the British Government was no longer of the opinion expressed in Lord Russell's note of September 1 as to its duties in regard to evidence such as that inclosed in Mr. Adams's previous notes, and no longer intended to regard the Foreign Enlistment Act, as expounded by the court in the Alexandra case, as the measure of its international duties.

[1] Russell to Adams, Vol. II, page 366.
[2] Layard to Stuart, Vol. II, page 363.

The contracts with Arman for the construction of vessels in France.

Extensive as were the arrangements made from Liverpool by the insurgent agents, at that time, for the construction in Great Britain of vessels of war intended to carry on war against the United States, their operations were not confined to Great Britain. Captain Bullock, without shifting his office from Liverpool, signed an agreement, "for the account of his principals," on the 16th of April, 1863, with Lucien Arman, ship-builder at Bordeaux, whereby Mr. Arman engaged "to construct four steamers of 400 horse-power, and arranged for the reception of an armament of from ten to twelve cannon." As it was necessary in France to obtain the consent of the Government to the armament of such vessels within the limits of the Empire, Mr. Arman informed the Government that these vessels were "intended to establish a regular communication between Shanghai, Yedo, and San Francisco, passing the strait of Van Dieman, and also that they are to be fitted out, should the opportunity present itself, for sale to the Chinese or Japanese Empire." On this representation permission was given to arm them, the armament of two to be supplied by Mr. Arman at Bordeaux, and that of the other two by Mr. Vorus at Nantes.

On the 16th of July, 1863, another agreement was made in Bordeaux between Mr. Arman and Mr. Bullock, "acting for the account of principals." Arman agreed to construct two screw steamships of wood and iron, with iron turrets, of 300 horse-power. Bullock was to supply the armament; the ships were to be finished in six months; one-fifth of the price was to be paid in advance.

Under these contracts Bullock is said to have paid Arman 5,280,000 francs.[1] But one of the vessels ever went into the possession of the insurgents, and that by fraud. It may interest the Tribunal of Arbitration to learn, in a few words,

---

[1] Mr. Moreau, counsel for the United States in a suit pending before the Cour d'Appel de Paris, growing out of these transactions, so states: "Il nous reste maintenant à indiquer à la cour ce que fit M. Arman, et des navires qu'il construisait et des capitaux qu'il avait reçus de M. Bullock, capitaux dont le montant, suivant le dire de M. Arman lui-même, ne s'élève pas à moins de 5,280,000 francs.

the result of these contracts and the course pursued by the French Government.

Conduct of the French Government. The authorization which had been obtained for Mr. Arman and Mr. Vorus to arm the four vessels, under the contract of the 15th April, and the doings of Mr. Arman under the contract of the 16th of July, were unknown to the Minister for Foreign Affairs. When they were brought to Mr. Drouyn de Lhuys's attention, by the Minister of the United States at Paris, he took immediate steps to prevent a violation of the neutrality of France. He wrote to Mr. Dayton, (October 22, 1863,) "Que M. le Ministre de la Marine vient de notifier à M. Vorus le retrait de l'autorisation qu'il avait obtenue pour l'armement de quatre navires en construction à Nantes et à Bordeaux. Il en a été donné également avis à M. Arman, dont l'attention a été en même temps appelée sur la responsabilité qu'il pourrait encourir par des actes en opposition avec la déclaration du 11 Juin, 1861."

Mr. Arman made many efforts to remove the injunctions of the Government, but without success. He was finally forced to sell to the Prussian Government two of the clippers constructed at Bordeaux under the contract of April 15. Two other clippers constructed at Nantes under that contract, were sold to the Peruvian Government. Of the two iron-clads constructed under the contract of July 16, one was sold to Prussia for 2,075,000 francs. A contract was made for the sale of the other to Denmark, which was then at war, and it was sent, under the Danish name of Stoerkodder, to Copenhagen for delivery. It arrived there after the time agreed upon for the delivery and after the war was over; and the Danish Government refused to accept it. The person in charge of the vessel in Copenhagen held at once the power of attorney of M. Arman and of Mr. Bullock; and in one capacity he delivered the vessel to himself in the other capacity, and took her to the Isle of Houat, off the French coast, where she was met by a steamer from England with an armament. Taking this on board, she crossed the Atlantic, stopping in Spain and Portugal on the way. In the port of Havana news was received of the suppression of the insurrection, and she was delivered to the authorities of the United States. The

Contrast between the conduct of France and of Great Britain. course pursued by France toward these vessels is in striking contrast with Great Britain's conduct in the cases of the Florida and the Alabama.

Bullock's operations in this way called for a great deal of money. On the 22d May, 1863, a "navy warrant on Messrs. Fraser, Trenholm & Co. for £300,000" was sent to him.[1] On the 25th June, 1863, "drafts for £26,000 and £38,962 13s. 4d., in favor of Commander James D. Bullock, on the C. S. Depositary in Liverpool, were forwarded to him."[2] Other funds were sent that the United States are not able to trace. In September, 1863, his contracts had been so heavy that he was low in funds. Maffitt sent to him at Liverpool a number of "men, discharged from the Florida, with their accounts and discharges."[3] He could not pay them, and the men "began to get restive." Mallory made an effort to send him further funds, and asked Memminger to instruct "the Depositary at Liverpool" to countersign certain cotton certificates "on the application of Commander Bullock."[4] In this, or in some other way, the funds were replenished, and large sums were spent after that time.

While these extensive preparations for a fleet were going on in England and France, an event took place at the Cape of Good Hope which tested afresh the purpose of Her Majesty's Government to maintain British neutrality and enforce the Queen's proclamation

The Tuscaloosa at the Cape of Good Hope. On the 5th of August, 1863, the Alabama arrived in Table Bay and gave information that the Tuscaloosa, a prize that had been captured off Brazil, would soon arrive in the character of a tender. On the 8th that vessel arrived in Simon's Bay, having her original cargo of wool on board. She lay in port about a week, and while there "overtures were made by some parties in Cape Town to purchase the cargo of wool."[5] The

---

[1] Bullock to Elmore, July 3, 1863, Vol. VI, page 129.
[2] Mallory to Elmore, June 25, 1863, Vol. VI, page 126.
[3] Maffitt to Bullock, September 3, 1863, Vol. II, page 639.
[4] Mallory to Memminger, September 12, 1863, Vol. VI, page 132.
[5] Walker to the Secretary of the Admiralty, Vol. IV, page 216; Vol. VI, page 456.

wool was disposed of to a Cape Town merchant, on condition that he should sent it to Europe for sale, and two-thirds of the price should be paid into the insurgent treasury; and it was landed for that purpose by the Tuscaloosa, on a wild spot, called Angra Pequena, outside of British jurisdiction.[1] When the Tuscaloosa made her appearance at Cape Town, Rear-Admiral Sir Baldwin Walker wrote to the Governor, desiring to know "whether this vessel ought still to be looked upon in the light of a prize, she never having been condemned in a prize court."[2] He was instructed to admit the vessel. The practical experience of the honest sailor rebelled at this decision, and he replied, "I apprehend that to bring a captured vessel under the denomination of a vessel of war, she must be fitted for warlike purposes, and not merely have a few men and a few small guns put on board her, (in fact nothing but a prize crew,) in order to disguise her real character as a prize. Now, this vessel has her original cargo of wool still on board, which cannot be required for warlike purposes, and her armament and number of her crew are quite insufficient for any services other than those of slight defense. Viewing all the circumstances of the case, they afford room for the supposition that the vessel is styled a tender, with the object of avoiding the prohibition against her entrance as a prize into our ports, where, if the captors wished, arrangements could be made for the disposal of her valuable cargo."[3]

She is released against the advice of Sir Baldwin Walker. The Governor replied that the Attorney General was of opinion that "if the vessel received the two guns from the Alabama or other Confederate vessel of war, or if the person in command of her has a commission of war, * * * there will be a sufficient setting forth as a vessel of war to justify her being held to be a ship of war."[4] The Admiral replied,

---

[1] Mountague Bernard's Neutrality of Great Britain, &c., page 421, note 1.
[2] Vol. IV, page 217; Vol. VI, page 458.
[3] Walker to Wodehouse, Vol. IV, page 218; Vol. VI, page 459.
[4] Wodehouse to Walker, Vol. IV, page 219; Vol. VI, page 459.

tersely, "As there are two guns on board, and an officer of the Alabama in charge of her, the vessel appears to come within the meaning of the cases cited in your communication."[1] He did not seem to think it worth while to repeat his opinion as to the frivolous character of such evidence, since it had been disregarded by the civil authorities.

The course of the Governor disapproved. The facts were in due course reported by the Governor to the Home Government at London[2] and the Colonial Minister wrote back that Her Majesty's Government were of opinion that the "Tuscaloosa" did not lose the character of a prize captured by the Alabama merely because she was at the time of her being brought within British waters armed with two small rifle guns, and manned with a crew of ten men from the Alabama, and used as a tender to that vessel under the authority of Captain Semmes.[3] He said that he "considered that the mode of proceeding in such circumstances most consistent with Her Majesty's dignity, and most proper for the vindication of her territorial rights, would have been to prohibit the exercise of any further control over the Tuscaloosa by the captors, and to retain that vessel under Her Majesty's control and jurisdiction until properly reclaimed by her original owners." These instructions were looked upon by the Governor as a censure;[4] and the Tuscaloosa having in the mean time come again into port and placed herself within the jurisdiction, was seized, and the facts reported to London.[5] Her Majesty's Government disavowed this act, and instructed the Governor "to restore the Tuscaloosa to the lieutenant of the Confederate States who

The Tuscaloosa comes again into the waters of the colony.

The Governor reverses his policy and seizes the vessel.

---

[1] Walker to Wodehouse, Vol. IV, page 19; Vol. VI, page 360.
[2] Wodehouse to Duke of Newcastle, Vol. VI, page 220; Vol. IV, page 460.
[3] Bernard's Neutrality of Great Britain during the American Civil War, page 425. See also Vol. III, page 207, and Vol. VI, page 463.
[4] Wodehouse to Newcastle, Vol. IV, page 229; Vol. VI, page 463.
[5] Vol. IV, page 230.

lately commanded her; or, if he should have left the Cape, then to retain her until she can be handed over to some person who may have authority from Captain Semmes, of the Alabama, or from the Government of the Confederate States, to receive her."[1] The Governor was also informed that the Home Government had not in any degree censured him for the course which he had pursued.[2]

His course is again disapproved.

The Duke of Newcastle placed his instructions to restore the vessel upon "the peculiar circumstances of this case." But the Tribunal of Arbitration will observe that, inasmuch as, notwithstanding his first decision of the 4th of November above cited, he did, in his second instructions, fully approve of the course of the Governor in receiving the vessel originally as a man-of-war, in violation of the Queen's Proclamation and of well-settled principles of International Law, and against the sensible and honest advice of Rear-Admiral Sir Baldwin Walker, he was in no position to shelter the British Government from responsibility for the hostile act of her officials, by pleading any special or peculiar circumstances.

Blockade running.

It is necessary now to go back and bring up the history of army purchases and blockade-running. Walker and Porter were left established as agents at Bermuda, and Heyliger at Nassau.

On the 28th of March, 1863, Fraser, Trenholm & Co. were notified that the insurgent Secretary of the Treasury had "appointed Mr. Lewis Heyliger a depositary of the treasury at Nassau, New Providence, and Colonel Norman S. Walker a depositary at Bermuda;"[3] and they were told that Messrs. Heyliger and Walker would forward shipments of cotton on account of the treasury, and would draw on them for funds to pay expenses of the vessels and to make purchases of return cargoes. They were also informed that shipments of

---

[1] Duke of Newcastle to Sir P. Woodhouse, Vol. IV, page 241; Vol. VI, page 468.

[2] Same to same, March 10, Vol. IV, page 242; Vol. VI, page 469.

[3] Memminger to Fraser, Trenholm & Co., March 28, 1863, Vol. VI, page 128.

cotton would be made by way of Nassau and Bermuda by the authorities at Richmond, and they were directed to pay the proceeds of such shipments to Mr. Huse. The cotton was sent forward as opportunity offered. Thus, for instance, in May, 1863, the navy transported to Nassau five hundred and seventy-five bales for the treasury.[1] The shipments were in fact going whenever there was opportunity.

Mr. J. M. Seixas was also appointed agent of the Insurgent War Department in the ports of Wilmington and Charleston, "to take charge of all that relates to the *running of the steamers of the Department* sailing from and arriving at those ports."[2]

Cotton shipments. On the 18th of April, 1863, Walker forwarded to Fraser, Trenholm & Co. 800 bales of cotton, drew against it for £20,000 for his own disbursements for commissary stores, and notified Huse that the balance would go to his credit with Fraser, Trenholm & Co. He also reported the arrival at Bermuda of "Confederate steamers," blockade-runners, with cotton, and he called Huse's attention to "the importance of sending to this place [Bermuda] one or two cargoes of Duffryne coal *for the Government steamers;*" and adds: "You will readily see the injurious delay which may result from the want of a proper supply of coal." He also says: *From all that I can learn, any Confederate man-of-war which may come to this port will have no difficulty in coaling and procuring supplies.*"[3]

The blockade-runners of the Richmond authorities were by this time well known, and were making regular voyages. The Cornubia was running before January, 1863.[4] The Giraffe and the Cornubia ran regularly to Bermuda and to Nassau,[5] in February, 1863. One or two more were thought "highly desirable." In March there was "enough to employ three steamers for some time to come," and Huse was

---

[1] Memminger to Mallory, May 6, 1863, Vol. VI, page 119.
[2] Seddon to Seixas, April 7, 1863, Vol. VI, page 113.
[3] Walker to Huse, April 18, 1862, Vol. VI, page 115.
[4] Gorgas to Huse, January 1, 1863, Vol. VII, page 48.
[5] Same to same, February 26, 1863, Vol. VII, page 48.

authorized "to add to the fleet two more good swift steamers,"[1] and was furnished with a credit of £200,000 on Fraser, Trenholm & Co.[2]

The insurgent government was all this while urging its agents to dispatch arms and munitions of war. In April, 1863, twenty thousand Enfield rifle bayonets were wanted as soon as possible.[3] On the 6th of May "one hundred and fifty thousand bayonets" were wanted, and "lead and saltpeter in large quantities."[4] On the 1st of June, Walker is ordered to send "paper for making cartridges by the first boat;" "if there is none on hand send immediately to Major Huse to buy a large quantity."[5] Two days later he was ordered to send "Colt's pistol-caps as soon as possible."[6] They were wanted for Lee, who was preparing to move toward Gettysburg.

Walker shows in all this emergency a fear of being crippled for want of coal. On the 21st of March he was arranging for a cargo in the port of Bermuda.[7] On the 29th of March he writes that he has purchased that cargo, and wants more.[8] On the 16th of May he urges Huse to send coal. "Every steamer takes from one hundred and sixty to one hundred and eighty tons." He has but six hundred tons left.[9] On the 23d of May he again calls attention "most earnestly to the importance of keeping him supplied with good steam coal." He "hopes that some are already on the way." His "stock is almost exhausted."[10] On the 30th of June he cries "send us coal, coal, coal! Each steamer takes one hundred and eighty tons, so that six hundred tons will be quickly consumed."[11] Again on

---

[1] Same to same, March 8, Vol. VII, page 48.
[2] Same to same, March 9, Vol. VII, page 49.
[3] Gorgas to Huse, Vol. VII, page 51.
[4] Same to same, May 6, Vol. VII, page 51.
[5] Gorgas to Walker, Vol. VII, page 54.
[6] Same to same, Vol. VII, page 54.
[7] Walker to Huse, 21 March, Vol. VII, **page 50.**
[8] Same to same, Vol. VII, page 50.
[9] Same to same, May 16, 1863, Vol. **VII, page 52.**
[10] Same to same, Vol. VII, page 53.
[11] Same to same, Vol. VII, page 55.

the 9th of July he writes "coal, coal, coal. Send me two thousand tons. The Lee, I fear, will be laid up for the want of it. You may calculate that each steamer will take one hundred and eighty tons."[1] He wrote also to Fraser, Trenholm & Co., to the same effect, saying that there should be a "reserve there of at least three or four thousand tons."[2] Shipments were made, and the supplies reached him before there was any serious detention of the blockade-runners. He was enabled to fulfill all the orders given in Richmond a short time before the advance of Lee's army into Pennsylvania.

The Insurgent Government interested in blockade running. In spite of the countenance given by the authorities in Bermuda and Nassau, funds could not be forwarded fast enough to Major Huse to meet the great demands made upon him at this time. On the 23d of July, 1863, "on behalf of the Confederate Government," he made an arrangement with the Mercantile Trading Company for an advance of £150,000, to be extended to £300,000, for the purchase of goods for the insurgents, and their shipment by the company, "via Bermuda, Nassau, or Havana;" "the Confederate Government to have two-thirds cargo space in each vessel, the company one-third each way;" "the cotton received from the Confederate States to be consigned to the company's agency in Liverpool."[3] Stringer, the managing director of the company, soon became doubtful of Huse's powers, and wrote Mr. Mason, saying that he had already advanced him £20,000 on saltpeter, and inquiring about the powers;[4] to which Mason replied that he did not know about the extent of Huse's powers, but that he had no doubt that the saltpeter would be taken by the insurgents.[5] Stringer's doubts were soon set at rest; for it would seem that about that time there must have been received in London an agreement

---

[1] Same to same, Vol. VII, page 56.
[2] Walker to Huse, Vol. VII, page 57.
[3] Memorandum made in London July 23, 1863, Vol. VI, page 136.
[4] Stringer to Mason, September 16, 1863, Vol. VI, page 134.
[5] Mason to Stringer, September 19, 1863, Vol. VI, page 136.

without date, executed in Richmond by "J. Gorgas, Colonel, Chief of Ordnance," and "approved" by "J. A. Seddon, Secretary of War," which probably replaced the temporary agreement of July 23. Five steamers were to be put on to run from Bermuda or Nassau to Charleston or Wilmington, two-thirds to be owned by the insurgents, and one-third by the British contractors. The insurgents were to pay for their two-thirds in cotton, at Charleston, and were to be allowed commissions for their part of the work, the other contracting parties having a similar allowance. The portion of the proceeds of cotton belonging to the insurgents was "to be paid to the credit of the War Department with Messrs. Fraser, Trenholm & Co., of Liverpool." The insurgents were to furnish officers to command the vessels. The document was signed by "C. E. Thorburn," and by "Chas. H. Reid & Co.," and by "The Mercantile Trading Co., Limited; Edgar P. Stringer, Managing Director, London, 23d September, 1863."[1] Mr. Thorburn was a shareholder in the Trading Company,[2] and on the 3d October Mr. Stringer is found corresponding with him about the purchase of these vessels.[3]

Meanwhile the operations of the insurgents at Nassau and Bermuda had gone on with even more vigor than during the previous year. Huse's credit had been strained to the utmost, but was now restored. The purchases and supplies for the Quartermaster's Department appear to have been transferred during this summer exclusively to Nassau. Seixas was instructed to place one thousand bales of cotton at Nassau for the Quartermaster's Department, before the close of the year, and was told that "the wants of the Quartermaster General are at Nassau, not Bermuda."[4]

Heyliger diligently complied with his instructions to forward quartermaster's stores. On the 29th October he sent 40 tons by the "Antonica," "Margaret," and "Jessie." On the 2d November he shipped by the "Hansa" 19 tons; the next day by the "Beauregard" 40 or 50 tons; and a

---

[1] Vol. VI, page 140. [2] Vol. VI, page 144. [3] Vol. VI, page 143.
[4] Bayne to Seixas, September 29, 1863, Vol. VI, page 139.

large quantity by the "Alice;" and on the 5th November he sent 20 tons by the "Banshee." The "Margaret" and the "Jessie" were captured; the others ran the blockade. The Quartermaster's Department was much employed in collecting and forwarding cotton to meet these purchases.[1]

Major Ferguson was in Liverpool at this time as an agent for the purchase of quartermaster's stores, and was sending large amounts forward. Fraser, Trenholm & Co. refused his drafts, because Heyliger had already overdrawn the Quartermaster's account.[2] Ferguson thereupon wrote, urging that cotton should be forwarded. "I have," he says, "more faith in cotton than I ever had. If we can but get that out, we can buy all England, for most of the men, as well as their merchandise, have a price."[3]

These facts brought to Earl Russell's notice. On the 3d. of November, 1863, Mr. Adams laid before Earl Russell "new proofs of the manner in which the neutrality of Her Majesty's ports is abused by the insurgents in the United States, in order the more effectually to procrastinate their resistance," which he contended showed the "establishment in the port of St. George's, in the island of Bermuda, of a depot of naval stores for their use and benefit in the prosecution of the war."[4] This information should have put Lord Russell on the track of all the facts in regard to Bermuda. Had Her Majesty's Government pursued the investigations to which it gave them the clew, it would have done so. Earl Russell, on the 27th of November, answered *He sees no offense in them.* that "Her Majesty's Government do not consider that they can properly interfere in this matter."[5] The dates would seem to indicate a possibility that no inquiries were made at Bermuda.

On the 29th of December, 1863, Mr. Adams wrote Earl Russell that he had "information entitled to credit," that Ralph Cator, "an officer in Her Majesty's naval service,"

---

[1] Bayle to Lawton, November 13, 1863, Vol. VI, page 147.
[2] Fraser, Trenholm & Co. to Lawton, November 26, 1863, Vol. VI, page 149.
[3] Ferguson to Lawton, December 23, 1863, Vol. VI, page 149.
[4] Vol. I, page 735.   [5] Vol. I, page 736.

was "engaged in violating the blockade;" and that there was "a strong disposition on the part of a portion of Her Majesty's navy to violate the neutrality of their Sovereign in aiding and assisting the enemies of the United States."[1] This, too, was answered in a week from its date, without taking the trouble to inquire in the West Indies.[2]

Again, upon the 25th day of January, 1864, Mr. Adams called attention to "the manner in which the insurgents habitually abuse the belligerent privileges which have been conceded to them by Great Britain." It would seem that he had lately had a conversation with Earl Russell on the subject, for he says that he "deems it almost superfluous to enlarge further on the difficulties which must grow out of a toleration of the outrageous abuses of the belligerent privileges that have been granted to the insurgents."[3] "It would be difficult," he adds, "to find an example in history of a more systematic and persistent effort to violate the neutral position of a country than this one has been from its commencement, that has not brought on a war. That this has been the object of the parties engaged in it I have never for a moment doubted." "It must be obvious," he says, "to your Lordship that, after such an exposition, all British subjects engaged in these violations of blockade must incur a suspicion strong enough to make them liable to be treated as enemies, and, if taken, to be reckoned as prisoners of war."[4]

Earl Russell's attention again called to these facts. Earl Russell replied to this note on the 9th of March.[5] He ignored the evidence and charges of the hostile use of the British West India ports. He alluded to a charge against Lieutenant Rooke, which he set aside as unimportant, and to a charge against one James Ash of a purpose to build ships for the insurgents. As to the latter charge, he reiterated the oft-repeated plea that there was no "legal and proper evidence" to sustain it; and having disposed of these, he confined

---

[1] Vol. I, page 739.   [2] Vol. I, page 740.   [3] Vol. I, page 746.
[4] Adams to Russell, Vol. I, page 745.
[5] Russell to Adams, Vol. I, pages 749—'51.

himself to a notice of Mr. Adams's intimation that it might become necessary to treat blockade-runners as prisoners of war. This, he said, could not be assented to.

A short discussion ensued, which was closed by a note of Mr. Adams, transmitting further evidence of the character of the trade between the British West Indian ports and the insurgent States, and calling Earl Russell's "particular attention to the express condition exacted from all vessels in trade with the insurgent ports, that one-half of the tonnage of each vessel may be employed by the so-called Government for its own use, both on the outward and homeward voyage;"[1] to which Earl Russell replied in an answer in which he said, in substance, that admitting all the facts stated to be true, there was nothing in them *He again sees no offence in them.* worthy of attention; for "the subjects of Her Majesty are entitled by International Law to carry on the operations of commerce equally with both belligerents, *subject to the capture of their vessels and to no other penalty.*"[2]

This discussion closed the correspondence which took place between the two Governments on this branch of the subject. It left Great Britain justifying all that took place, after actual knowledge of much, and possible knowledge of all, had been brought within its reach. It left, too, the Queen's Proclamation as to this subject virtually revoked, and Her Majesty's subjects assured that it was no violation of international duty to break the blockade. It is worthy of remark that Lord Westbury, the Lord High Chancellor, gave a judicial decision to the same effect,[3] which was soon after followed by the High Court of Admiralty.[4] The executive and judicial branches of the British Government were thus a second time brought into accord in construing away Her Majesty's Proclamation.

---

[1] Adams to Russell, Vol. I, page 756.
[2] Russell to Adams, Vol. I, page 757.
[3] 11 Jurist N. S., 400.
[4] Law Reports Admiralty and Ecclesiastical Courts, Browning, Vol. I, page 1.

Blockade-running in partnership with the Insurgent Government.
Blockade-running throve, and Nassau and Bermuda prospered under these repeated decisions of Her Majesty's Government. The Florida, too, arrived at Bermuda on the 16th of July, 1864, and remained there until the 27th, taking coal and supplies on board; and this at a time when like permission was refused to the vessels of the United States.

It was a favorite idea of the insurgent authorities from the beginning to become interested with Englishmen as partners in blockade-running. One contract to that effect has already been alluded to.

In July, 1864, McRae reported other contracts.[1] Captain Bullock, "with whom (he said) I [McRae] am directed by the Secretary of the Treasury to consult," was a party to the transaction. These contracts "made provision for fourteen steamers, four to leave during the month of August, eight in December, and two in April, 1865." They were to be "built of steel, and to carry one thousand bales of cotton each, on a draught of seven feet water, and with an average speed of thirteen knots per hour." Arrangements were at the same time made for the purchase of supplies for Huse and Ferguson pending the finishing of the vessels. The "Owl" was the first of these vessels to arrive. The insurgent Navy Department claimed the right "to place a naval officer in charge of her in conformity with regulations."[2] The treasury doubted this, but Mallory insisted upon his right.[3] This drew from Bullock an indignant letter, complaining that the navy had taken these vessels. Good ships were building for the navy; why take these vessels, which were not suited for naval purposes.[4]

On the 5th of October, 1864, orders were given for more arms, and McRae was ordered to supply Huse with £50,000 for the purpose.[5] On the 26th of November, Ferguson reports his doings in the purchase of woolen goods,

[1] McRae to Seddon, July 4, 1864, Vol. VI, page 163.
[2] Mallory to Trenholm, September 21, 1864, Vol. VI, page 171.
[3] Same to same, September 22, 1864, Vol. VI, page 172.
[4] Bullock to McRae, November 1, 1864, Vol. VI, page 173.
[5] Gorgas to Seddon, October 5, 1864, Vol. VI, page 172.

and gives the reason for "making Liverpool his headquarters."[1] As late as the 7th of January, 1865, McRae is ordered to pay to Bullock £105,000. The steamer "Laurel," the same which took the arms and men to the Shenandoah, was then in Wilmington. She was sent out with a cargo of cotton, with instructions to the officer in command to sell the steamer and the cotton, and to pay Bullock £12,000 out of the proceeds, putting the balance to the credit of the treasury, with Fraser, Trenholm & Co.[2] No efforts seem to have been spared to sustain the dying fortunes of the insurrection. The insurgents, at the last, fell into the unaccountable error of supposing that the British Government intended to interfere with their blockade-running. They changed the apparent ownership of the Stag into the name of John Fraser & Co., lest it should be seized as "a transport owned by the Confederate States, engaged in the blockade."[3] It is needless to say that the precaution was not required. Evidence had over and over again been laid before Lord Russell that these blockade-runners were, in fact, transports of the insurgents, carrying their funds for Liverpool, and bringing back their arms and munitions of war, and that the operations of these vessels were brought clearly within the terms of the Foreign Enlistment Act; but he ever turned a deaf ear to the charges.

Continued partiality. On the 15th of March, 1865, Mr. Adams complained of this matter for the last time. The United States steamer San Jacinto having been wrecked on the Bahamas, and her officers and crew having found shelter at Nassau, the "Honduras," also a man-of-war, was sent there for the purpose of paying in coin the claims for salvage. The Consul asked permission for the "Honduras" to enter the port, which was refused, although the "Florida" had, less than six months before, remained eleven days at Bermuda, and taken on board a full supply of coal. In bringing this breach of hospitality to the notice of Earl

---

[1] Ferguson to Lawton, November 26, 1864, Vol. VI, page 175.
[2] Trenholm to Fraser, Trenholm & Co., December 24, 1864, Vol. VI, page 177.
[3] Trenholm to Mallory, December 17, 1864, Vol. VI, page 176.

Russell Mr. Adams said: "I shall not seek to dwell on the painful impression this proceeding has made in the Naval Department of the United States, which at the same time laid too much reason to be cognizant of the abuse made of that port by persons practically engaged in hostilities in violation of Her Majesty's Proclamation. There was no single day during the month in which this incident happened that thirty-five vessels, engaged in breaking the blockade, were not to be seen flaunting their contraband flags in that port. Neither has its hospitality been restricted to that hybrid class of British ships running its illegal ventures on joint account with the insurgent authorities in the United States. The Chameleon, not inaptly named, but before known as the Tallahassee, and still earlier as a British steamer fitted out from London to play the part of a privateer out of Wilmington, was lying at that very time in Nassau, relieved indeed of her guns, but still retaining all the attributes of her hostile occupation. But a few days earlier the steamer Laurel, whose history is already too well known to your Lordship, by my note of the 7th instant, had re-appeared after its assumption of the name of the Confederate States, and had there been not only received, but commissioned with a post mail to a port of Her Majesty's Kingdom."[1] Lord Russell took no notice of Mr. Adams's charge, that many of these blockade-runners were in fact transports in the insurgent service, and that the ports of Nassau and Bermuda were depots of ordnance and quartermasters' stores. His only reply, made four days after the surrender of Lee at Appomattox, was a repetition of the old story, "there is nothing in the law of nations which forbids the attempt of neutral ship-owners or commanders to evade the blockade."[2] To the last the British Government refused to interfere. The fears which induced the insurgents to try to cover up the ownership of the "Stag" were groundless. The partnership continued until the United States interfered, and closed the business, before the English partners could deliver the last vessels under the contract.

[1] Adams to Russell, Vol. I, page 709.
[2] Russell to Adams, Vol. I, page 714.

It is necessary to add a few words in regard to the closing operations of Bullock's department, before bringing this imperfect outline of Great Britain's violation of its duties as a neutral to a close.

The Rappahannock. On the 30th of November, 1863, the London Times announced that "the screw gun-vessel 'Victor,' recently purchased from the Admiralty, has, *as had been expected*, passed into the hands of the Confederate Government."[1] "The 'Victor,' an old dispatch-boat belonging to Her Majesty's Navy, was one of a number of ships ordered by the Admiralty to be sold as worn out and unserviceable. An offer for her was accepted on the 14th September, 1863, and on the 10th November the hull was delivered to the order of the purchasers, Messrs. Coleman & Co., the masts, sails, and rigging having been previously removed, as the pivots and other fittings for guns."[2] The steamer, instead of being taken away, remained at Sheerness, "refitting, under the direction of persons connected with the royal dock-yards."[3] Many facts came to the knowledge of Mr. Adams, indicating that the vessel was intended for the insurgents. In pursuing his inquiries, however, the suspicions of the parties concerned were probably excited; for the vessel, "by no means prepared for sea, and with no adequate force to man her," was carried, with the workmen actually engaged upon her, across the English Channel and taken into Calais. Mr. Adams called Lord Russell's attention to these proceedings,[4] and furnished him with evidence tending to show the guilt of the purchasers, and also that one Rumble, inspector of machinery afloat of Her Majesty's dock-yard, Sheerness, had been the principle person concerned in enlisting the crew. Rumble was subsequently tried and acquitted, although the proof against him was clear. As to the vessel, any doubt of her character was at once removed. The insurgent flag was hoisted, and she went into commission under the name of the Rappahannock in crossing the Channel, and she entered the port of Calais

---
[1] Vol. II, page 725.
[2] Bernard's Neutrality of Great Britain, page 357.
[3] Mr. Adams to Mr. Seward, Vol. II, page 726.
[4] Vol. II, pages 727, 735, 738, 747, 751, 754, 771, 776, 787.

claiming to be an insurgent man-of-war. What was done there is described in the statement of the Solicitor General to the jury on the trial of Rumble. "The preparations for equipping, which had been interrupted, were proceeded with; a number of boiler-makers were sent for from England, and many of them were induced to leave their employment in the dock-yard without leave, and when they returned they were discharged as being absent without leave; attempts were made to enlist more men; a large store of coals was taken in; but at this point the French Government stepped in. The French Government, not choosing their ports to be made the scene of hostile operations, interposed, and prevented any further equipment of the vessel, and, by the short and summary process of mooring a man-of-war across her bows, prevented her going out of the port, and she has been kept a prisoner in the harbor ever since."[1] Contrast again the course of the French Government with that of the British Government in like cases. What vessel bearing a commission from the Richmond authorities was ever disturbed by a British gun-boat, no matter how flagrant might have been her violations of British sovereignty?

The Shenandoah. In the summer or autumn of the year 1864, there was in London a vessel called the Sea King. She was a merchant steamer which had belonged to a Bombay company, and had been employed in the East India trade.[2] On the 20th of September in that year she was sold in London to Richard Wright, of Liverpool,[3] the father-in-law of Prioleau, of South Carolina, the managing partner in the Liverpool house of Fraser, Trenholm & Co.

On the 7th of October Wright gave a power of attorney to one Corbett, an Englishman, "to sell her at any time within six months for a sum not less than £45,000 sterling. On the next day she cleared for Bombay, and sailed with a large supply of coal and about fifty tons of metal and a crew of forty-seven men."[4] Corbett sold her to the insurgents

---
[1] Vol. IV, page 583.
[2] Bernard's British Neutrality, page 359.
[3] Vol. III, page 319.
[4] Dudley to Seward, Vol. III, page 319.

on the high-seas, or rather made the form of transfer comply with the facts of the original transaction which took place in England.¹ On the day after the Sea King left London, the Laurel, a screw-steamer, "nearly new built, very strong, and admirably adapted for a privateer,"² left Liverpool, clearing for Matamoras via Nassau. She took on board "a number of cases containing guns and carriages;" and she had "twenty-one seamen, six stewards, besides deck-hands and firemen,"² as first reported by the Consul at Liverpool. Further information after she left led him to write that she had taken "about one hundred men, forty or fifty of whom were on the pirate Alabama, and all Englishmen."⁴ The two vessels met off Madeira. On the morning of the 18th of October they went together to the barren island of Porto Santo near Madeira, and there, with eighteen hours' work, transferred to the Sea King the arms and ammunition from the Laurel, "guns, gun-carriages, shot, shell, powder, clothing, goods, &c."⁵ The insurgent commander of the Sea King and about forty men came out of the Laurel and took possession of the vessel, and named her the Shenandoah; the insurgent flag was hoisted, the Laurel hoisted the English flag, and took on board some of the men of the Shenandoah, who could not be induced, even by "a bucketful of sovereigns," to aid in violating the Queen's Proclamation; and the two vessels separated.

The next appearance of the Shenandoah in a British port was at Melbourne in January, 1865. Her character and history were well known, and were at once brought to the notice of the Governor by the Consul of the United States.⁶ The evidence was so clear that the authorities evidently felt they must go through the form of arresting and examining her. This was the shell conceded to the United States. The kernel was reserved for the insurgents. The vessel was di-

---

¹ Wilson's affidavit, Vol. III, page 326.
² Dudley to Seward, Vol. III, page 316.
³ Dudley to Adams, Vol. III, page 317.
⁴ Dudley to Seward, Vol. III, page 318.
⁵ Wilson's affidavit, Vol. III, page 325.
⁶ Vol. III, pages 393, 394, 396, 398.

charged and allowed to make extensive repairs; to go upon
a dry-dock; to take on board three hundred tons of coal,
having at the time four hundred tons on board; and the
authorities deliberately shut their eyes while she enlisted
about fifty men.[1]

The Shenandoah, with its British crew, continued its career
of destruction until long after the insurgents had abandoned
the contest in America. It was not until the 19th of June,
1865, that Bullock, managing things to the last, issued his
instructions to Captain Waddell to desist.[2] This communication the Foreign Office undertook to forward to him.[3]
Captain Waddell arrived with his ship in the Mersey in
November, 1865, and surrendered his ship to the British
Government, by whom it was handed over to the United
States.

Mr. Mountague Bernard's list of vessels detained by Great Britain. It is due to Great Britain to say that, in
addition to the rams, some other vessels were
detained by Her Majesty's Government. Mr.
Mountague Bernard, one of Her Majesty's High Commissioners
at Washington, in his able and courteous, but essentially
British, "Historical Account of the Neutrality of Great Britain
during the American Civil War,"[4] thus recapitulates the action
of the British Government in the cases which have not been
hitherto noticed in this paper. From his position, it may
reasonably be assumed that the list is a complete one:

"November 18, 1862—The *Hector*. Mr. Adams's application referred to the Admiralty November 18. This was
an inquiry whether the Hector was building for Her Majesty's
Government. On reference to the Admiralty it was answered
in the affirmative.—January 16, 1863—The *Georgiana*.
Referred to Treasury and Home Office January 17. Ship
said to be fitting at Liverpool for the Confederates. Mr.
Adams could not divulge the authority on which this statement was made. Reports from the customs, sent to Mr.

---

[1] Vol. III, pages 384—444.
[2] Bullock to Waddell, Vol. III, page 457.
[3] Hammond to Mark, Vol. III, page 459.
[4] Bernard's Neutrality, page 352.

Adams on the 18th, 19th, and 27th of January, tended to show that she was not designed for war. She sailed on the 21st January for Nassau, and on the 19th March was wrecked in attempting to enter Charleston Harbor.—March 26, 1863 —The *Phantom* and the *Southerner*. Referred to the Treasury and the Home Office March 27, to the Law Officers of the Crown June 2. The *Phantom* was fitting at Liverpool, the *Southerner* at Stockton-on-Tees. Both proved to be intended for blockade-runners. * * * *—March 19, 1864—The *Amphion*. Referred to Home Office March 18. This vessel was said to be equipped for the Confederate service. The Law Officers reported that no case was made out. She was eventually sent to Copenhagen for sale as a merchant ship.—April 16, 1864—The *Hawk*. Referred to the Home Office, to the Lord Advocate, and the Treasury April 18. This case had been already (April 4) reported on by the customs, and the papers sent to the Lord Advocate. On the 13th April the ship, which was suspected of having been built for the Confederates, left the Clyde without a register, and came to Greenkittle. The Law Officers decided that there was no evidence to warrant a seizure. She proved to be a blockade-runner. * * * —January 30, 1865— The *Virginia* and the *Louisa Ann Fanny*. Referred to Treasury February 1. Vessels said to be in course of equipment at London. No case was established, and they proved to be blockade-runners, as reported by the Governor of the Bahamas, who had been instructed to watch their proceedings. —February 7, 1865—The *Hercules* and *Ajax*. Referred to Treasury and Home Office February 8 and 9. Both vessels built in the Clyde. The *Ajax* first proceeded to Ireland, and was detained at Queenstown by the mutiny of some of the crew, who declared she was for the Confederate service. She was accordingly searched, but proved to be only fitted as a merchant ship. The Governor of the Bahamas was instructed to watch her at Nassau. On her arrival there she was again overhauled, but nothing suspicious discovered, and the Governor reported that she was adapted, and he believed intended, for a tug-boat. The *Hercules* being still in the Clyde, inquiries were made by the customs officers there, who reported that she was undoubtedly a tug-boat, and the sister ship to the *Ajax*."

This is the whole catalogue of good works, additional to those already alluded to, which the accomplished advocate of Great Britain is able to put in as an offset to the simple story of injuries which has been told in this paper. Comment upon it is unnecessary.

The United States have now completed what they have to say in this connection of the conduct of Great Britain during the insurrection. Some of the narrative may, in its perusal, appear minute, and to refer to transactions which will be claimed on the part of Great Britain to have been conducted in conformity with some construction of alleged International Law. These transactions are, however, historically narrated; and even those which come the nearest to a justification, as within some precedent, or some claim of neutral right, exhibit a disinclination to investigate, not to say a foregone conclusion of adverse decision. British municipal statute rather than recognized International Law was the standard of neutral duty; and the rigid rules of evidence of the English common law were applied to the complaints made in behalf of the United States, in striking contrast to the friendliness of construction, the alacrity of decision, and the ease of proof in the interest of the insurgents.

Before proceeding to relate in detail the acts of the several cruisers, which will constitute specific claims against Great Britain, the United States ask the Tribunal to pause to see what has been already established.

The charges in Mr. Fish's instruction of September 25, 1869, sustained by this evidence.
In a dispatch from Mr. Fish to Mr. Motley, on the 25th of September, 1869, in which the Government of the United States, for the last time, recited diplomatically its grievances against Great Britain, certain statements were made which were esteemed to be of sufficient importance to be transferred to Mr. Mountague Bernard's book. Mr. Bernard was pleased to say of these statements, that a "rhetorical color, to use an inoffensive phrase, [was] thrown over the foregoing train of assertions, which purport to be statements of fact." The United States now repeat those

statements which Her Majesty's High Commissioner did them
the honor to incorporate into his able work, and to comment
upon, and they confidently insist that every statement therein
contained has been more than made good by the evidence
referred to in this paper. Those statements were as follows,*
the references to the proof being inserted for the convenience of the Tribunal:—

"As time went on; as the insurrection from political
came at length to be military; as the sectional controversy
in the United States proceeded to exhibit itself in the organization
of great armies and fleets, and in the prosecution of hostilities on a scale of gigantic magnitude, then it was that the
spirit of the Queen's Proclamation showed itself in the event,
seeing that in virtue of the Proclamation maritime enterprises in the ports of Great Britain, which would otherwise
have been piratical, were rendered lawful, [see *Lord Campbell's speech in the House of Lords, May 16, 1864;
cited ante, page 14.*] and thus Great Britain became, and
to this end continued to be, the arsenal, [see *Huse and
Ferguson's letters, and Gorgas's report of Huse's purchases,*] the navy yard [see *the foregoing account of Bullock's doings,*] and the treasury, [see *the foregoing evidence
as to Fraser, Trenholm & Co.'s acts as depositaries,*]
of the insurgent Confederates.

"A spectacle was thus presented without precedent or
parallel in the history of civilized nations. Great Britain,
although the professed friend of the United States, yet, in
time of avowed international peace, permitted [see *the decision in the Alexandra case; also the refusals to proceed against the Florida, Alabama, and the rams*] armed
cruisers to be fitted out and harbored and equipped in her
ports to cruise against the merchant ships of the United
States, and to burn and destroy them, until our maritime
commerce was swept from the ocean. [See *Mr. Cobden's
speech in the House of Commons, May 13, 1864.*] Our
merchant vessels were destroyed piratically by captors who
had no ports of their own [see *Earl Russell's speech in

---
* Bernard's Neutrality of Great Britain, 378—380.

the *House of Lords, April* 26, 1864] in which to refit or to condemn prizes, and whose only nationality was the quarter-deck of their ships, built, dispatched to sea, and, not seldom in name, still professedly owned in Great Britain. [*See the evidence in regard to the transfers of the Georgia, and of the Shenandoah.*]

* * * * * *

"The Queen's Ministers excused themselves by alleged defects in the municipal law of the country. [*See Earl Russell's constant pleas of want of sufficient proof to convict criminals.*] Learned counsel either advised that the wrongs committed did not constitute violations of the municipal law, or else gave sanction to artful devices of deceit, to cover up such violations of law. [*See the decision as to the Florida; as to the Alabama until she was ready to sail; as to the rams; and as to the operations at Nassau, Bermuda, and Liverpool.*] And, strange to say, the courts of England or of Scotland, up to the very highest, were occupied month after month with juridical niceties and technicalities of statute construction, in this respect, [*see the Alexandra case,*] while the Queen's Government itself, including the omnipotent Parliament, which might have settled these questions in an hour by appropriate legislation, sat with folded arms, as if unmindful of its international obligations, and suffered ship after ship to be constructed in its ports to wage war on the United States. [*See the decision of the Cabinet, communicated to Mr. Adams, February* 13, 1863, *and Lord Palmerston's speech in the House of Commons, March* 27, 1863.]

* * * * * *

"When the defects of the existing laws of Parliament had become apparent, the Government of the United States earnestly entreated the Queen's Ministers to provide the required remedy, as it would have been easy to do, by a proper act of Parliament; but this the Queen's Government refused. [*See the account of Lord Russell's interview with Mr. Adams, February* 13, 1863.]

* * * * * *

"On the present occasion, the Queen's Ministers seem to

have committed the error of assuming that they needed not to look beyond their own local law, enacted for their own domestic convenience, and might, under cover of the deficiencies of that law, disregard their sovereign duties toward another sovereign Power. Nor was it, in our judgment, any adequate excuse for the Queen's Ministers to profess extreme tenderness of private rights, or apprehension of actions for damages, in case of any attempt to arrest the many ships which, either in England or Scotland, were, with ostentatious publicity, being constructed to cruise against the United States. *See the evidence as to the Florida, the Georgia, the Alabama, the rams, the Bermuda, the Tallahassee, the Pampero, the Rappahannock, the Laurel, and other vessels.*]

*   *   *   *   *   *

"But although such acts of violation of law were frequent in Great Britain, and susceptible of complete technical proof, notorious, flaunted directly in the face of the world, varnished over, if at all, with the shallowest pretexts of deception, yet no efficient step appears to have been taken by the British Government to enforce the execution of its municipal laws or to vindicate the majesty of its outraged sovereign power. [*The Alabama, the Florida, the Georgia, and the Shenandoah escaped. The rams were seized, but never condemned; no guilty party was ever punished; Bullock and Prioleau were never interfered with.*]

"And the Government of the United States cannot believe—it would conceive itself wanting in respect for Great Britain to impute—that the Queen's Ministers are so much hampered by juridical difficulties that the local administration is thus reduced to such a state of legal impotency as to deprive the Government of capacity to uphold its sovereignty against local wrong-doers, or its neutrality as regards other Sovereign Powers. [*Contrast with this the course of the British Government and Parliament during the Franco-German war.*]

"If, indeed, it were so, the causes of reclamation on the part of the United States would only be the more positive and sure, for the law of nations assumes that each Government is capable of discharging its international obligations; and, perchance, if it be not, then the absence of such capability is itself a specific ground of responsibility for consequences. [*This statement probably will not be denied.*]

"But the Queen's Government would not be content to admit, nor will the Government of the United States presume to impute to it, such political organization of the British Empire as to imply any want of legal ability on its part to discharge, in the amplest manner, all its duties of sovereignty and amity toward other Powers.

"It remains only in this relation to refer to one other point, namely, the question of *negligence;* neglect on the part of officers of the British Government, whether superior or subordinate, to detain Confederate cruisers, and especially the Alabama, the most successful of the depredators on the commerce of the United States.

"On this point the President conceives that little needs now to be said, for various cogent reasons:

"First, the matter has been exhaustively discussed already by this Department, or by the successive American Ministers.

"Then, if the question of negligence be discussed with frankness, it must be treated in this instance as a case of extreme negligence, which Sir William Jones has taught us to regard as equivalent or approximate to evil intention. The question of negligence, therefore, cannot be presented without danger of thought or language disrespectful toward the Queen's Ministers; and the President, while purposing, of course, as his sense of duty requires, to sustain the rights of the United States in all their utmost amplitude, yet intends to speak and act in relation to Great Britain in the same spirit of International respect which he expects of her in relation to the United States, and he is sincerely desirous that all discussions between the Governments may be so conducted as not only to prevent any aggravation of existing differences, but to tend to such reasonable and amicable determination as best becomes two great nations of common origin and conscious dignity and strength.

"I assume, therefore, pretermitting detailed discussion in this respect, that the negligence of the officers of the British

Government in the matter of the Alabama, at least, was gross and inexcusable, and such as indisputably to devolve on that Government full responsibility for all the depredations committed by her. Indeed, this conclusion seems in effect to be conceded in Great Britain. [*See the preface to Earl Russell's Speeches and Dispatches.*] At all events, the United States conceive that the proofs of responsible negligence in this matter are so clear that no room remains for debate on that point, and it should be taken for granted in all future negotiations with Great Britain."

PART V.

WHEREIN GREAT BRITAIN FAILED TO PERFORM ITS DUTIES AS A NEUTRAL.—THE INSURGENT CRUISERS.

"In the first place, I am sorry to observe that the unwarrantable practice of building ships in this country, to be used as vessels of war against a State with which Her Majesty is at peace, still continues. Her Majesty's government had hoped that this attempt to make the territorial waters of Great Britain the place of preparation for warlike armaments against the United States might be put an end to by prosecutions and by seizure of the vessels built in pursuance of contracts made with the confederate agents. But facts which are unhappily too notorious, and correspondence which has been put into the hands of Her Majesty's government by the minister of the Government of the United States, show that resort is had to evasion and subtlety in order to escape the penalties of the law; that a vessel is bought in one place, that her armament is prepared in another, and that both are sent to some distant port beyond Her Majesty's jurisdiction, and that thus an armed steamship is fitted out to cruise against the commerce of a power in amity with Her Majesty. A crew, composed partly of British subjects, is procured separately; wages are paid to them for an unknown service. They are dispatched, perhaps, to the coast of France, and there or elsewhere are engaged to serve in a confederate man of-war.

Now, it is very possible that by such shifts and stratagems, the penalties of the existing law of this country, nay, of any law that could be enacted, may be evaded; but the offense thus offered to Her Majesty's authority and dignity by the *de facto* rulers of the confederate States, whom Her Majesty acknowledges as belligerents, and whose agents in the United Kingdom enjoy the benefit of our hospitality in quiet security, remains the same. It is a proceeding totally unjustifiable, and manifestly offensive to the British Crown."—*Earl Russell's Letter to Messrs. Mason, Slidell, and Mann, February 13, 1865. Vol. 1, page 630.*

Earl Russell denounces the acts of which the United States complain as unwarranted and totally unjustifiable.

The Tribunal of Arbitration will probably agree with Earl Russell in his statement to the insurgent agents, that "the practice of building ships" in Great Britain "to be used as vessels of war" against the United States, and the "attempts to make the territorial waters of Great Britain the place of preparation for warlike armaments against the United States" in pursuance of contracts made with the Confederate agents," were "unwarrantable" and "totally unjustifiable."

British territory the base of the naval operations of the insurgents.

British territory was, during the whole struggle, the base of the naval operations of the insurgents. The first serious fight had scarcely taken place before the contracts were made in Great Britain for the Alabama and the Florida. The contest was nearly over when Waddell received his orders in Liverpool to sail thence in the Laurel in order to take command of the Shenandoah and to visit the Arctic Ocean on a hostile cruise.[1]

Their arsenal.

There also was the arsenal of the insurgents, from whence they drew their munitions of war, their arms, and their supplies. It is true that it has been said, and may again be said, that it was no infraction of the law of nations to furnish such supplies. But, while it is not maintained that belligerents may infringe upon the rights which neutrals have to manufacture and deal in such military supplies in the ordinary course of commerce, it is asserted with confidence that a neutral ought not to permit a belligerent to use the neutral soil as the main, if not the only base of its military supplies, during a long and bloody contest, as the soil of Great Britain was used by the insurgents.

---

[1] Vol. III, page 461.

The systematic operations of the insurgents a violation of the duties of a neutral.   It may not always be easy to determine what is and what is not lawful commerce in arms and munitions of war; but the United States conceive that there can be no doubt on which side of the line to place the insurgent operations on British territory. If Huse had been removed from Liverpool, Heyliger from Nassau, and Walker from Bermuda; or if Fraser, Trenholm & Co. had ceased to sell insurgent cotton and to convert it into money for the use of Huse, Heyliger, and Walker, the armies of the insurgents must have succumbed. The systematic operations of these persons, carried on openly and under the avowed protection of the British Government, made of British territory the "arsenal" of which Mr. Fish complained in his note of September 25, 1869.[1] Such conduct was, to say the least, wanting in the essentials of good neighborhood, and should be frowned upon by all who desire to so establish the principles of International Law, as to secure the peace of the world, while protecting the independence of nations.

It is in vain to say that both parties could have done the same thing. The United States were under no such necessity. If they could not manufacture at home all the supplies they needed, they were enabled to make their purchases abroad openly, and to transport them in the ordinary course of commerce. It was the insurgents who, unable to manufacture at home, were driven to England for their entire military supplies, and who, finding it impossible to transport those supplies in the ordinary course of commerce, originated a commerce for the purpose, and covered it under the British flag to Bermuda and Nassau. Under the pressure of the naval power of the United States, their necessities compelled them to transport to England a part of the executive of their Government, and to carry on its operation in Great Britain. They were protected in doing this by Her Majesty's Government, although its attention was called to the injustice thereof.[2] This conduct deprived the United States of the

---

[1] Vol. VI, page 4.
[2] Lord Russell to Mr. Adams, Vol. I, page 578.

benefit of their superiority at sea, and to that extent British neutrality was partial and insincere. The United States confidently submit to the Tribunal of Arbitration that it is an abuse of a sound principle to extend to such combined transactions as those of Huse, Heyliger, Walker, and Fraser, Trenholm & Co., the well-settled right of a neutral to manufacture and sell to either belligerent, during a war, arms, munitions, and military supplies. To sanction such an extension will be to lay the foundation for international misunderstanding and probable war, whenever a weaker party hereafter may draw upon the resources of a strong neutral, in its efforts to make its strength equal to that of its antagonist.

Continuing partiality for the insurgents. From the Queen's proclamation of neutrality to the close of the struggle, Great Britain framed its rules, construed its laws and its instructions, and governed its conduct in the interest of the insurgents. What could tend more to inspirit them than the news that on the eve of Mr. Adams's arrival in London, as if to show in the most public manner a purpose to overlook him, and to disregard the views which he might have been instructed by his Government to present, it had been determined to recognize their right to display on the ocean a flag which had not then a ship to carry it? How they must have welcomed the parliamentary news,[1] on the heels of this proclamation, that the effect of this recognition would be to employ British subjects in warring upon the commerce of the United States, with a protection against piracy promised in advance! How great must have been their joy, when they found British laws construed so as to confer upon them the right to use the workshops and dockyards of Liverpool, for building ships which, without violating the municipal law of England, might leave British ports in such warlike state that they could be fitted for battle in twenty-four hours! How they must have been cheered by the official legalization of the operations of those who had been sent to Liverpool in anticipation of the proclamation,

---

[1] Vol. V, pages 486 to 91.

to be in readiness to act! And if these welcome sights inspirited and cheered the insurgents, as was doubtless the case, how relatively depressing must have been their effect upon the loyal people and upon the Government of the United States! The correspondence of Mr. Seward and of Mr. Adams, running through the whole of the volumes of evidence accompanying this case, bears testimony to the depth of this feeling.

Recapitulation of hostile acts tolerated in British possessions. When Great Britain carried into practice its theory of neutrality, it was equally insincere and partial.

Its municipal laws for enforcing its obligations as a neutral, under the law of nations, were confessedly inadequate, and, during the struggle, were stripped of all their force by executive and judicial construction. Yet Great Britain refused to take any steps for their amendment, although requested so to do.[1]

The Queen's proclamation inhibited blockade-running; yet the authorities encouraged it by enacting new laws or making new regulations which permitted the transshipment of goods contraband of war within the colonial ports: by officially informing the colonial officers that "British authorities ought not to take any steps adverse to merchant vessels of the Confederate States, or to interfere with their free resort to British ports:"[2] by giving official notice to the United States that it would not do to examine too closely, on the high seas, British vessels with contraband of war:[3] and by regulations which operated to deter the United States vessels of war from entering the British ports from which the illicit trade was carried on.

The Foreign Enlistment Act of 1819 forbade the employment of a British vessel as a transport: and yet vessels known to be owned by the insurgent authorities, and engaged in carrying munitions of war for them, were allowed to carry the British flag and were welcomed in British ports. Still further, the same vessel would appear one day as a blockade-runner, and

---

[1] Ante, page 251.
[2] Duke of Newcastle to Governor Ord, Vol. II, page 558.
[3] Earl Russell to Lord Lyons, Vol. II, page 591.

another day as a man-of-war, receiving an equal welcome in each capacity.

The instructions of January 31, 1862, forbade both belligerents alike to enter the port of Nassau except by permission of the governor, or in stress of weather. That permission was lavishly given to every insurgent cruiser, but was granted churlishly, if at all, to the vessels of the United States.

The same instructions forbade the granting to a steam man-of-war of either belligerents in British ports a supply of coal in excess of what would be necessary to take the vessel to the nearest port of its own country or some nearer destination. This rule was enforced upon the vessels of the United States, but was utterly disregarded as to the vessels of the insurgents.

Those instructions also forbade the granting of any supply of coal to such a vessel if it had been coaled in a British port within three months. Yet in three notable instances this salutary rule was violated, that of the Nashville at Bermuda in February, 1862; the Florida at Barbadoes, in February, 1863; and the Alabama at Capetown in March, 1864.

These facts throw suspicion upon the acts of British officials toward insurgent cruisers. These admitted facts were repeatedly, and in detail, brought to the notice of the British Government, and as repeatedly, the answer was given that there was no cause for interference. At length they were, as a system, brought to Lord Russell's attention, by Mr. Adams, with the threads of evidence, which furnished him with the proof of their truth. Yet he declined to act, saying that "this correspondence does not appear to Her Majesty's Government to contain any sufficient evidence of a system of action in direct hostility to the United States;" that it furnished no proof as to the building of iron-clads that "could form matter for a criminal prosecution;" and that the other acts complained of were "not contrary to law."[1] In other words, he declared that the only international offense of which Her Majesty's Government would take notice was the building of iron-clads; and that no steps would be taken, even against persons guilty of that violation of neutrality, until the officials of the United States would act the part of

---

[1] Earl Russell to Mr. Adams, Vol. I, page 578.

detectives, and secure the proof which a British court could hold competent to convict the offender of a violation of a local law. It is important, in considering the evidence which is about to be referred to, to bear in mind these constant demonstrations of partiality for the insurgents. They show a persistent absence of real neutrality, which, to say the least, should throw suspicion upon the acts of the British officials as to those vessels, and should incline the Tribunal to closely scrutinize their conduct.

They show an abnegation of all diligence to prevent the acts complained of.
The United States, however, go farther than this. They insist that Her Majesty's Government abandoned, in advance, the exercise of that due diligence which the Treaty of Washington declares that a neutral is bound to observe. They say that the position of Her Majesty's Government just cited, taken in connection with the construction put upon the Foreign Enlistment Act by the British courts in the Alexandra case, was a practical abandonment of all obligation to observe diligence in preventing the use of British territory by the insurgents, for purposes hostile to the United States. They aver that it was a notice to them that no complaints in this respect would be listened to, which were not accompanied by proof sufficient to convict the offender as a criminal under the Foreign Enlistment Act. To furnish such proof was simply impossible. The Tribunal will remember that it was judicially said in the case of the Alexandra, that what had been done in the matter of the Alabama was no violation of British law, and therefore constituted no offense to be punished. Well might Earl Russell say that the Oreto and the Alabama were a scandal to English laws.

They throw upon Great Britain the burden of proof to show that the acts complained of could not have been prevented.
The United States with great confidence assert that the facts which have been established justify them in asking the Tribunal of Arbitration, in the investigations now about to be made, to assume that in the violations of neutrality which will be shown to have taken place, the burden of proof will be upon Great Britain to establish that they could not have been prevented. Her Majesty's Government declined to investigate charges and to examine evidence submitted by Mr. Adams as to repeated violations of British

territory, which subsequent events show were true in every respect. It placed its refusal upon principles which must inevitably lead to like disregard in future—principles which rendered nugatory thereafter any measure of diligence to discover violations of neutrality within Her Majesty's dominions. Thereby Great Britain assumed and justified all similar acts which had been or might be committed, and relieved the United States from the necessity of showing that due diligence was not exercised to prevent them.

Of what use was it to exercise diligence to show the purpose for which the Florida, the Alabama, or the Georgia was constructed, or the Shenandoah was purchased, if the constructing, fitting out, or equipping, or the purchase for such objects was lawful, and could not be interfered with? What diligence could have prevented the excessive supplies of coal and other hospitalities to the insurgent cruisers, or the protection of transports, all of which made those ports bases of operations, if such acts were no violation of the duties of a neutral, of which the United States might justly complain?

List of the insurgent cruisers. The cruisers for whose acts the United States ask this Tribunal to hold Great Britain responsible are (stating them in the order in which their cruises began) the Sumter; the Nashville; the Florida and her tenders, the Clarence, the Tacony, and the Archer; the Alabama and her tender, the Tuscaloosa; the Retribution; the Georgia; the Tallahassee; the Chicamauga; and the Shenandoah. The attention of the Tribunal of Arbitration is now invited to an account of each of these vessels.

THE SUMTER.

The Sumter. The Sumter escaped from the passes of the Mississippi on the 30th of June, 1861, and on the 30th of the following July arrived at the British port of Trinidad. She remained there six days, taking in a supply of coal.[1] Complaint being made of this act as a "violation of Her

---

[1] Bernard to Seward, Vol. II, page 485.

Majesty's Proclamation of Neutrality."[1] Lord Russell replied, that, "the conduct of the Governor was in conformity to Her Majesty's Proclamation;" that "Captain Hillyar, of Her Majesty's Ship Cadmus, having sent a boat to ascertain her nationality, the commanding officer showed a commission signed by Mr. Jefferson Davis, calling himself the President of the so-styled Confederate States."[2] Her Majesty's Government thus held this vessel to be a man-of-war as early as the 30th of July, 1861.

Having got a full supply of coal and other necessary outfit, the Sumter sailed on the 5th of August, 1861, and, after a cruise in which she destroyed six vessels carrying the flag of the United States, she arrived in Gibraltar on the 18th of the following January. Before she could again be supplied with coal and leave that port, she was shut in by the arrival of the Tuscarora, a vessel of war of the United States, which "anchored off Algeciras."[3] The Tuscarora was soon followed by the Kearsarge, both under the instructions of the Government of the United States.

Finding it impossible to escape, an attempt was made to sell the Sumter, with her armament, for £4000.[4] The consul of the United States at Gibraltar, by direction of Mr. Adams, protested against this sale.[5] The sale was finally made "by public auction" on the 19th of December, 1862.[6] Mr. Adams notified Earl Russell that the sale would not be recognized by the United States, and called upon Great Britain not to regard it, as it had been made in violation of principles of law that had been adopted by British courts and publicists.[7] He maintained that "Her Majesty's Government, in furnishing shelter for so long a period to the Sumter in the harbor of Gibraltar, as a ship of war of a belligerent, had determined the character of the vessel;"[8]

---

[1] Adams to Russell, Vol. II, page 484.
[2] Russell to Adams, Vol. II, page 486.
[3] Sprague to Seward, Vol. II, page 502.
[4] Sprague to Adams, Vol. II, page 507.
[5] Sprague to Codrington, Vol. II, page 509.
[6] Sprague to Adams, Vol. II, page 515.
[7] Adams to Russell, **Vol. II**, page 522.
[8] Adams to Russell, **Vol. II**, page 523.

and that "the purchase of ships of war belonging to enemies is held in the British courts to be invalid."[1]

After reflecting upon this simple proposition for more than five weeks, Earl Russell denied it. He said, "The British Government, when neutral, is not bound to refuse to a British subject the right to acquire by purchase a vessel which a belligerent owner may desire to part with, but it would not deny the right of the adverse belligerent to ascertain, if such vessel were captured by its cruisers, whether the vessel had rightfully, according to the law of nations, come into the possession of the neutral."[2] Mr. Adams also maintained that the sale was fictitious,[3] to which Earl Russell replied that he "could not assume that the Sumter had not been legally and *bona fide* sold to a British owner for commercial and peaceful purposes."[3] Mr. Adam's insisted (and the result proved that he was correct) that the sale of the Sumter was fictitious, and that the purchaser was an agent of Fraser, Trenholm & Co., the treasury agents and depositaries, &c., for the insurgent authorities at Richmond.[4] His representations were disregarded, and the vessel was taken to Liverpool and thoroughly repaired. She then took on board a cargo of arms and munitions of war, and, under the name of the Gibraltar, fortified with a British register, became an insurgent transport.[5]

In all these proceedings on the part of British officials the United States find a partiality toward the insurgents, which is inconsistent with the duties of a neutral.

1. The Sumter was permitted to receive at Trinidad a full supply of coal. The United States, however, were forbidden by Great Britain even to deposit coal in the British

---

[1] Russell to Adams, Vol. II, page 526.
[2] Adams to Russell, Vol. II, page 520.
[3] Russell to Adams, Vol. II, page 521.
[4] The nominal purchasers were M. G. Klingerder & Co. (Vol. II, page 529.) This house was connected with Fraser, Trenholm & Co., and paid regularly a portion of the wages of the men on the Alabama, to their families in Liverpool. (See Dudley to Adams, Vol. III, page 210.)
[5] Vol. II, pages 521—538.

West Indies for their own use, under such regulations as might be prescribed by Her Majesty's Government. What took place at Nassau in December, 1861, has already been told. In Bermuda, on the 19th of February, 1862, their consul was officially informed that "the Government of Her Britannic Majesty had determined not to allow the formation in any British colony of a coal-depot for the use of their vessels of war, either by the Government of the United States or of the so-styled Confederate States." [1] Before this Case is finished it will be seen how thoroughly this determination was disregarded as to the "so-styled Confederate States."

If it should be thought that the habitually insincere neutrality of Great Britain, as already detailed, did not constitute such a violation of the duties of a neutral as would entail responsibility for the acts of all the insurgent cruisers, (which the United States, with confidence, maintain that it did,) it is clear that the Sumter was furnished with an excessive supply of coal at Trinidad, which supply enabled her to inflict the subsequent injuries on the commerce of the United States. It is not contended that at that time there were any precedents which settled absolutely the quantity of coal which might be furnished to a belligerent steam man-of-war by a neutral. When the proclamation of neutrality was issued, it seemed to be the opinion of leading members of the House of Lords, (Lords Brougham and Kingsdown, for instance,) that coal for the use of vessels of war might be regarded as contraband of war. [2] The instructions issued by Her Majesty's Government a few months later permitted this article to be furnished, provided the supply should be measured by the capacity of the vessel to consume it, and should be limited to what might be necessary to take it to the nearest port of its own country, or to some nearer

---

[1] Ord to Allen Vol. II, page 590. See also the reports of the officers of the Keystone and the Quaker City, who, in December, 1861, were refused supplies of coal at this port. Vol. VI, pages 52 and 53. See also the case of the Florida, *post*, where this subject is more fully discussed.

[2] Vol. IV, pp. 486—491.

destination. This rule, as subsequently modified by the United States,[1] appears to be a just medium between the excessive supply furnished to the Sumter in Trinidad and the absolute refusal to permit the United States to supply itself. Under this rule the Sumter would have been entitled to receive only what would be necessary to take her to New Orleans or to Galveston.

2. The Sumter was in the port of Gibraltar when the instructions of January 16, 1862. (Vol. IV, p. 175,) were published there,[2] on the 11th February. By their terms they were to go into effect six days after that date. Under those instructions the Sumter, having been recognized as a man-of-war, ought to have been required to leave the port of Gibraltar within twenty-four hours, or, if without coal, within twenty-four hours after getting a supply of coal. Instead of that she was allowed to remain there for twelve months, while Lord Russell's instructions were rigidly enforced against the vessels of the United States. The reason for this partiality may be easily gathered from the correspondence of the United States Consul at Gibraltar.[3] The vessels of war of the United States were on her track, and had the instructions of Earl Russell been complied with, the well-laid schemes of the United States officers for her destruction would have been successful. But the Tribunal will observe that the instructions, which were so offensively enforced against the United States vessels Connecticut and Honduras, were ignored as to the insurgent vessel Sumter.

3. The sale of the Sumter was palpably an evasion. She went into the hands of Fraser, Trenholm & Co.; and, knowing the connection between that firm and the insurgents, it is not too much to ask the Tribunal to assume as a pro-

---

[1] The President's Proclamation of October 8, 1870, issued during the Franco-German war, limited the supply of coal to the war vessels or privateers of the belligerents to so much as might be sufficient, if without sail power, to carry the vessel to the nearest European port of its own country; if with sail power, to half that quantity.

[2] Vol. II, pages 502—503.

[3] Sprague to Adams, Vol. II, pages 502, 503, 506, 507.

bability that there was never any change of ownership. But if it should be thought that the transaction was made *bona fide*, then there is an equal probability that the money found its way to the credit of the insurgents in their Liverpool transactions.

By reason of these repeated acts of insincere neutrality, or of actual disregard of the duties of a neutral, the United States were great sufferers. Before arriving at Trinidad, the Sumter captured eleven American vessels.[1] After leaving that port, and before arriving at Gibraltar, she captured six other vessels belonging to citizens of the United States. The injury did not stop there. The United States made diligent efforts to capture this vessel which was destroying their commerce. For this purpose they dispatched across the Atlantic two of their men-of-war, the Kearsarge and the Tuscarora. These vessels followed on the track of the Sumter, and the plans of the United States would have been successful had Earl Russell's instructions of January 31, 1862, been carried out toward the Sumter in the port of Gibraltar, as they were carried out toward the vessels of the United States in all the colonial ports of Great Britain.

Under these circumstances, the United States ask the Tribunal to find and certify as to the Sumter that Great Britain, by the acts or omissions hereinbefore recited or referred to, failed to fulfill the duties set forth in the three rules in Article VI of the Treaty of Washington, or recognized by the principles of International Law not inconsistent with such rules. Should the Tribunal exercise the power conferred upon it by Article VII of the Treaty, to award a sum in gross to be paid to the United States, they will ask that, in considering the amount so to be awarded, the losses of individuals in the destruction of their vessels and cargoes by the Sumter, and also the expenses to which the United States were put in the pursuit of that vessel, may be taken into account.

---

[1] Bernard to Seward, Vol. II, page 485.

THE NASHVILLE.

The Nashville. The Nashville, a large paddle-wheel steamer, formerly engaged on the New York and Charleston line, lightened to diminish her draught, armed with two guns, and commanded by an officer who had been in the Navy of the United States, ran out from Charleston on the night of the 26th of October, 1861.[1] She arrived at the British port of St. George, Bermuda, on the afternoon of the 30th[2] of the same month, having been about three and a half days making the passage. She took on board there, by the permission of the Governor, six hundred tons of coal,[3] and this act was approved by Her Majesty's principal Secretary of State for the Colonies.[4] This approval seems to have been elicited by the complaints which had been made to the Governor by the Consul of the United States at that port.[5] It may also be that Her Majesty's Government preferred to have the question settled, before it could be made the subject of diplomatic representation on the part of the United States.

In view of the rule as to supplies of coal which was soon after adopted by Her Majesty's Government, the United States insist, as they have already insisted in regard to the Sumter, that a supply of six hundred tons was greatly in excess of the needs of the Nashville. There are no means of knowing whether she had any coal on board at the time she arrived in the port of St. George. Assuming that she had none, the utmost she should have received was enough to take her back to Charleston, from which port she had just come in three days and a half. Instead of that, she received more than a supply for a voyage to Southampton. She left Bermuda on the afternoon of the 5th of November,[6] and anchored in Southampton waters on

---

[1] Bernard's Neutrality of Great Britain, page 267.
[2] Wells to Seward, Vol. II, page 538.
[3] Governor Ord to the Duke of Newcastle, Vol. II, page 557.
[4] Duke of Newcastle to Governor Ord, Vol. II, page 558.
[5] Wells to Ord, Vol. II, page 539.
[6] Wells to Seward, Vol. II, page 540.

the morning of the 21st of the same month,[1] having destroyed at sea the United States merchant ship Harvey Birch[1] on the passage.

A correspondence ensued between Earl Russell and Mr. Adams as to the character of this vessel, in which Lord Russel said, "The Nashville appears to be a Confederate vessel of war."[2] She was received as such, was "taken into dock for calking and other repairs," and "received one hundred and fifty tons of coal" on the 10th of January. On the 25th "Captain Patey, of Her Majesty's Navy, reported the Nashville coaled and necessary repairs completed."[4]

On the 4th of the following February the Nashville left Southampton and proceeded to Bermuda, where she arrived on the evening of the 20th. On the day previous to that (the 19th) the Consul had received from the Governor the official notice already alluded to, that the Government of Her Britannic Majesty had determined not to allow the formation, in any British Colony, of a coal depot for the use of the vessels of war of the United States.[5] The Government of the United States was, therefore, not a little astonished to learn from the Consul at Bermuda that the Nashville had taken on board one hundred and fifty tons of coal at that place, and that she left "under the escort of Her Majesty's steamer Spiteful."[6]

These circumstances, in accordance with the principles hereinbefore stated, justify the United States in asking the Tribunal of Arbitration as to this vessel, to find and certify that Great Britain, by the acts or omissions hereinbefore recited or referred to, failed to fulfill the duties set forth in the three rules in Article VI of the Treaty of Washington or recognized by the principles of international law not inconsistent with such rules. Should the Tribunal exercise

---

[1] Captain Patey to the Secretary of the Admiralty, Vol. II, pages 543, 544.
[2] Russell to Adams, Vol. II, page 555.
[3] Vol. II, page 587.
[4] Ord to Allen, Vol. II, page 590.
[5] Adams to Seward, Vol. II, page 542.
[6] Allen to Seward, Vol. II, page 591.

the power conferred upon it by Article VII of the Treaty, to award a sum in gross to be paid to the United States, they will ask that, in considering the amount so to be awarded, the losses of individuals in the destruction of their vessels and cargoes by the Nashville, and also the expenses to which the United States were put in the pursuit of that vessel, may be taken into account.

THE FLORIDA, AND HER TENDERS, THE CLARENCE, THE TACONY, AND THE ARCHER.

The Florida and her tenders. The Florida, originally known as the Oreto, was an iron screw gun-boat, of about seven hundred tons burden, bark-rigged, and had two smoke-stacks and three masts.[1] The contract for her construction was made with Fawcett, Preston & Co., of Liverpool, by Bullock, soon after he came to England in the summer of 1861. He was introduced to them by Prioleau, of the firm of Fraser, Trenholm & Co., in order that he might make the contract.[2]

It was pretended, for form's sake, that she was constructed for the Italian Government; but it was a shallow pretense, and deceived only those who wished to be deceived. The Italian Consul at Liverpool disclaimed all knowledge of her,[3] and people at that port who were familiar with ship-building understood from the first that she was being built for the Southern insurgents.[4]

The precise date of the making of the contract cannot

---

[1] Dudley to Adams, Vol. II, page 594.
[2] Prioleau's evidence, Vol VI, page 181.
[3] Dudley to Seward, Vol. II, page 592.
[4] See Mr. Dudley's dispatches of January 24 and 31, and of February 4, 12, 17, 19, 21, 22, 26, and 27, and of March 1, 5, 12, 15, 19, and 22, in the year 1862, Vol. VI, page 214 et seq.

be given by the United States. The range of time within which it must have been made can be determined. Bullock left England in the autumn of 1861, at or about the time that the Bermuda sailed with Huse's first shipment of stores; and returned in March, on the Annie Childs, which ran the blockade from Wilmington.[1] The contract was made before he left, and the Florida was constructed during his absence.

The contract for the construction of the hull was sub-let by Fawcett, Preston & Co. to Miller & Sons, of Liverpool.[2] The payments to Miller & Sons were made by Fawcett, Preston & Co.; the payments to Fawcett, Preston & Co. were made by Fraser, Trenholm & Co.

By the 4th of February the Florida was taking in her coal, and appearances indicated that she would soon leave without her armament.[3] She made her trial trip on the 17th of February. By the 1st of March she had taken in her provisions, "a very large quantity, enough for a long cruise," and was getting as many Southern sailors"[4] as possible. She was registered as an English vessel.[5] Although apparently ready to sail, she lingered about Liverpool, which gave rise to some speculations in the minds of the people of that town. It was said that she had "injured herself and was undergoing repairs."[6] The mystery was solved by the arrival, on the 11th of March, in the Mersey, of the Annie Childs from Wilmington, bringing as passengers Captain Bullock[7] and four other insurgent naval officers, who came on board of her "some twenty miles down the river from Wilmington,"[8] and who were to take commands on the vessels which were contracted for in Liverpool. As soon as they arrived they went on board the Florida, and were entertained there that evening.[7] On the 22d of March the Florida took her final

---

[1] Dudley to Seward, March 12, 1862, Vol. VI, page 223.
[2] Same to same, February 12, 1862, Vol. VI, page 215.
[3] Dudley to Seward, Vol. II, page 592; Vol. VI, page 215.
[4] Same to same, Vol. II, page 596; Vol. VI, page 220.
[5] Same to same, Vol. II, page 597; Vol. VI, page 221.
[6] Dudley to Seward, March 7, 1862, Vol. VI, page 222.
[7] Same to same, March 22, 1862, Vol. VI, page 224.
[8] Dudley to Adams, Vol. II, page 601.

departure from the Mersey,[1] with "a crew of fifty-two men, all British, with the exception of three or four, one of whom only was an American."[2] She was consigned by Bullock to Heyliger. Another account says that she was consigned to Adderley & Co.

Simultaneously with these proceedings, shipments were being made at Hartlepool, on the eastern coast of England, of cannon, rifles, shot, shells, &c., intended for the Florida. They were sent from Liverpool to Hartlepool by rail, and there put on board the steamer Bahama for Nassau.

It was a matter of public notoriety that this was going on.[3] All the facts about the Florida, and about the hostile expedition which it was proposed to make against the United States, were open and notorious at Liverpool. Mr. Dudley's correspondence, already cited, was full of it. The means of intelligence were as accessible to British authorities as to the consular officers of the United States. Nevertheless, it was esteemed to be the duty of the officers of the United States to lay what had come to their knowledge before Her Majesty's Government. Mr. Dudley, the Consul at Liverpool, wrote to Mr. Adams that he had information from many different sources as to the Oreto, "all of which goes to show that she is intended for the Southern Confederacy."[4] Mr. Adams transmitted the intelligence to Earl Russell, and said that he "entertained little doubt that the intention was precisely that indicated in the letter of the Consul, the carrying on war against the United States." * * * He added, "Should further evidence to sustain the allegations respecting the Oreto be held necessary to effect the object of securing the interposition of Her Majesty's Government, I will make an effort to procure it in a more formal manner."[5]

The United States ask the Tribunal to observe that, notwithstanding this offer, *no objection was taken as to the*

---

[1] Vol. II, page 604.
[2] Customs Report, Vol. II, page 605; Vol. VI, page 231.
[3] See Mr. Dudley's dispatches of March 7, 12, and 15, Vols. II and VI.
[4] Dudley to Adams, Vol. II, page 594; Vol. VI, page 216.
[5] Adams to Russell, Vol. II, page 593; Vol. VI, page 216.

form of the information submitted by Mr. Adams, nor was he asked by Earl Russell for further particulars. Lord Russell, however, in reply, transmitted to Mr. Adams a report of the British Commissioners of Customs, in which it was stated that the Oreto was a vessel of war "pierced for four guns;" that she was "built by Miller & Sons for Fawcett, Preston & Co.," and was "intended for the use of Messrs. Thomas Brothers, of Palmero;" that she "had been handed over to Messrs. Fawcett & Preston; that Miller & Son stated their belief that the destination was Palmero;" and that "the examiners had every reason to believe that the vessel was destined for the Italian Government."[1] Further representations being made by Mr. Adams, the same officers subsequently reported that, having received directions "to inquire into the further allegations made in regard to the Oreto," they found "that the vessel in question was registered on the 3d of March in the name of John Henry Thomas, of Liverpool, as sole owner; that she cleared on the following day for Palermo and Jamaica, in ballast, but did not sail until the 22d, * * * having a crew of fifty-two men, all British, with the exception of three or four, one of whom only was an American."[2]

The Tribunal of Arbitration will observe that even from the reports of these British officers it is established that the Florida was a vessel of war, "pierced for four guns;" and also that notwithstanding their alleged belief that she was intended for the King of Italy, she was allowed to clear for Jamaica in ballast. Attention is also invited to the easy credulity of these officials, who, to the first charges of Mr. Adams, replied by putting forward the "belief" of the builders as to the destination of the vessel, and who met his subsequent complaints by extracting from the custom-house records the false clearance which Bullock, and Fraser, Trenholm & Co., had caused to be entered there. Such an examination and such a report can scarcely be regarded as the exercise of the "due diligence" called for by the rules of the Treaty of Washington.

---

[1] Vol. II, pages 595—96; Vol. VI, page 218.
[2] Vol. II, page 605; Vol. VI, page 231.

The Florida arrived at Nassau on the 28th of April, and was taken in charge by Heyliger, who was then a well-known and recognized insurgent agent. The Bahama arrived a few days later at the same port by preconcerted arrangement. The two branches of the hostile expedition, which had left Great Britain in detachments, were thus united in British waters. They were united in their conception in the contracts with Fawcett, Preston & Co. They were temporarily separated by the shipment of a portion of the ammunition and stores by rail to Hartlepool, and thence by the Bahama. They were now again united, and the vessels went together to Cochrane's Anchorage, a place about nine miles from the harbor of Nassau, not included in the port limits.

While there Captain Hickley, of Her Majesty's ship Greyhound, thought it his duty to make a careful examination of the vessel, and he reported her condition to the Governor. In a remarkable certificate, signed by himself, and by the officers of the Greyhound, dated June 13, 1862, it is stated that he "asked the captain of the Oreto whether the Oreto had left Liverpool in all respects as she was then; his answer was yes; in all respects."[1] As, therefore, no changes had been made in her after leaving Liverpool, Captain Hickley's report may be taken to be the official evidence of a British expert as to her character, at the time of Mr. Adams's complaints, and of the customs examinations. He says, "I then proceeded to examine the vessel, and found her in every respect fitted as a war vessel, precisely the same as vessels of a similar class in Her Majesty's Navy. She has a magazine and light-rooms forward, handing-rooms and handing-scuttles for powder as in war vessels; shell-rooms aft, fitted as in men-of-war; a regular lower deck with hammock-hooks, mess-shelves, &c., &c., as in our own war vessels, her cabin accommodations and fittings generally being those as fitted in vessels of her own class in the Navy. * * * She is a vessel capable of carrying guns; she could carry four broadside-guns forward, four broadside-guns aft, and two pivot-guns amidships. Her ports are fitted to ship and unship;

---

[1] Vol. VI, page 246.

port-bars cut through on the upper part to unship also. The construction of her ports, I consider, are peculiar to vessels of war. I saw shot-boxes all round her upper deck, calculated to receive Armstrong shot, or shot similar. She had breeching bolts and shackles, and side-tackle bolts. Magazine, shell-rooms, and light-rooms are entirely at variance with the fittings of a merchant ship. She had no accommodation whatever for the stowage of cargo; only stowage for provisions and stores. She was in all respects fitted as a vessel of war of her class in Her Majesty's Navy. * * * *The Oreto, as she now stands, could, in my professional opinion, with her crew, guns, arms, and ammunition, going out with another vessel alongside of her, be equipped in twenty-four hours for battle."*[1]

The judge before whom the case was tried, commenting on this evidence, said: "Captain Hickley's evidence as to the construction and fittings of the vessel I should consider conclusive even had there been no other; *but that construction and those fittings were made, not here, but in England.*"[2]

This was, therefore, the condition of the Florida when she left Liverpool. That she was then "intended to cruise and carry on war" against the United States there can be no reasonable doubt; that she was "fitted out" and "equipped" within the jurisdiction of Great Britain, with all the fittings and equipments necessary to enable her to carry on such war, is equally clear from Captain Hickley's professional statement. "Arming" alone was necessary to make her ready for battle. By the rules of the Treaty of Washington either the "fitting out" or the "equipping" constitute an offense without the "arming." That Great Britain had reasonable ground to believe that the fitting out and the equipping had been done within its jurisdiction, with intent that she should carry on such a war, the United States claim to have substantiated. That she had been specially adapted within British jurisdiction, to wit, at Liverpool, to warlike use, will scarcely be questioned after the positive testimony

---

[1] Vol. VI, pages 264 and 266.
[2] Vol. V, page 513.

of Captain Hickley. That her departure from the jurisdiction of Great Britain might have been prevented after the information furnished by Mr. Adams would seem to be beyond doubt. And that a neglect to prevent such departure was a failure to use the "due diligence" called for by the second clause of the first rule of the Treaty obviously follows the last conclusion. If these several statements are well founded, Great Britain, by permitting the construction of the Florida, at Liverpool, under the circumstances, and by consenting to her departure from that port, violated its duty as a neutral Government toward the United States.

The United States Consul, soon after the arrival of the Oreto at Nassau, called the attention of the Governor to her well-known character.[1] The Governor declined to interfere, and with an easy credulity accepted the statements of the insurgent agents that the vessel was not and would not be armed,[2] and he made no further inquiries. She was then permitted to remain at Cochrane's Anchorage. A second request to inquire into her character was made on the 4th of June, and refused.[3] On the 7th of June both the Oreto and the Bahama were arrested and brought up from Cochrane's Anchorage into the harbor of Nassau. On the 8th the mail-steamer Melita arrived from England, with Captain Raphael Semmes and his officers from the Sumter as passengers. They "became lions at once."[4] The Oreto was immediately released. The Consul reported this fact to his Government, and said that "the character of the vessel had become the theme of general conversation and remark among all classes of the citizens of Nassau for weeks."[5] On the same day Captain Hickley, whose professional eye had detected the purpose of the vessel from the beginning, signed with his officers the certificate quoted above.

The Consul, finding that renewed representations to the

---

[1] Consul Whiting to Governor Bayley, May 9, 1862, Vol. VI, page 235.
[2] Nesbitt to Whiting, May 13, 1862, Vol. VI, page 236.
[3] Vol. VI, pages 238—239.
[4] Whiting to Seward, June 19, 1862, Vol. VI, page 241.
[5] Whiting to Seward, June 13, 1862, Vol. VI, page 242.

Governor[1] were met by an answer that the agents of the Oreto assured him of their intention to clear in ballast for Havana, and that he had given his assent to it,[2] applied to Captain Hickley, of the Greyhound, and laid before him the evidence which had already been laid before the civil authorities. He answered by sending a file of marines on board the Oreto and taking her into custody.[3]

The civil authorities at Nassau were all actively friendly to the insurgents. With the Consul of the United States they had only the formal relations made necessary by his official position. With the insurgents it was quite different. We have already seen how Heyliger thought they regarded him. Maffitt, Semmes, and many other insurgent officers were there, and were often thrown in contact with the Government officials. Adderley, the correspondent of Fraser, Trenholm & Co., and the mercantile agent of the insurgents, was one of the leading merchants of the colony. Harris, his partner, was a member of the Council, and was in intimate social relations with all the authorities. The principal law officer of the colony, who would have charge of any prosecution that might be instituted against the Oreto and the cross-examination of the witnesses summoned in her favor, was the counsel of Adderley. All these circumstances, combined with the open partiality of the colonial authorities for the cause of the South, threw the insurgent agents and officers at that critical moment into intimate relations with those local authorities.[4]

If it had been predetermined that the Oreto should be released by going through the form of a trial under the Foreign Enlistment Act,[5] the steps could not have been better directed for that purpose. The trial commenced on the 4th of July, 1862.[6] The prosecution was conducted by a gentle-

---

[1] Whiting to Bayley, June 12, 1862, Vol. VI, page 243.
[2] Nesbitt to Whiting, June 13, 1862, Vol. VI, page 244.
[3] Whiting to Seward, June 13, 1862, Vol. VI. page 250.
[4] Kirkpatrick to Seward, Vol. VI, page 327.
[5] This seemingly harsh statement is fully borne out by the report of the trial. See Vol. V. page 509.
[6] Governor Bayley to Captain Hickley, June, 1862.

man who was at once Crown Counsel, Advocate General, and confidential counsel of Adderley & Co., and who, in a speech made in a trial in another court, which took place after the Oreto was libeled and before the decree was rendered, said that the Union of the United States was "a myth, a Yankee fiction of the past, now fully exploded."[1] The temper with which he would manage the prosecution of the Oreto may be imagined from this speech. He hurried on the trial before evidence could be obtained from Liverpool. He conducted his cross-examinations so as to suppress evidence unfavorable to the Oreto, when it could be done. He neglected to summon witnesses who must have been within his control, who could have shown conclusively that the Oreto was built for the insurgents, and was to be converted into a man-of-war.[2] Maffitt knew it, but was not called.[3] Heyliger knew it, but was not called. Adderley knew it, but was not called. Evans and Chapman were both there-officers in the insurgents' navy, under the direction of Maffitt, drawing pay from him as an officer in that navy, and giving receipts as such.[4] They knew all about it, but were not called. Harris,[5] a member of the firm of Adderley & Co., was called, but his cross-examination was so conducted as to bring out nothing damaging to the vessel.[6] He said, for instance, that the Oreto was consigned to him by Fraser, Trenholm and Co., and was to clear for St. John's, New

---

[1] Whiting to Seward, August 1, 1862, Vol. VI, page 261.

[2] If the Tribunal will read the summary of this case in the opinion of the court, which may be found at page 509 of Vol. V, it will be found that this statement is not too strong.

[3] The Oreto had in fact been ordered by Bullock, as agent of the Confederate Government, from one ship-building firm, as the Alabama had been ordered by him from another; and Captain Maffitt, the officer appointed to command her, was all this while at Nassau, awaiting the result of the trial.—*Bernard's Neutrality of Great Britain*, page 351.

[4] See Evans and Chapman's vouchers, Nassau, July 28th, Vol. VI, page 330.

[5] See Consul Kirkpatrick's dispatch to Mr. Seward, July 7, 1865 as to the standing of these men, Vol. VI, page 327.

[6] Vol. V, page 517.

Brunswick. It might have been supposed that counsel desirous of ascertaining the truth would have followed up these clews, and would have shown from this witness the origin and the real purposes of the vessel; but that was not done.

The direct examination of Captain Hickley, of the Greyhound, disclosed that officer's opinion of the character and destination of the Oreto. His cross-examination was conducted by a gentleman who was represented to be the Solicitor General of the Colony, but who, in this case, appeared against the Crown. The testimony of sailors was also received to show that the vessel carried Confederate flags, and that Semmes and the other insurgent officers were in the habit of visiting her.

The judge, in deciding the case, disregarded the positive proof of the character, intent, and ownership of the vessel. He said that he did not believe the evidence as to the insurgent flags, coming from common sailors, and he added, "Had there been a Confederate flag on board the Oreto, I should not consider it as very powerful evidence." The overwhelming testimony of Captain Hickley and his officers was summarily disposed of. To this he said, "I have no right whatever to take it into consideration; the case depends upon what has been done since the vessel came within this jurisdiction." While thus ruling out either as false or as irrelevant evidence against the vessel which events proved to be true and relevant, he gave the willing ear of credence to the misstatements of the persons connected with the Oreto. He could see no evidence of illegal intent in the acts of those who had charge of the Oreto. It is no wonder that the trial ended on the 2d of August with a judgment that, "Under all these circumstances I do not feel that I should be justified in condemning the Oreto. She will therefore be restored."[1]

The United States call the attention of the Arbitrators to the important fact that the principal ground on which this vessel was released, namely, the irrelevancy of the evidence of Captain Hickley and his associates, was believed by

---

[1] Vol. V, page 521, Vol. VI, page 285.

Her Majesty's Government not to be in accordance with British law. When the news of the seizure of the Oreto arrived at London, Earl Russell directed inquiries to be made, "in order that a competent officer should be sent to Nassau in order to give evidence as to what occurred at Liverpool in the case of that vessel."[1] Her Majesty's Government evidently considered that it would be relevant and proper to show the condition of the vessel when she left Liverpool; and should it appear, as it did appear in Captain Hickley's testimony, that at the time of her leaving she was fitted out as a man-of-war, with intent to cruise against the United States, then it would be entirely within the scope of the powers of the court in Nassau to condemn her for a violation of the Foreign Enlistment Act of 1819. Had the trial not been hurried on, such probably would have been the instructions from London.

Both before and after the release of the Oreto, Maffitt was shipping a crew at Nassau. One witness deposes[2] to shipping forty men. On the 8th of August she cleared for St. John's, New Brunswick. This was on its face a palpable fraud. On the 9th the schooner Prince Alfred went to the wharf of Adderley & Co., the Nassau correspondents of Fraser, Trenholm & Co., and there took on board eight cannon and a cargo of shot, shells, and provisions, and then went over the bar and laid her course for Green Cay, one of the British Bahama Islands, about sixty miles distant from Nassau. The Oreto, having been thoroughly supplied with coal while at the island of New Providence, lay outside with a hawser attached to one of Her Majesty's ships of war. When the Prince Alfred appeared she cast off the hawser, and followed and overtook the Prince Alfred, and gave her a tow. It was a bright moonlight night, with a smooth sea, and the voyage was soon made. The arms and ammunition, and so much of the supplies as she had room for, were then transferred to the Oreto; the rest were taken back to Nassau, where the Prince Alfred went unmolested for her

---

[1] Vol. II, pages 610—611.
[2] Solomon's deposition, Vol. VI, page 310.

violation of the law. The two vessels parted company, and the Oreto, now called the Florida, made for the coast of Cuba.

The United States ask the Tribunal of Arbitration to find that in these proceedings which took place at Nassau and in the Bahamas, Great Britain was once more guilty of a violation of its duty, as a neutral, toward the United States, in regard to this vessel.

The Oreto had been, within the jurisdiction of Great Britain at Liverpool, specially adapted to warlike use, with intent that she should cruise or carry on war against the United States. She had come again at Nassau within the jurisdiction of Her Majesty, and no steps were taken to prevent her departure from that jurisdiction. This alone was a violation of the duties prescribed by the second clause of the first rule of the Treaty; but it was not the only failure of Her Majesty's officials to perform their duties at that time as the representative of a neutral Government.

The Oreto was armed within British jurisdiction; namely, at Green Cay. The arrangements for arming, however, were made in the harbor of Nassau; and the two vessels left that port almost simultaneously, and proceeded to Green Cay together. The purpose for which they went was notorious in Nassau. This was so palpable an evasion that the act should be assumed as having taken place in the harbor of Nassau. In either event, however, the act was committed within British jurisdiction, and was therefore a violation of the first clause of the first rule of the Treaty.

In like manner, the same acts, and the enlistment of men at New Providence, were violations of the second rule of the Treaty. There was no diligence used to prevent any of these illegal acts.

From Green Cay the Florida went to Cardenas, in the island of Cuba, and attempted to ship a crew there. "The matter was brought to the notice of the Government, who sent an official to Lieutenant Stribling, commanding during Lieutenant Commanding J. N. Maffitt's illness, with a copy of the [Spanish] Queen's Proclamation, and notification to him that the Florida had become liable to seizure."[1] This

---

[1] Copy of voucher of Manuel Corany, Vol. VI, page 331.

efficient conduct of the Spanish authorities made the officers of the Florida feel at once that they were no longer in British waters. She left Cuba, and on the 4th of September she ran through the blockading squadron of Mobile, pretending to be a British man-of-war, and flying British colors.

During the night of the 16th of January, 1863, the Florida left Mobile. On the morning of the 26th of the same month she reentered the harbor of Nassau. Between Mobile and Nassau she had destroyed three small vessels, the Corris Ann, the Estelle, and the Windward. At Nassau she was received with more than honor. She "entered the port without any restrictions,"[1] and "the officers landed in the garrison boat, escorted by the post adjutant, Lieutenant Williams, of the Second West India Regiment."[2] The Governor made a feint of finding fault with the mode in which she had entered, but ended by giving her all the hospitality which her commander desired. She was at Nassau for thirty-six hours,[2] and while there she took in coal and provisions to last for three months.[3] This coal was taken on board by "permission of the authorities."[4]

The attention of the Tribunal of Arbitration is also invited to the excess of these and all similar hospitalities, as violations of the instructions issued on the 31st of January, 1862.[5]

"These orders required every ship of war or privateer of either belligerent, which should enter British waters, to depart within twenty-four hours afterward, except in case of stress

---

[1] Whiting to Seward, January 26, 1863, Vol. VI, page 333.
[2] Whiting to Seward, January 27, 1863, Vol. VI, page 333.
[3] Journal quoted ante. See also Vol. II, page 617. See also Vol. VI, page 335, the disposition of John Demerith, who says, "We filled her bunkers with coal; and placed some on deck and in every place that could hold it. I suppose that she had on board over one hundred and eighty tons that we put there. She did not have less than that quantity. The coal was taken from the wharves and from vessels in the harbor. The money for coaling her was paid from Mr. Henry Adderley's store."
[4] Whiting to Wells, Vol. II, page 616.
[5] Vol. IV, page 175.

of weather, or of her requiring provisions or things necessary for the subsistence of her crew, or repairs. In either of these cases she was to put to sea as soon after the expiration of the twenty-four hours as possible, taking in no supplies beyond what might be necessary for immediate use, and no more coal than would carry her to the nearest port of her own country, or some nearer destination, nor after coaling once in British waters was she to be suffered to coal again within three months, unless by special permission."[1]

These rules were rigidly enforced against the United States. They were not only relaxed, but they were oftentimes utterly disregarded in the treatment of the insurgent vessels.

The Florida when at Nassau, in the months of May, June, and July, 1862, and again in the month of January, 1863, was distant from Wilmington, Charleston, or Savanah, only two, or at most three, days' steaming. She ordinarily sailed under canvas. Even when using steam in the pursuit and capture of vessels her consumption of coal, as shown by her log-book, did not average four tons a day. Thirty tons, (more than the amount taken by the United States Steamer Dacotah in September, 1862,) was all that she should have been allowed to take on board under the instructions, even had she been an honest vessel, and one that Great Britain was not bound to arrest and detain. Yet in July, 1862, she received all the coal she wanted, and in January, 1863, she took on board a three months' supply.

The Tribunal also will note that in January, 1863, the entry into the harbor, though made without permission, was condoned; that the visit lasted thirty-six hours instead of twenty-four; and that the "supplies" exceeded largely what was immediately necessary for the subsistence of the crew.

This excessive hospitality was in striking contrast with the receptions given to vessels of the United States at that port. It has already been shown that in December, 1861, the United States had been forbidden to land coals at Nassau or Bermuda, except on condition that it should not be used for their vessels of war. It has also been shown that in

---

[1] Bernard's Neutrality of Great Britain, pages 265 and 266.

September, 1862, the United States war steamer Dacotah was forbidden to take more than twenty tons of coal, and that only upon condition that for ten days she would not re-appear in British waters. On the 20th of the previous November the commander of the Wachusett was informed that he could not be allowed even to anchor, or to come within three miles of the shore, without permission of the Governor. In fact, the indignities to which the vessels of the United States were subjected were so great that the Rear-Admiral in command of the fleet, on the 2d January, 1863, wrote to the Secretary of the Navy, "I have not entered any British port except Bermuda, nor do I intend to enter, or permit any of the vessels of the squadron to ask permission to enter, or subject myself and those under my command to the discourtesies those who had entered heretofore had received."[1]

The United States insist that these excessive hospitalities to the Florida and these discourtesies to the vessels of war of the United States constituted a further violation of the duties of Great Britain as a neutral. By furnishing a full supply of coal to the Florida, after a similar hospitality had been refused to the vessels of the United States, the British officials permitted Nassau to be made a base of hostile operations against the United States; and for this, as well as for other violations of duty as to that vessel, which have been already noticed, Great Britain became liable to the United States for the injuries resulting from her acts.

The Florida left the port of Nassau on the afternoon of the 27th of January, 1863. By the middle of the following month her coal was getting low. On the 26th day of February Admiral Wilkes, in command of the United States Squadron in the West Indies, wrote to his Government thus: "The fact of the Florida having but a few days' coal makes me anxious to have our vessels off the Martinique, which is the only island at which they can hope to get any coal or supplies, the English islands being cut off under the rules

---

[1] Rear-Admiral Wilkes to the Secretary of the Navy, January 2, 1862.

of Her Majesty's Government for some sixty days yet, which precludes the possibility, unless by chicanery or fraud, of the hope of any coal or comfort there."[1] Admiral Wilkes's hopes were destined to disappointment. On the 24th of February, two days before the date of his dispatch, the Florida had been in the harbor of Barbadoes, and had taken on board about one hundred tons[2] of coal in violation of the instructions of January 31, 1862.

Rear-Admiral Wilkes, hearing of this new breach of neutrality, visited Barbadoes ten days later to inquire into the circumstance. He addressed a letter to the Governor, in which he said, "I have to request your Excellency will afford me the opportunity of laying before my Government the circumstances under which the Florida was permitted to take in a supply of coal and provisions to continue her cruise and operations, after having so recently coaled and provisioned at Nassau, one of Her Majesty's Colonies in the West Indies, ample time having been afforded, some thirty days, for the information to have reached this island and Government; and if any cause existed why an investigation was not instituted after the letter to Your Excellency was received from the United States Consul."[3] The Governor evaded the question. He "doubted very much whether it would be desirable to enter into correspondence upon the points adverted to," and said that "in sanctioning the coaling of the Florida, he did no more than what he had sanctioned in the case of the United States steamer of war San Jacinto."[4] There was no parallel or even resemblance between the treatment of the San Jacinto and that of the Florida. On the 18th of November, 1863, the San Jacinto received seventy-five tons of coal and some wood of Barbadoes. With that exception she received no coal or other fuel from a British port during that cruise.[5]

Under these circumstances the United States must ask the

---

[1] Admiral Wilkes to Mr. Welles, Vol. VI, page 338.
[2] Trowbridge to Seward, Vol. II, page 619, Vol. VI, page 339.
[3] Wilkes to Walker, Vol. II, page 628; Vol. VI, page 343.
[4] Walker to Wilkes, Vol. II, page 629; Vol. VI, page 344.
[5] Robeson to Fish, Vol. VI, page 345.

Tribunal to declare that the burden is upon Great Britain to establish that this express violation of Her Majesty's proclamation was innocently done. Whether done innocently or designedly, they insist, for the reasons already set forth, that the act was a new violation of the duties of a neutral, and furnished to the United States fresh cause of complaint against Great Britain.

Before completing the history of this vessel, the United States desire to show to the Tribunal how the vessels of the United States were received at Barbadoes, the port at which the Florida received the last-mentioned supply of coal. They have already referred to the treatment of their vessels at Nassau and Bermuda. Captain Charles Boggs arrived at Barbadoes in April, 1865, in the United States war steamer Connecticut, and made application for permission to remain there "a few days for the purpose of overhauling the piston and feedpump of the engine."[1] The Governor replied, "It will be necessary for you, before I can give my sanction to your staying here longer than twenty-four hours, to give a definite assurance of your inability to proceed to sea at the expiration of that time, and as to the period within which it would be possible for you to execute the necessary repairs."[2] Captain Boggs replied, "Your letter virtually refuses the permission requested, inasmuch as it requires me to give a definite assurance of my inability to proceed to sea at the termination of twenty-four hours. This I cannot do, as an American man-of-war can always go to sea in some manner. I shall do this, although with risk to my vessel and machinery. Regretting that the national hospitality of remaining at anchor for the purposes named in my letter of this morning is refused, I have the honor to inform you that I shall depart from this port to-morrow at 10 A. M."[3]

Barbadoes as well as Nassau having been thus made a base of hostile operations against the United States, the

---

[1] Captain Boggs to Governor Walker, Vol. VI, page 178.
[2] Governor Walker to Captain Boggs, Vol. VI, page 178.
[3] Captain Boggs to Governor Walker, Vol. VI, page 179.

Florida again sailed out on her work of destruction on the evening of the 26th of February, 1863, and in a short time captured or destroyed the following vessels of the commercial marine of the United States, viz.: the Aldebaran, the Clarence, the Commonwealth, the Crown Point, the General Berry, the Henrietta, the M. J. Colcord, the Lapwing, the Oneida, the Rienzi, the Southern Cross, the Star of Peace, the William B. Nash, and the Red Gauntlet. An intercepted letter from her commander to Bullock, dated April 25, 1863, says, "The Florida has thus far done her duty. Six million dollars will not make good the devastation this steamer has committed." [1]

On the 16th of July, 1863, the Florida arrived at Bermuda. She remained nine days in that port, and was thoroughly repaired both in her hull and machinery. She also took on board a full supply of the best Cardiff coal, which had been brought to her from Halifax by the transport Harriet Pinckney.[2] This was permitted notwithstanding the general order that neither belligerent was to be permitted to make coal depots in British colonial ports.

Here, again, were fresh-recurring violations of the duties of Great Britain as a neutral, to be added to the accumulated charges that have already been made as to this vessel.

With the improvements, repairs, and supplies obtained at Bermuda the Florida started for Brest. In crossing the Atlantic she destroyed the Francis B. Cutting on the 6th of August, and the Avon on the 20th. On the 3d of September Maffit reports from Brest to Bullock, at Liverpool, "a list of men discharged from the Florida, with their accounts and discharges," and he asks him "to provide them situations in the service."[3] We have already seen that when Bullock received this letter he was low in funds. He was, however, able to send from Liverpool to Brest for the

---

[1] Vol. II, page 629; Vol. VI, page 346.
[2] Consul's report to Mr. Seward.
[3] Vol. II, page 630; Vol. VI, page 349.

Florida some new machinery and armament,[1] and also a crew.[2]

The Florida left Brest in January, 1864, and entered the port of Bermuda in the following May, remaining, however, only long enough to land a sick officer. In June she returned to that port and made application for permission to repair. The Governor directed an examination to be made by experts, who reported;[3] "1. She can proceed to sea with such repairs as can be made good here, which, as far as we can judge, will require five days for one man, viz.: a diver for two days and a fitter for three days; or three complete days in all. 2. She can proceed to sea with safety in her present state under steam, but under sail is unmanageable with her screw up in bad weather, and her defects aloft (cross-trees) render maintop-mast unsafe. This could be made good in two days." On this report, the Florida received permission to remain there five days; she actually remained nine days. While there she took on board one hundred and thirty-five tons of coal, half a ton of beef, half a ton of vegetables, a large supply of bread, provisions and medicines, a large supply of clothing and other stores, and twenty days of carpenter's work were done upon the vessel.[4] Morris, the new commander, then drew upon Bullock, in Liverpool, in order to pay these bills and provide himself with means for a cruise; and on the 27th of June, 1864, the Florida, being thus completely fitted out, left the port of Bermuda, and cruised off the harbor, boarding all vessels approaching the island.[5]

The breach of neutrality and violation of the instructions issued for the observance of British officials involved in these transactions were brought to Earl Russell's notice by Mr.

---

[1] Dudley to Seward, January 21, 1864. Fraser, Trenholm & Co. to Barney, September 22, 1863, Vol. VI, page 352.
[2] Morse to Seward, January 8, 1864, Vol. VI, page 353.
[3] Vol. VI, page 357.
[4] See the vouchers for their payments, Vol. VI, page 358, et seq.
[5] Welles to Seward, Vol. II, page 652.

Adams.[1] Earl Russel replied that "although some disposition was manifested by the commander of the Florida to evade the stringency of Her Majesty's regulations, the most commendable diligence and strictness in enforcing those regulations was observed on the part of the authorities, and no substantial deviation, either from the letter or from the spirit of those regulations, was permitted to or did take place."[2]

With the evidence now submitted to the Tribunal, which are the original vouchers for the purchases made at Bermuda by the Florida, it is evident that Earl Russell must have been misinformed when he stated that there had been no deviation from the regulations. The five days' stay which was granted was extended to nine. Twenty days' carpenter work were done instead of five; supplies for a cruise were taken instead of supplies for immediate use; clothing, rum, medicines, and general supplies were taken, as well as supplies for the subsistence of the crew; one hundred and thirty-five tons of coal were taken instead of twenty. In all this the United States find fresh and cumulative cause of complaint on account of this vessel.

They also call the particular attention of the Tribunal to the fact that at that time there was no necessity of making any repairs to the Florida. The experts employed by the Governor to make the examination reported, "*She can proceed to sea with safety in her present state under steam.*" The repairs, therefore, were only necessary to enable her to use her sails, banking her fires,[3] and laying to for the purpose of watching and destroying the commerce of the United States. Permitting any repairs to be made at that time was another violation of the duties of Great Britain as a neutral toward the United States.

The Florida left Bermuda on the 27th of June, 1864. On the 1st of July she destroyed the Harriet Stevens; the Golconda on the 8th; the Margaret Y. Davis on the 9th; the Electric Spark on the 10th; and the Mondamin on the

---
[1] Adams to Russell, Vol. II, page 651.
[2] Russell to Adams, Vol. II, page 653.
[3] Maffitt to Barney, Vol VI, pages 351—2.

26th of September, all being vessels belonging to the commercial marine of the United States. On the 7th of October, 1864, her career as an insurgent cruiser terminated at Bahia.

During her cruise, three tenders were fitted out and manned from her officers and crew. The Clarence was captured by her off the coast of Brazil on the 6th of May, 1863. She was then fitted out with guns, officers, and men, and during the first part of the month of June, 1863, captured and destroyed the Kate Stewart, the Mary Alvina, the Mary Schindler, and the Whistling Wind. On the 10th of that month she captured the Tacony. The Clarence was then destroyed and the Tacony was converted into a tender, and, in the same month, destroyed the Ada, the Byzantian, the Elizabeth Ann, the Goodspeed, the L. A. Macomber, the Marengo, the Ripple, the Rufus Choate, and the Umpire.[1] On the 25th she captured the Archer. The crew and armament were transferred to that vessel and the Tacony burned. On the 27th the United States revenue cutter Caleb Cushing was destroyed by the Archer.

The amount of the injury which the United States and its citizens suffered from the acts of this vessel and of its tenders will be hereafter stated. The United States, with confidence, assert, that they have demonstrated that Great Britain by reason of the general principles above stated, and in consequence of the particular acts or omissions hereinbefore recited, failed to fulfill all of the duties set forth in the three rules of the sixth article of the Treaty, or recognized by the principles of International Law not inconsistent with such rules, and they ask the Tribunal to certify that fact as to the Florida and as to its tenders. Should the Tribunal exercise the power conferred upon it by Article VII of the Treaty, to award a sum in gross to be paid to the United States, they ask that in considering the amount so to be awarded, the losses of individuals in the destruction of their vessels and cargoes, by the Florida, or by its tenders, and also the expenses to which the United States were put in the pursuit of either of those vessels, may be taken into account.

---

[1] Vol. VI, page 370.

THE ALABAMA, AND HER TENDER, THE TUSCALOOSA.

The Alabama and her tender, the Tuscaloosa. The Alabama, a vessel which has given the generic name to the claims before this Tribunal, is thus described by Semmes, her commander: "She was of about 900 tons burden, 230 feet in length, 32 feet in breadth, 20 feet in depth, and drew, when provisioned and coaled for cruise, 15 feet of water. She was barkentine-rigged, with long lower masts, which enabled her to carry large fore and aft sails, as jibs and try-sails. The scantling of the vessel was light compared with vessels of her class in the Federal Navy, but this was scarcely a disadvantage, as she was designed as a scourge of the enemy's commerce rather than for battle. Her engine was of 300 horsepower, and she had attached an apparatus for condensing from the vapor of sea-water all the fresh water that her crew might require. * * * Her armament consisted of eight guns; six 32-pounders in broadside, and two pivot-guns amidship, one on the forecastle, and the other abaft the mainmast, the former a 100-pounder rifled Blakeley and the latter a smooth-bore 8-inch."[1]

The Alabama was built, and from the outset was "intended for, a Confederate vessel of war."[2] The contract for her construction was "signed by Captain Bullock on the one part and Messrs. Laird on the other." The date of the signature cannot be given exactly. The drawings were signed October 9, 1861, and it is supposed that the contract was signed at or about the same time. "The ship cost in United States money about $255,000." The payments were made by the agents of the insurgents. Bullock "went almost daily on board the gun-boat, and seemed to be recognized in authority;" in fact, "he superintended the building of the Alabama."[3]

On the 15th of May she was launched under the name

---

[1] Semmes's Adventures Afloat, pages 402, 403.
[2] Journal of an officer of the Alabama. See Vol. IV, page 181.
[3] Dudley to Edwards, Vol. III, page 17; Vol. VI, page 389.

of the 290.[1] Her officers were in England awaiting her completion, and were paid their salaries "monthly, about the first of the month, at Fraser, Trenholm & Co.'s office in Liverpool."[2]

The purpose for which this vessel was being constructed was notorious in Liverpool. Before she was launched she became an object of suspicion with the Consul of the United States at that port, and she was the subject of constant correspondence on his part with his Government and with Mr. Adams.[3]

The failure of Mr. Adams to secure in the previous March the interference of Her Majesty's Government to prevent the departure of the Florida, appears to have induced him to think that it would be necessary to obtain strictly technical proof of a violation of the municipal law of England before he could hope to secure the detention of the then nameless Alabama. That he had good reason to think so is not open to reasonable doubt. On the 23d of June he thought he had such proof. He wrote Earl Russell that day,[4] recalling to his recollection the fact that notwithstanding the favorable reports from the Liverpool customs in regard to the Florida, there was the strongest reason for believing that she had gone to Nassau, and was there "engaged in completing her armament, provisioning, and crew," for the purpose of carrying on war against the United States.[5] He continued, "I am now under the painful necessity of apprising your Lordship that a new and still more powerful war-steamer is nearly ready for departure from the port of Liverpool on the same errand."[4] The parties engaged in the enterprise are persons well known at Liverpool to be agents and officers of the United States."

---

[1] Dudley to Seward, Vol. III, page 1; Vol. VI, page 371.
[2] Vol. III, page 146; Vol. VI, page 435.
[3] See Vol. III, *passim*.
[4] Adams to Russell, Vol. III, page 5; Vol. VI, page 375.
[5] The Florida arrived at Nassau April 28, and the Bahama with her armament a few days later. These facts were undoubtedly known, to Lord Russell and to Mr. Adams when this letter was written.

"'This vessel has been built and launched from the dockyard of persons, one of whom is now sitting as a member of the House of Commons, and is fitting out for the especial and manifest object of carrying on hostilities by sea." He closed by soliciting such action as might "tend either to stop the projected expedition, or to establish the fact that its purpose is not inimical to the people of the United States."

Earl Russell replied that he had referred "this matter to the proper department of Her Majesty's Government,"[1] and on the 4th of July, 1862, he inclosed the customs report on the subject, in which it is stated that "the officers have at all times free access to the building yards of the Messrs. Laird, at Birkenhead, where the vessel is lying, and *that there has been no attempt, on the part of her builders, to disguise, what is most apparent, that she is intended for a ship of war*." It was further said that "the description of her in the communication of the United States Consul is most correct, with the exception that her engines are not constructed on the oscillatory principle." "With reference to the statement of the United States Consul that the evidence he has in regard to this vessel being intended for the so-called Confederate Government in the Southern States is entirely satisfactory to his mind," it was said that "the proper course would be for the Consul to submit such evidence as he possesses to the collector at that port, who would thereupon take such measures as the Foreign Enlistment Act would require;" and the report closed by saying "that the officers at Liverpool will keep a strict watch on the vessel."[2] The point that the vessel was intended for a vessel of war being thus conceded, Mr. Adams thereupon, at once, relying upon the promise to keep watch of the vessel, instructed the Consul to comply with the directions indicated in the report of the Commissioners and furnish all the evidence in his possession to the Collector of Customs at Liverpool.[3]

---
[1] Russell to Adams, Vol. III, page 6; Vol. VI, page 376.
[2] Vol. III, page 7; Vol. VI, page 379.
[3] Adams to Wilding, Vol. III, page 8; Vol. VI, page 381.

Mr. Dudley did so on the 9th of July, in a letter to the Collector of Liverpool,[1] and the attention of the Tribunal of Arbitration is called to the fact that every material allegation in that letter has been more than borne out by subsequent proof. The Collector replied that he was "respectfully of opinion that the statement made was not such as could be acted upon by the officers of the revenue unless legally substantiated by evidence."[2] And again, a few days later, he said to Mr. Dudley, "The details given by you in regard to the said vessel are not sufficient, in a legal point of view, to justify me in taking upon myself the responsibility of the detention of this ship."[3]

Thus early in the history of this cruiser the point was taken by the British authorities—a point maintained throughout the struggle—that they would originate nothing themselves for the maintenance and performance of their international duties, and that they would listen to no representations from the officials of the United States which did not furnish technical evidence for criminal prosecution under the Foreign Enlistment Act.

The energetic Consul of the United States at Liverpool was not disheartened. He caused a copy of his letter to be laid before R P. Collier, Esq., one of the most eminent barristers of England, who, a few months later, became Solicitor General of the Crown, under Lord Palmerston's administration, and who is now understood to be the principal law adviser of the Crown.

Mr. Collier advised that "the principal officer of the customs at Liverpool * * * be applied to to seize the vessel, with a view to her condemnation," and, "at the same time, to lay a statement of the fact before the Secretary of State for Foreign Affairs, coupled with the request that Her Majesty's Government would direct the vessel to be seized, or ratify the seizure if it has been made."[4]

It was useless to attempt to induce the collector to seize

---

[1] Dudley to Edwards, Vol. III, page 17; Vol. VI, page 383.
[2] Edwards to Dudley, Vol. III, page 19; Vol. VI, page 385.
[3] Vol. VI, page 389.
[4] Vol. III, page 16; Vol. VI, page 386.

the vessel. Mr. Dudley thereupon set about to get the direct proof required by the authorities as to the character of the Alabama or 290. "There were men enough," he said, "who knew about her, and who understood her character, but they were not willing to testify; and, in a preliminary proceeding like this, it was impossible to obtain process to compel them. Indeed, no one in a hostile community like Liverpool, where the feeling and sentiment are against us, would be a willing witness, especially if he resided there, and was any way dependent upon the people of that place for a livelihood".[1] At last Mr. Dudley succeeded in finding the desired proof. On the 21st day of July, he laid it in the form of affidavits before the Collector at Liverpool in compliance with the intimations which Mr. Adams had received from Earl Russell.[2] These affidavits were on the same day transmitted by the Collector to the Board of Customs at London, with a request for instructions by telegraph, as the ship appeared to be ready for sea and might leave any hour.[3] Mr. Dudley then went to London, and on the 23d of July laid the affidavits before Mr. Collier for his opinion.[4] Copies of the affidavits will be found in Vol. III, page 21 to 28, and Vol. VI, page 391, et seq.

It is not necessary to dwell upon the character of this proof, since it was conclusively soon passed upon by both Mr. Collier and by Her Majesty's Government. It is sufficient to say that it showed affirmatively that the 290 was a "fighting vessel;" that she was "going out to the Government of the Confederate States of America to cruise and commit hostilities against the Government and people of the United States of America;" "that the enlisted men were to join the ship in Messrs. Laird & Co.'s yard;" that they were enlisting men "who had previously served on fighting ships;" that the enlistments had then been going on for over a month, and that there was need of immediate action by the British

---
[1] Dudley to Seward, Vol. III, page 13.
[2] Dudley to Seward, Vol. III, page 13; Vol. VI, page 390.
[3] Collector to Commissioners, Vol. III, page 20; Vol. VI, page 395.
[4] Vol. III, page 20; Vol. VI, page 398.

Government, if action was to be of any service in protecting its neutrality against violation.

Mr. Collier said immediately, "It appears difficult to make out a stronger case of infringement of the Foreign Enlistment Act, which, if not enforced on this occasion, is little better than a dead letter. It well deserves consideration whether, if the vessel be allowed to escape, the Federal Government would not have serious grounds of remonstrance."[1]

The 290 was at this time nearly ready for sea, and time was important. Mr. Dudley, through his counsel, in order that no time might be lost, on the same day laid Mr. Collier's new opinion before the Under Secretary of State for Foreign Affairs and before the Secretary of the Board of Customs. The Under Secretary "was not disposed to discuss the matter, nor did he read Mr. Collier's opinion."[2] The Secretary of the Board of Customs said that the Board could not act without orders from the Treasury Lords.[3] The last of these answers was not communicated until the 28th of July.

The additional proof and the new opinion of Mr. Collier were also officially communicated to Her Majesty's Government through the regular diplomatic channels. On the 22d of July copies of the depositions of Dudley, Maguire, DaCosta, Wilding, and Passmore were sent to Lord Russell by Mr. Adams;[4] and on the 24th of July copies of the depositions of Roberts and Taylor were in like manner sent to Lord Russell. These were acknowledged by Earl Russell on the 28th.

On that day "these papers were considered by the law officers of the Crown; on the same evening their report was agreed upon, and it was in Lord Russell's hands early on the 29th. Orders were then immediately sent to Liverpool to stop the vessel."[5]

Thus it appears that this intelligence, which Great Britain

---

[1] Vol. III, page 29; Vol. IV, page 398.
[2] Squary to Adams, Vol. III, page 29; Vol. VI, page 397.
[3] Vol. III, page 31; Vol. VI, page 406.
[4] Vol. III, page 21; Vol. VI, page 397.
[5] A speech delivered in the House of Commons on Friday, August 4, 1871, by Sir Roundell Palmer, M. P. for Richmond, page 16.

regarded as sufficient to require the detention of the 290, was communicated to Her Majesty's Government in three ways: first, on the 21st of July, through the channel at Liverpool which had been indicated by Earl Russell; second, on the 22d by the solicitor of Mr. Dudley in person to the Customs and to the Under Secretary of State for Foreign Affairs at the Foreign Office; and thirdly, on the 23d and on the 24th by Mr. Adams officially. It also appears that the information communicated on the 21st was transmitted to London by the collector, with the statement that the vessel might sail at any hour, and that it was important to give the instructions for detention by telegraph; and it still further appears that notwithstanding this official information from the collector, the papers were not considered by the law advisers until the 28th, and that the case appeared to them to be so clear that they gave their advice upon it that evening. Under these circumstances, the delay of eight days after the 21st in the order for the detention of the vessel was, in the opinion of the United States, gross negligence on the part of Her Majesty's Government. On the 29th the Secretary of the Commission of the Customs received a telegram from Liverpool saying that "the vessel 290 came out of dock last night, and left the port this morning."[1] Mr. Adams was justly indignant at the failure of the customs authorities to redeem their voluntary promise to watch the vessel.[2]

On the 31st of July Mr. Adams had a "conference with Lord Russell at the Foreign Office," at which "his Lordship first took up the case of the 290, and remarked that a delay in determining upon it had most unexpectedly been caused by the sudden development of a malady of the Queen's Advocate, Sir John D. Harding, totally incapacitating him for the transaction of business. This had made it necessary to call in other parties, whose opinion had been at last given for the retention of the gun-boat, but before the order got down to Liverpool the vessel was gone. *He should, however, send directions to have her stopped* if she went, as was probable, to Nassau."[3] The judgment of Her Majesty's

---
[1] Vol. III, page 36. [2] Adams to Russell, Vol. III, page 536.
[3] Vol. III, pages 35, 36; Vol. VI, page 414.

Government upon the character of the Alabama and upon the duty of Great Britain toward her was, therefore, identical with that of Mr. Collier.

The departure of the 290 from Birkenhead was probably, it may be said certainly, hastened by the illicit receipt of the intelligence of the decision of the Government to detain her.[1]

After leaving the dock she "proceeded slowly down the Mersey. Both the Lairds were on board, and also Bullock. On the way down the river Laird settled with the paymaster for some purchases for the vessel, and paid into his hands a small sum of money.[2]

At the bell-buoy the Lairds and the ladies left by a tug, and returned to Liverpool. The 290 slowly steamed on to Moelfra Bay, on the coast of Anglesey, where she remained "all that night, all the next day, and the next night." No effort was made to seize her.

During this time the tug Hercules, which had returned from the bell-buoy with the Lairds and the ladies, took on board at Liverpool a number of new hands for the 290. One account says there were as many as forty.[3] The master of the Hercules admits that there might have been thirty.[4] This was done publicly—so publicly that the United States Consul knew of it, and notified the Collector. The Collector had his orders to seize the 290, and had only to follow the Hercules to get the information which would enable him to obey those orders. He did cause the Hercules to be examined. The Surveyor who did that work reported to him that there were a number of persons on board, who admitted "that they were a portion of the crew, and were going to join the gun-boat,"[5] and yet he neither stopped

---

[1] Semmes says in his Adventures, "Fortunately for the Confederate vessel tidings of the projected seizure were conveyed to Birkenhead." "Our unceremonious departure was owing to the fact of news being received to the effect that the customs authorities had orders to board and detain us that morning." Vol. IV, page 181.

[2] Vol. III, page 147; Vol. VI, page 437.

[3] Vol. VI, page 408.   [4] Vol. VI, page 411.

[5] Vol. VI, page 409.

the Hercules, nor followed it. In an emergency when, if ever, the telegraph ought to have been employed, he wrote a letter by mail to the Commissioners of Customs at London,[1] which could not be received until the following day. When this letter was received the Commissioners took no notice of the admitted recruitment of men, but ordered inquiries to be made as to powder and guns.[2] Before these inquiries could be commenced, the offender was at sea.[3] Under the circumstances this hesitation and delay, and the permitting the Alabama to lie unmolested in British waters for over two days, is little short of criminal in the officials who were or should have been cognizant of it.

When the Alabama left Moelfra Bay her crew numbered about ninety men.[4] She ran part way down the Irish Channel, then round the north coast of Ireland, only stopping near the Giant's Causeway. She then made for Terceira, one of the Azores, which she reached on the 10th of August.[5]

On the 13th of August, while she was at Terceira, a sail was observed making for the anchorage. It proved to be the "Agrippina of London, Captain McQuoen, having on board six guns, with ammunition, coals, stores, &c., for the Alabama." Preparations were immediately made to transfer this important cargo. On the afternoon of the 20th, while employed discharging the bark, the screw-steamer Bahama, Captain Tessier, (the same that had taken the armament to the Florida, whose insurgent ownership and character were well known in Liverpool,) arrived, "having on board Commander Raphael Semmes and officers of the Confederate States steamer Sumter."[6] There were also taken from this steamer two 32-pounders and some stores,[7] which occupied all the remainder of that day and a part of the next.

[1] Vol. VI, page 410. [2] Vol. IV, page 410. [3] Vol. VI, page 413.
[4] Vol. III, page 46. Two crew-lists are in the accompanying volumes. One will be found in Vol. III, page 150; the other, in Vol. III, page 213.
[5] Vol. IV, page 182.
[6] Journal of an Officer of the Alabama. See Vol. IV, page 182.
[7] The Bahama cleared from Liverpool on the 12th of August. Fawcett, Preston & Co. shipped on board of her "nineteen

The 22d and 23d of August were taken up in transferring coal from the Agrippina to the Alabama. It was not until Sunday (the 24th) that the insurgents' flag was hoisted. Bullock and those who were not going in the 290 went back to the Bahama, and the Alabama, now first known under that name, went off with "twenty-six officers and eighty-five men."

If it be necessary for the Tribunal to ascertain and determine what was the condition of the Alabama when she left Liverpool on the 29th of July, 1862, the affidavits of various witnesses, printed in the accompanying Volume, (III,) will enable them to do so with accuracy.[1] If any details are wanting, they can easily be supplied from the account which her commander has given of his Adventures Afloat.[2]

It is clear from all these statements that when she left Liverpool she was even more completely fitted out as a man-of-war than the Florida, at the time of her departure. The Tribunal will recall what Captain Hickley, a competent expert, said of that vessel: *"She was in all respects fitted out as a vessel of war of her class* in her Majesty's Navy." "As she now stands she could, in my professional opinion, be equipped in twenty-four hours for battle." This is not too strong language to be used concerning the Alabama. She was, in fact, equipped for battle in little more than twenty-four hours after the Bahama joined her.

---

cases containing guns, gun-carriages, shot, rammers, &c., weighing in all 156 cwt. 1 qr. 27 lbs. There was no other cargo on board, except five hundred and fifty-two tons of coal for the use of the ship." Vol. III, page 54; see also Vol. III, page 141, for further details.

[1] See particularly Younge's deposition, Vol. III, page 145; Passmore's deposition, Vol. III, page 25; and Latham's deposition, Vol. III, page 211. See also Vol. VI, pages 435 and 472.

[2] I had arrived on Wednesday, [at Terceira,] and on Saturday night we had, by dint of great labor and perseverance, drawn order out of chaos. * * * The ship having been properly prepared, we steamed out on this bright Sunday morning; the flag of the Confederate States was unfurled for the first time from the peak of the Alabama.—*Semmes's Adventures Afloat,* pages 408, 409.

It is not necessary, however, to consider this question; for her guilty status at that time is conclusively established against Great Britain.

1st. By the opinion of Mr. Collier, who, soon after giving it, became a member of Her Majesty's Government, under the lead of Lord Palmerston, and with Earl Russell as a colleague. They must, therefore, be held to have adopted his views on one of the most important questions, half legal and half political, that came before Lord Palmerston's Government for determination.

2d. Her Majesty's Government, by ordering the detention of the 290, admitted her illegal character. Earl Russell himself hints that it is not impossible that "the officers of the customs were misled or blinded by the general partiality to the cause of the South known to prevail at Liverpool, and that a *prima facie* case of negligence could be made out.[1]

3d. Earl Russell stated to Mr. Adams in an official note that "it is undoubtedly true that the Alabama was partly fitted out in a British port."[2] This is all that is necessary to be said in order to bring it within the operation of the rules of the Treaty of Washington.

Thus constructed, equipped, fitted out, and manned as a ship-of-war in Liverpool, and armed under the original contract made at the same place with arms and munitions there collected by the contractors of the vessel, but sent out from Great Britain by a separate vessel in order to comply with the official construction of British municipal law, the Alabama commenced a career of destruction which proved highly disastrous to the commerce of the United States.

She was found to be a "fine sailor under canvas," "a quality of inestimable advantage," as it enabled Captain Semmes "to do most of his work under sail."[3] "She carried but an eighteen days' supply of fuel," which induced her commander "to adopt the plan of working under sail in the very beginning," and "to practice it unto the end." "With the ex-

---
[1] Speeches and dispatches of Earl Russell, Vol. II, pages 259, 260.
[2] Earl Russell to Mr. Adams, Vol. III, page 299.
[3] Semmes's Adventures Afloat, page 419.

ception of half a dozen prizes, all captures were made with the screw hoisted and ship under sail."[1]

The United States will confine their comments to the official treatment which this vessel received within British jurisdiction. Her history for a large part of her career may be found in Vol. IV, between pages 181 and 201. It has also been made the subject of an elaborate volume, from which some short extracts have been quoted above.

From Terceira she crossed to the West Indies, taking at Martinique coal again from the bark Agrippina, which had been sent from England for the purpose;[2] and she passed up thence into the Gulf of Mexico, marking her course by the destruction of vessels of the merchant marine of the United States, and of their war-steamer Hatteras. On the 18th of January, 1862, she arrived at Jamaica. Three British men-of-war were in the harbor, but the promised orders of Earl Russell to detain her for a violation of British sovereignty were not there. In lieu of that, "the most cordial relations were at once established between the officers of all these ships and of the Alabama,"[3] and the Governor of the island promptly granted Semmes's request to be permitted to repair his ship.[4] On the 25th of January, having been refitted and furnished with supplies, she left Jamaica, "bound to the coast of Brazil, and thence to the Cape of Good Hope."[5]

On the 30th of the previous November, after Captain Semmes's mode of carrying on war was known in England, Mr. Adams made to Lord Russell the first of a long series of representations concerning this vessel. This communication

---

[1] Semmes's Adventures Afloat, page 420.
[2] Same, page 514. The Agrippina is the same vessel that took coal and supplies to her at Terceira.
[3] Semmes's Adventures Afloat, page 555.
[4] Ibid. "By the act of consenting to receive the Alabama in Kingston, and permitting her to refit and supply herself at that, we had considered the British Government as having given her a positive recognition, and having assumed the responsibility for the consequences of that sanction."—Mr. Adams's statement to Lord Russell, described in a dispatch to Mr. Seward. Vol. III, page 247.
[5] Semmes's Adventures Afloat, page 563.

contains a summary of all that the United States deem it
necessary to say about the Alabama in this place. "It now
appears," Mr. Adams says, "from a survey of all the evidence,
First. That this vessel was built in a dock-yard belonging
to a commercial house in Liverpool, of which the chief member,
down to October of last year, is a member of the House of
Commons. Secondly. That from the manner of her construction,
and her peculiar adaption to war purpose, there could have
been no doubt by those engaged in the work, and familiar
with such details, that she was intended for other purposes
than those of legitimate trade; and, Thirdly. That during
the whole process and outfit in the port of Liverpool, the
direction of the details, and the engagement of persons to
be employed in her, were more or less in hands known to
be connected with the insurgents in the United States. It
further appears that since her departure from Liverpool, which
she was suffered to leave without any of the customary
evidence at the custom-house to designate her ownership, she
has been supplied with her armament, with coals, and stores,
and men, by vessels known to be fitted out and dispatched
for the purpose from the same port, and that although commanded by Americans in her navigation of the ocean, she
is manned almost entirely by English seamen, engaged and
forwarded from that port by persons in league with her
commander. Furthermore it is shown that this commander,
claiming to be an officer acting under legitimate authority,
yet is in the constant practice of raising the flag of Great
Britain, in order the better to execute his system of ravage
and depredation on the high seas. And lastly, it is made
clear that he pays no regard whatever to the recognized law
of capture of merchant vessels on the high seas, which requires the action of some judicial tribunal to confirm the
rightfulness of the proceedings, but, on the contrary, that
he resorts to the piratical system of taking, plundering, and
burning private property, without regard to consequences, or
responsibility to any legitimate authority whatever."[1]

The course of conduct so forcibly sketched by Mr. Adams

[1] Vol. III, pages 70, 71.

was continued by the officers of the Alabama until that vessel was sunk by the Kearsarge off Cherbourg.

The Alabama went from the West Indies to Bahia, where she met the Georgia. She then crossed to the Cape of Good Hope, and entered Table Bay, as has already been seen. It is not necessary to say again what took place as to the Tuscaloosa: to speak of the evident character of the vessel with the captured cargo on board; of the honest indignation of Rear-Admiral Sir Baldwin Walker at the flimsy attempt to convert the prize into a cruiser; of the partiality of the Governor and the Attorney General; of the decision of Her Majesty's Government that she must be regarded as a prize and not as a cruiser; of the reluctant enforcement of the decision of the Government by the Colonial Authorities; or of the reversal of that decision by Her Majesty's Government, when they found that it had been enforced. These facts have all been sufficiently set forth. It only remains to add, that, when Her Majesty's Government had determined to send the instructions to disregard in similar cases such attempts to change the character of a prize, Earl Russell informed Mr. Adams of the fact, and added "Her Majesty's Government hope that under those instructions nothing will for the future happen to admit of a question being raised as to Her Majesty's orders having been strictly carried out."[1] Earl Russell could not have anticipated that the first and only attempt of the authorities at Cape Town to carry out those instructions, would be disavowed by Her Majesty's Government, and that restoration would be ordered to the insurgents of the only vessel ever seized under them.

From Cape Town the Alabama pushed into the Indian Ocean, and, "within a day or two of six months,"[2] returned again to Cape Town on the 20th of March, 1864. During her absence she had coaled at Singapore, with the consent of the authorities, at the wharf of the Peninsular and Oriental Steamship Company.[3]

---

[1] Vol. III, page 203.
[2] Semmes's Adventures Afloat, page 737.
[3] Semmes's Adventures Afloat, page 715.

On the 21st of March the Alabama began taking on board fresh supplies of coal in Cape Town.[1] The last coal from a British port (and, in fact, the last supply) had been taken on board at Singapore on the 23d day of the previous December.[2] The new supply was allowed to be put on board within three months from the time when the last supply was received in a British port. This was a fresh violation of the duties of Great Britain as a neutral.

On the 25th of March the Alabama "got up steam and moved out of Table Bay for the last time, amidst lusty cheers and the waving of handkerchiefs from the boats by which they were surrounded."[3] "Military and naval officers, governors, judges, superintendents of boards of trade, attorneys-general, all on their way to their missions in the far East, came to see her."[4]

She now made her way to northern waters, and on the 11th of June, 1864, cast anchor in the harbor of Cherbourg. Her career was now finished. The United States war-steamer Kearsarge was in those waters, and on the 19th of the same June, within sight of Cherbourg, this British-built, British-armed, and British-manned cruiser went down under the fire of American guns.

During her career the Alabama fitted out one tender, the Tuscaloosa. The "Conrad of Philadelphia, from Buenos Ayres for New York, with part of a cargo of wool," was captured on the 20th of June, 1863, in latitude 25° 48' south.[5] It has already been seen that this prize was taken into the port of Cape Town, under the name of the Tuscaloosa, and under pretense of a commission; and that the pretense was recognized as valid. When the Alabama left to cruise in the Indian Ocean, Semmes "dispatched this vessel from Angra Pequeña back to the coast of Brazil, to make a cruise on

---

[1] Semmes's Adventures Afloat, page 744.
[2] This is evident from Semmes's account of his voyage on leaving Singapore, page 715, et seq.
[3] Semmes's Adventures Afloat, page 744.
[4] Semmes's Adventures Afloat, page 745.
[5] Semmes's Adventures Afloat, page 627.

that coast."[1] It has also been seen how, on her return to Cape Town, she was seized by the Governor of Cape Town, and held until the close of the struggle.

The United States ask the Tribunal of Arbitration, as to the Alabama and as to her tender, to determine and to certify that Great Britain has, by its acts and by its omissions, failed to fulfill its duties set forth in the three rules of the Treaty of Washington, or recognized by the principles of law not inconsistent with such rules. Should the Tribunal exercise the power conferred upon it by Article VII of the Treaty, to award a sum in gross to be paid to the United States, they ask that, in considering the amount to be awarded, the losses of the United States, or of individuals, in the destruction of their vessels, or their cargoes by the Alabama, or by its tender, and also the expense to which the United States were put in the pursuit of either of those vessels, or in the capture and destruction of the Alabama, may be taken into account.

In addition to the general reasons already stated, they ask this for the following reasons:

1. That the Alabama was constructed, was fitted out, and was equipped within the jurisdiction of Great Britain, with intent to cruise and carry on war against the United States, with whom Great Britain was then at peace; that Great Britain had reasonable ground to believe that such was the intent of that vessel, and did not use due diligence to prevent such construction, fitting out, or equipping.

2. That the Alabama was constructed and armed within British jurisdiction. The construction of the vessel and the construction of the arms; the dispatch of the vessel and the dispatch of the arms—all took place at one British port; and the British authorities had such ample notice that they must be assumed to have known all these facts. The whole should be regarded, therefore, as one armed hostile expedition, from a British port, against the United States.

3. That the Alabama, having been specially adapted to warlike use at Liverpool, and being thus intended to cruise

---

[1] Semmes's Adventures Afloat, page 738.

and carry on war against the United States, Great Britain did not use due diligence to prevent her departure from its jurisdiction at Liverpool; nor subsequently from its jurisdiction at Kingston; nor, subsequently, from its jurisdiction at the Cape of Good Hope; nor, subsequently, from its jurisdiction at Singapore; nor lastly, from its jurisdiction again at the Cape of Good Hope, as required by the rules of the Treaty of Washington.

4. That Great Britain did not, as Earl Russell had promised, send out orders for her detention.

5. That the Alabama received excessive hospitalities at Cape Town on her last visit, in being allowed to coal before three months had expired after her coaling at Singapore, a British port.

6. That the responsibility for the acts of the Alabama carries with it responsibility for the acts of her tender.

THE RETRIBUTION.

The Retribution. The steam-propeller Uncle Ben, built at Buffalo, in New York, in 1856, was sent to the southern coast of the United States just prior to the attack on Fort Sumter. Entering Cape Fear River in stress of weather, she was seized by the insurgents. Her machinery was taken out, and she was converted into a schooner, and cruised, under the name of the Retribution, about the Bahama Banks. On the 19th day of December, 1862, she captured, near the island of San Domingo, the United States schooner Hanover, and took the prize to Long Cay, (Fortune Island,) Bahamas, and there sold the cargo "without previous judicial process."[1] Representations being made of these facts, an answer was made by the Colonial Authorities, claiming that they were deceived, and that they supposed that the person making the sale was the master of the vessel.[2] Mr. Seward

---

[1] Mr. Seward to Lord Lyons, Vol. I, page 701.
[2] Burnside to Nesbitt, Vol. I, page 702.

replied that this answer was not "deemed altogether conclusive." Subsequently one Vernon Locke was represented as the person who had, "by fraudulent personations and representations procured the admission of that vessel [the Hanover] to entry at the Revenue Office and effected the sale of her cargo there."[1] Locke was indicted, and bail accepted in the sum of £200. The United States are not aware that he was ever brought to trial. Mr. Seward thought the bail "surprisingly small and insignificant."[1] On the 19th of February, 1863, when off Castle Island, one of the Bahamas, she captured the American brig Emily Fisher, freighted with sugar and molasses. This prize also "was taken to Long Cay, one of the Bahama Islands, and notwithstanding the protest of Captain Staples, [the master,] and in the presence of a British magistrate, was despoiled of her cargo; a portion of which was landed, and the balance willfully destroyed."[2] The Retribution then went to the harbor of Nassau, where she was sold, assuming the name of the Etta.[2]

The United States, with confidence, ask the Tribunal to find and certify as to this vessel, that Great Britain failed to fulfill the duties set forth in the three rules of Article VI of the Treaty, or recognized by the principles of International Law not inconsistent with such rules. They ask this, not only for the general reasons heretofore mentioned as to this class of vessels, but because, in the case of each of the captured vessels above named, the acts complained of were done within Her Majesty's jurisdiction.

THE GEORGIA.

The Georgia. The Georgia was built for the insurgents at Dumbarton, below Clyde, on the Glasgow. She was launched on the 10th day of January, 1863, at which time, as has already been said, "a Miss North, daughter of

---

[1] Governor Bayley to Duke of Newcastle, Vol. I, page 706.
[2] Affidavit of Thomas Sampson, Vol. VI, page 736.

a Captain North, of one of the Confederate States, officiated as priestess, and christened the craft Virginia."[1] It was notorious that she was being constructed for this service.[2] When finished she was a "screw-steamer of about five hundred tons register, clipper-built; figure-head, fiddle-bow; short thick funnel; with a number of compartments forward on both sides, from eight to ten feet square, and stronger than a jail, strong doors to them, with hinges about three inches thick, and brass padlocks accordingly, and a strong magazine forward in the bow." On Friday, the 27th of March, she left for Greenock. By this time had parted with her name Virginia, and had the name Japan "written in small letters on her bow;" and it was pretended that her voyage was to be to China.

On the evening of Monday, the 30th of March, some seventy or eighty men who had been shipped at Liverpool for this vessel were sent to Greenock.[3] The agreements with this crew were made by the house of Jones & Co., of Liverpool,[4] who advanced money to them.[5] The vessel was registered in the name of Thomas Bold, of Liverpool, a member of the house of Jones & Co., and a near connection of Maury, who afterward commanded her. It remained registered in his name until the 23d day of the following June.[6] When the men arrived in the Clyde from Liverpool, the Japan was "lying in the river opposite Greenock," and they were taken on board in a tug. On the morning of the 2d of April they ran out toward the sea, but returned in the afternoon, and remained near the light-house down the Clyde, taking on board more men and provision from Greenock. They started again, and next morning they were

---

[1] Unterwood to Seward, January 16, 1863, Vol. VI, page 503.
[2] Extracts from London Daily News, February 12 and 17, 1863, Vol. VI, page 503, et seq.
[3] Dudley to Seward, Vol. II, page 665; Vol. VI, page 509.
[4] Vol. II, page 681; Vol. VI, page 516; Vol. VII, page 88.
[5] Vol. II, page 672; Vol. VI, page 512; Vol. VII, page 88.
[6] Mr. Adams to Earl Russell, Vol. II, pages 677—8; Vol. VII, page 88.

off Castleton, Isle of Man.¹ Here they changed their course, and went into the Atlantic, through the northern passage, between Ireland and Scotland. On the 6th of April they reached the coast of France. Ushant light was the first place they sighted. Here they turned their steps toward St. Malo, proceeding under slow steam, and in the morning they sighted, off Morleaux², the steamer Alar, with arms, ammunition, and supplies for the Georgia, under charge of Jones, a partner in the Liverpool house of Jones & Co.³

It happened that these proceedings were afterward made the subject of judicial investigation before Sir Alexander Cockburn, Lord Chief Justice of England. Highatt and Jones, two of the members of the firm of Jones & Co., were indicted at Liverpool, for a violation of the Foreign Enlistment Act of 1819, in causing these men to be enlisted to serve in a war against the United States. The case came on for trial at the Liverpool Assizes, in August, 1864. In his address to the jury, after the evidence was in, the Lord Chief Justice said: "There was no doubt that Matthews, Stanley, and Glassbrook did enter themselves and enlist on board the steamer, which was immediately afterward employed as a war steamer in the Confederate service, for the purpose of waging war against the Northern States of America; and there seemed to be very little doubt that both the defendants had to do with the men's leaving the port of Liverpool, for the purpose of joining the Japan, afterward called the Georgia. * * * Now came the question, whether the defendants had procured the men to be engaged in war against a country toward which this country was bound to maintain a strict neutrality. No doubt it was possible that the defendants might have been under a delusion that the ship was engaged for a voyage to China. It was for the jury to say whether they believed that to have been the case. If they believed the witnesses Conolly and Glassbrook, the defendant Jones could not have been of that opinion,

---

[1] Mahon's affidavit, Vol. II, page 672; Vol. VI, page 513.
[2] Thompson's affidavit, Vol. II, page 671; Vol. VI, page 511.
[3] Speech of Thomas Baring, Esq., M. P., Hansard, 3d series, Vol. 175, page 467.

because he was on board the small steamer which was an important agent in the transaction; and when he found out what the vessel really was, he manifested no surprise or horror. It was true that the jury had to rely on the evidence of men who had turned traitors to the people they had sworn to serve, and who had since played the spy upon the persons who, as they alleged, had engaged them. But, on the other hand, there was no attempt to show them that, on the day when these men signed articles at Brest, Mr. Jones was not on board, and if he was on board it was difficult to suppose he could have got there with the innocent intention described by the defense. It seems strange that if they were acting as agents for Mr. Bold, they did not now call upon him to come into court, and state that they were innocently employed, and perfectly unconscious that the vessel was intended to go on a warlike expedition. Although sometimes it was an inconvenience and a hardship that a man, charged as the defendants were, could not be called to give his own evidence, sometimes it was a vast convenience to persons accused that they could not be called, because if they were, they would be constrained to admit, unless they committed perjury, that the truth was on the other side."[1]

The Alar, with her cargo, had cleared at Newhaven for St. Malo. When the two vessels met, the Georgia took the Alar in tow, and they floated about on those waters during the whole day. At night they came to anchor, probably off the island of Ushant, and the Georgia commenced taking in arms and ammunition and supplies. Three days passed in this way. There were nine breech-loading guns to be mounted on decks, and "guns, shot, shells, rockets, ammunition, rifles, cutlasses, and all sorts of implements of war."[2]

All were put on board before Friday, the 10th of April; the insurgents' flag was then hoisted; Maury, the insurgent officer destined for the command, produced his commission;

---

[1] Vol. IV, page 567.
[2] Vol. II, page 671; Vol. VI, page 511.

the Japan was changed into the Georgia; fifteen sailors who refused to cruise in her were transferred to the Alar, and the Georgia continued her cruise.

On the 8th of April Mr. Adams called Earl Russel's attention to the departure from the Clyde and Newhaven of this hostile expedition, "with intent to depredate on the commerce of the United States,"[1] and he stated his belief that the destination of the vessel was the island of Alderney. Earl Russell replied, on the same day, that copies of his letter "were sent, without loss of time, to the Home Department and to the Board of Treasury, with a request that an immediate inquiry might be made into the circumstances stated in it, and that if the result should prove the suspicions to be well founded, *the most effective measures might be taken which the law admits of for defeating any such attempts to fit out a belligerent vessel from a British port.*"[2]

Had Her Majesty's Government taken the measures which Earl Russell suggested, it is probable that the complaints of the United States, as to this vessel, might not have been necessary. The sailing and the destination of the Japan were so notorious as to be the subject of newspaper comment.[3] No time, therefore, was required for that investigation. It could have been very little trouble to ascertain the facts as to the Alar. The answer to a telegram could have been obtained in a few minutes. Men-of-war might have been dispatched on the 8th from Portsmouth and Plymouth, to seize both these violators of British sovereignty. In doing this Her Majesty's Government need only have exercised the same powers which were used against General Saldanha's expedition, arrested at Terceira in 1827, and whose use in that case was sustained by a vote of both Houses of Parliament.[4] The island of Alderney and the other Channel

---

[1] Vol. II, page 666; Vol. VI, page 509.
[2] Vol. II, page 667; Vol. VI, page 510.
[3] Vol. II, page 668.
[4] Hansard, new series, Vols. XXIII and XXIV; Annual Register, History, &c., A. D. 1829, Vol. LXXII, page 187.

islands were on the route to St. Malo and Brest, and it is not at all probable, scarcely possible, that the Alar and the Georgia would not have been discovered. The purposes of the latter vessel, thus taken *flagrante delicto*, would then have been exposed.

This was not done. Instead of directing *action* to be taken by the *Navy*, Lord Russell caused *inquiries* to be made by the *Home* Office and the *Treasury*, and the Georgia escaped.

On the 1st of December, 1863, Mr. Adams called Lord Russell's attention to the fact of "the existence of a regular office in the port of Liverpool for the enlistment and payment of British subjects, for the purpose of carrying on war against the Government and people of the United States;" and he expressed the hope that "the extraordinary character of these proceedings, as well as the hazardous consequence to the future peace of all nations of permitting them to gain any authority under the international law, will not fail to fix the attention of Her Majesty's Government."[1] The depositions inclosed in this communication furnished conclusive proof that the members of the firm of Jones & Co. were still engaged at Liverpool in procuring and shipping men for the Georgia, and that the payments of the wages of the crew of that vessel were regularly made through the same firm.[2] It was also proved that Jones had superintended the shipping of the armament of the Georgia off Brest; that he had been standing by the side of Maury when he assumed command, and that he had told the men, as an inducement to them to remain, that "of course they would get the prize money."[3]

On the 11th of January, 1864, Mr. Adams inclosed to Lord Russell copies of papers which he maintained went "most clearly to establish the proof of the agency of Messrs. Jones & Co. in enlisting and paying British subjects in this

---

[1] Vol. II, page 682; Vol. VI, page 519.
[2] Vol. II, pages 683, 684, 686, 689, &c.
[3] Stanley's affidavit, Vol. II, page 684; Vol. VI, page 522. See also Charles Thompson's affidavit, Vol. III, page 57.

Kingdom to carry on war against the United States."[1]
Proceedings were taken against Jones & Highatt, as has
already been shown. They were convicted, and were fined
but fifty pounds each—manifestly a punishment not calculated
to deter them from a repetition of the offense.[2]

After all this information was before Lord Russell, the
Georgia, on the 1st day of May, 1864, reappeared in the
port of Liverpool. During her absence she had been busy
in destroying such of the commerce of the United States in
the Atlantic as had escaped the depredations of the Florida
and the Alabama. She had been to the Western Islands,
and from thence to the Brazilian port of Bahia. From
thence she went to the Cape of Good Hope. On the way
she fell in with the Constitution, a merchant vessel of the
United States, laden with coal. "We filled our vessel with
coal from her," says one of the witnesses. In a few days
after that she entered Simon's Bay, Cape of Good Hope.
There she staid a fortnight, having repairs done and getting
more coal. She left Simon's Bay on the 29th of August.
It is not probable that the supply from the Constitution
was exhausted at that time.[3] She then worked her way to
Cherbourg, and in a short time after came again into the
port of Liverpool. Her career and character were rapidly
but forcibly sketched by Thomas Baring, Esq., in a speech
in the House of Commons on the 13th of May, 1864.
He said: "At the time of her departure the Georgia was

---

[1] Vol. II, page 698; Vol. VI, page 534.
[2] "Five prosecutions were instituted at different times against persons charged with having enlisted or engaged men for the naval service of the Confederate States. Of these, three were successful. Five of the accused were convicted or pleaded guilty. * * No prosecution appears to have been instituted against Bullock himself." (*Bernard's Neutrality*, pages 361—2.) This is a terribly small record, considering the magnitude of the offenses committed, and considering the zeal shown in repressing enlistments for the service of the United States. (*See Vol. IV, page 547, and Vol. IV, page 540.*) It is to be observed, too, that Mr. Adams furnished Lord Russell with evidence to sustain a prosecution against Bullock. (*Mr. Adams to Earl Russell, March 30, 1863, Vol. III, page 130.*)
[3] See the affidavits in Vol. II, page 684, et seq.

registered as the property of a Liverpool merchant, a partner
of the firm which shipped the crew. She remained the
property of this person until the 23d of June, when the
register was canceled, he notifying the Collector of her sale
to foreign owners. During this period, namely, from the
1st of April to the 23d June, the Georgia being still
registered in the name of a Liverpool merchant, and thus
his property, was carrying on war against the United States,
with whom we were in alliance. It was while still a
British vessel that she captured and burned the Dictator,
and captured and released, under bond, the Griswold, the
same vessel which had brought corn to the Lancashire
sufferers. The crew of the Georgia were paid through the
same Liverpool firm. A copy of an advance note used is
to be found in the Diplomatic Correspondence. The same
firm continued to act in this capacity throughout the cruise
of the Georgia. After cruising in the Atlantic, and burning
and bonding a number of vessels, the Georgia made for
Cherbourg, where she arrived on the 28th of October. There
was, at the time, much discontent among the crew; many
deserted, leave of absence was given to others, and their
wages were paid all along by the same Liverpool firm. In
order to get the Georgia to sea again, the Liverpool firm
enlisted in Liverpool some twenty seamen, and sent them to
Brest. The Georgia left Cherbourg on a second cruise, but
having no success she returned to that port, and thence to
Liverpool, where her crew have been paid off without any
concealment, and the vessel is now laid up. Here, then, is
the case of a vessel, clandestinely built, fraudulently leaving
the port of her construction, taking Englishmen on board
as her crew, and waging war against the United States, an
ally of ours, without once having entered a port of the power
the commission of which she bears, but being, for some time,
the property of an English subject. She has now returned
to Liverpool—and has returned, I am told, with a British crew
on board, who, having enlisted in war against an ally of ours,
have committed a misdemeanor in the sight of the law.[1]

---

[1] Hansard, third series, Vol. 175, page 467; Vol. V, page 577.

The Attorney General, Sir Roundell Palmer, replied on behalf of the Government to this speech. He did not seriously dispute the facts as stated by Mr. Baring. "The whole of the honorable gentleman's argument," he said, "assumes that the facts, and the law applicable to the facts, are substantiated, that we are in a position, as between ourselves and the Confederates, to treat the matter as beyond controversy, and to assume that the Georgia was, in fact, fitted out in violation of our neutrality. Now we may have very strong reason to suspect this, and may even believe it to be true; but to say that we are to act upon strong suspicion or belief against another state, upon certain facts which have never been judicially established, and which it is not easy to bring to the test as between Government and Government, that is a proposition which is not without grave consideration to be accepted."[1] He found a defense for the irresolution and inactivity of the Government, in the fact that the United States were unwilling to abandon their claims for compensation for the losses by the acts of the Alabama. "I have no hesitation," he said, "in saying that the United States by advancing such demands, and by seeking to make our Government responsible for pecuniary compensation for prizes taken by the Alabama upon the high seas, and never brought within our ports or in any way whatever under our control, are making demands directly contrary to the principles of International Law laid down by their own jurists, and thereby they render it infinitely more difficult for us at their request to do anything resting on our own discretion."[2]

When it was apparent that the Georgia was to be allowed to remain in Liverpool, and that she was not to be made subject to the rules of January 31, 1862, Mr. Adams addressed a note to Lord Russell in which he said: "I learn that she is about to remain for an indefinite period, the men having been discharged. I scarcely need to suggest to your Lordship that it has become a matter of interest to my

---

[1] Hansard, 3d series, Vol. CLXXV, pages 484—5.
[2] Same, page 488.

Government to learn whether this vessel assumes the right to remain in virtue of her former character, or, if received in a later one, why she is permitted to overstay the period of time specified by the terms of Her Majesty's proclamation. * * I cannot but infer, from the course previously adopted toward the armed vessels of the United States, that any such proceeding, if taken by one of them, would have been attended by an early request from your Lordship to myself for an explanation."[1]

Having received no answer to these questions, Mr. Adams, on the 7th of June, 1864, informed Lord Russell that he had received from the Consul of the United States, at Liverpool, information that a transfer purporting to be a sale had been made of the Georgia by the insurgents or their agents at Liverpool, and on behalf of the Government of the United States he "declined to recognize the validity of the sale."[2]

While Mr. Adams was vainly endeavoring to ascertain from Lord Russell whether the Georgia entered the port of Liverpool as a merchant ship or as a man-of-war, that vessel went into dock at Birkenhead and had her bottom cleaned and her engines overhauled.[3] The insurgent agents went through the form of selling her to a person who was supposed to be in collusion with them. All this was communicated to Earl Russell by Mr. Adams.[4] Lord Russell, in his reply to these notes, took no notice of Mr. Adams's protest against the validity of the sale, or of his inquiries as to the character the vessel enjoyed in the port of Liverpool. He said that the evidence failed to satisfy him that the steamer Georgia would be again used for belligerent purposes; and he added that, "with a view to prevent the recurrence of any question such as that which has arisen in the case of the Georgia, Her Majesty's Government have given directions that in future no ship of war, of either

---

[1] Vol. II, page 703; Vol. VI, page 538.
[2] Vol. II, page 710; Vol. VI, page 543.
[3] Wilding to Seward, Vol. II, page 711; Vol. VI, page 543.
[4] Vol. II, page 713; Vol. VI, page 545.

belligerent, shall be allowed to be brought into any of Her Majesty's ports for the purpose of being dismantled or sold." [1]

This terminated the discussion on the questions raised by Mr. Adams. A few days later, the career of the Georgia itself was terminated by its capture by the United States vessel of war Niagara.

The United States ask the Tribunal of Arbitration to also certify as to this vessel, that Great Britain has, by its acts and omissions, failed to fulfill the duties set forth in the three rules of the sixth article of the Treaty, or recognized by the principles of International Law not inconsistent with such rules. Should the Tribunal exercise the power conferred upon it by Article VII of the Treaty, to award a sum in gross to be paid to the United States, they ask that, in considering the amount to be awarded, the losses of the United States and of individuals, and the expense to which the United States were put in the pursuit and capture of the Georgia, may be taken into account.

They ask this, in addition to the general reasons already assigned, for the following reasons applicable to this particular vessel:

1. That, though nominally cruising under the insurgent flag, and under the direction of an insurgent officer, the Georgia was essentially a British vessel. The evidence on this point cannot be better stated than in the words to which Mr. Thomas Baring gave the great weight of his name in the House of Commons. When she returned to Liverpool, in May, 1864, she was received as a British vessel. Mr. Adams's inquiries of Earl Russell failed to elicit a response that she was not. No steps were taken against her or against the parties concerned in fitting her out, equipping and arming her, or against any one concerned in the destruction of the commerce of the United States, with the exception of the proceedings as to enlistments. The United States insist that by reason of the origin and history

---

[1] Earl Russell to Mr. Adams, Vol. II, page 719; Vol. VI, page 650.

of the vessel, and by reason of this negligence of Her Majesty's Government, Great Britain became justly liable to the United States for the injuries done by this vessel.

2. Great Britain did not use due diligence to prevent the fitting out and equipping of the Georgia within its jurisdiction. It was notorious that she was being constructed for use under the insurgent flag. *(See the extract from the News, and Underwood's dispatch.)* Her fittings were of such a nature and character as to have afforded of themselves a reasonable ground to believe that she was intended to cruise or to carry on war; and her destination rendered it certain that that war was to be carried on against the United States. It was therefore the duty of Great Britain to prevent her departure from the Clyde.

3. It was the duty of Her Majesty's Government, on the receipt of Mr. Adams's note of the 8th of April, to take the most effectual measures which the law admitted of for defeating the attempt to fit out the Georgia from a British port. Lord Russell admitted this measure of duty in his reply to Mr. Adams's note. The most effectual, and in fact the only effectual remedy, was not taken, so far as known to the United States. Vessels of war dispatched from Plymouth and Portsmouth, immediately on the receipt of Mr. Adams's note, into the waters about Brest and the Channel Islands, would have afforded a complete remedy. This was a measure sanctioned by British precedent and by British law. [*See the Terceira case, above cited.*] The failure to adopt that "effectual measure," taken in connection with the original fitting out and equipping of the Georgia, in the Clyde, and with the arming her through the Alar, at Newhaven, constitute a violation of the duties of Great Britain as a neutral toward the United States, which entails upon it the obligation to make full compensation for the injuries caused by the acts of the Georgia.

4. When the Georgia arrived at Cape Town, Great Britain failed to detain her. This was a violation of the duties of a neutral as set forth in the second clause of the first rule of the Treaty of Washington.

THE TALLAHASSEE, OR THE OLUSTEE.

The Tallahassee or Olustee. The Tallahassee was "a British steamer fitted out from London to play the part of a privateer out of Wilmington."[1] She was originally called the Atlanta.[2] Under that name she arrived in Bermuda from England on the 18th day of April, 1864. She made two trips as a blockade-runner between there and Wilmington, and then went out for a cruise as a vessel of war. Her captures were principally made under the name of the Tallahassee. Some were made under the name of the Olustee. It is not quite clear whether she made two trips, one under each name, or whether the name was changed in one trip in order to blind the pursuers.[3] On the 19th of August, 1864, she arrived in Halifax after destroying several vessels near Cape Sable. The Consul of the United States at Halifax reported her as "about six hundred tons burden," "an iron double-screw steamer," having "about one hundred and twenty men."[4] He also said that the insurgents had established a coal depot there. On arrival, the officer in command called upon the Admiral and Lieutenant Governor. He gives the following account of what took place. "My reception by the first [the Admiral] was very cold and uncivil; that of the Governor less so. I stated that I was in want of coal, and that as soon as I could fill up I would go to sea; that it would take from two to three days. No objection was made at the time—if there had been I was prepared to demand forty-eight hours for repairs. The Governor asked me to call next day and let him know how I was progressing and when I would leave. I did so, and then was told that he was surprised that I was still in port; that we must leave at once; that we could leave the harbor with only one hundred tons of coal on board. I protested

---

[1] Mr. Adams to Earl Russell, Vol. I, page 709; see Vol. VI, page 728.
[2] Morse to Seward, Vol. VI, page 727.
[3] Boreham's affidavit, Vol. VI, page 732.
[4] Mr. Jackson to Mr. Seward, 19th August, 1864, Vol. VI, page 728.

against this, as being utterly insufficient. He replied that the Admiral had reported that quantity sufficient (and in such matters he must be governed by his statement) to run the ship to Wilmington. The Admiral had obtained this information by sending on board three of his officers, ostensibly to look at our machinery and the twin-screw, a new system, but really *to ascertain the quantity of coal on board, that burned daily, &c.* * * I am under many obligations to our agent, Mr. Weir, for transacting our business, and through his management about one hundred and twenty tons of coal were put aboard instead of half that quantity. * * Had I procured the coal needed I intended to have struck the coast at the capes of the Delaware and followed it down to Cape Fear, but I had only coal enough to reach Wilmington on the night of the 25th."[1]

Had the British authorities at Nassau, Bermuda, Barbadoes, Cape Town, Melbourne, and other colonial ports, pursued the same course that the Lieutenant Governor at Halifax did, under the wise advice of the Admiral, the grievances of the United States would have been much less, and this case would have been shorter by many pages. The first time that the rule of January 31st, 1862, as to the supply of coal, was fairly carried out, the operations of the insurgent cruiser, to which it was applied, were arrested on the spot, and the vessel was obliged to run for a home port.

The Tallahassee apparently remained in Wilmington for some months. On the 13th of January, 1865, she arrived in Bermuda again, under the name of the Chameleon. On the 19th she sailed again, taking a cargo to Liverpool, where at the close of the war she was claimed by the United States.

From the fact that she was fitted out in London to be used as a privateer from Wilmington, and that she did go out from Wilmington with what purported to be a commission from the insurgent authorities, and did prey upon the commerce of the United States, and for the reasons already given, the United States ask the Tribunal to find and certify as to this vessel as they have been asked to find and certify

---

[1] Wood to Mallory, 31st August, 1864, Vol. VI, page 729.

as to the Sumter and the Nashville, the Florida, and the Alabama, and the Georgia.

THE CHICKAMAUGA.

The Chickamauga. Among the New British-built blockade-runners reported by the United States Consul at Liverpool on the 5th of March, 1864, was "the Edith, new double-screw; two pole masts; forecastle raised one foot higher than bulwark; two funnels; marked to draw nine feet forward and ten aft; no figure-head."[1] She arrived at Bermuda from England, on the 7th day of April, 1864. On the 23d of the following June she sailed for Wilmington, and on the 7th of the next July arrived from there with cotton. On the 23d of July she again went to Wilmington.

The Edith was one of that class of blockade-runners, like the Tallahassee, which was owned by the insurgent authorities. In the year 1864 other parties as well as the insurgent authorities were largely engaged in the business of running cotton out of the blockaded ports. Thus, in the quarter in which the Edith left Liverpool, 34,754 bales of cotton were imported into Liverpool from the Southern States, via Bermuda, Nassau, Havana, and Matamoras, of which only 7,874 were consigned to Fraser, Trenholm & Co.[2] The Edith, however, was a vessel belonging to the so-called government at Richmond, and, being found to be fast, and adapted for the sort of war that was carried on against the commerce of the United States, it was determined to put her in commission as a man-of-war.

The attention of the Tribunal of Arbitration is invited to the facile manner in which these vessels were permitted to adapt themselves to circumstances. The Sumter cruised as a man-of-war, and received hospitalities as such. She was allowed to change her character in a British port, and then

---

[1] Manuscripts in Department of State; see Vol. VI, pages 723—4—5.

[2] Dudley to Seward, 1st April, 1864. Only 697 bales came by way of Havana.

to sail under the British flag as a blockade-runner, owned and operated by the insurgents. The same thing would undoubtedly have been done with the Georgia had she not been captured by the Niagara. The Atlanta started her career as a blockade-runner, owned by the insurgents; she was converted into a man-of-war under the name of the Tallahassee. When unable to pursue further her work of destruction, she became again a carrier for the benefit of the insurgents, and was accepted by Great Britain in her new character. The Edith was now to go through similar transformations.

On the 17th of September she was in commission as a man-of-war. Between that date and the 28th of October she took on board large supplies of coal from blockade-runners. On the 28th of October, having waited for a month for a night dark enough to run the blockade, she put to sea from Wilmington, and ran northward toward Long Island. On the 30th she destroyed the bark Mark L. Potter, of Bangor, Maine; on the 31st, the Emily L. Hall, the Shooting Star, the Goodspeed, and the Otter Rock, all vessels under the flag of the United States; on the 2d of November, the bark Speedwell, also a vessel of the United States; and on the 7th of November she reached Bermuda. On the 8th of November she was allowed to come into the harbor, and permission was given for a stay of five days for repairs, and also to take on board twenty-five tons of coal, although she had at that time one hundred tons in her bunkers. She actually staid seven days and took on board eighty-two tons.[1] On the 15th of November she sailed from Bermuda, and on the 19th arrived at Wilmington.

For the reason already given the United States ask the Tribunal, as to this vessel, to find and certify as they have been asked to find and certify as to the Sumter, the Nashville, the Florida, the Alabama, the Georgia, and the Tallahassee.

---

[1] Manuscript diary in the Department of State.

THE SHENANDOAH.

The Shenandoah. The British steamer Sea King, a merchant vessel which had belonged to a Bombay Company, and had been employed in the East India trade,[1] was "a long rakish vessel of seven hundred and ninety tons register, with an auxiliary engine of two hundred and twenty nominal horse-power, with which she was capable of steaming ten knots an hour. She was the handiwork of celebrated builders on the river Clyde, in Scotland, and had made one voyage to New-Zealand as a transport for British troops, when she proved herself one of the fastest vessels afloat, her log showing at times over three hundred and twenty miles in twenty-four hours."[2]

In the year 1863, before the voyage to New Zealand, Mr. Dudley had seen her at Glasgow, and had reported her as a most likely steamer for the purposes of a privateer.[3]

On the 20th of September, in the year 1864, she was sold in London to Richard Wright, of Liverpool, a British subject, and the father-in-law of Mr. Prioleau, of South Carolina, the managing partner in the house of Fraser, Trenholm & Co.,[4] and the transfer was registered the same day.

The United States assert that the notorious connection of the firm of Fraser, Trenholm & Co. with the insurgents, and their repeated violations of the sovereignty of Great Britain in purchasing, constructing, equipping, arming, and contracting for vessels of war to be used in carrying on hostilities against the United States, ought by that time to have made them objects of suspicion to every British official, connected with the construction or the transfer of steamers capable of being adapted to warlike use. The acquisition, by a near connection of a member of their firm, of a fast-going steamer, capable of being so converted, and the proposition to send her to sea in ballast, with nothing on board but two mounted guns and a supply of provisions and coal, ought of itself to

---

[1] Bernard's British Neutrality, page 359.
[2] Cruise of the Shenandoah, page 9.
[3] Dudley to Seward and Morse to Seward, Vol. VI, page 555.
[4] Dudley to Seward, Vol. III, page 319; Vol. VI, page 560.

have attracted the attention of the British officials. The omission to take notice of the fact is a proof of want of the due diligence required by the Treaty. Under the circumstances, it would have been the exercise of but the most ordinary diligence to supervise the transfers of this class of vessels in the Government records, and to follow up so palpable a clew as was given in the case of the Sea King.

On the 7th of October, Wright gave a power of attorney to one Corbett to "sell her at any time within six months for a sum not less than £45,000 sterling."[1] Corbett was an Englishman who had commanded the Douglas, afterward known as the Margaret and Jessie, one of the kaleidoscopic blockade-runners owned by the insurgents and carrying the British flag.

The next day the Sea King cleared for Bombay, and sailed "with a crew of forty-seven men."[2] Before sailing, while she "lay in the basin," she "took in coal and provisions sufficient for a twelve-months' cruise."[3] She "had two 18-pounders mounted on the decks," which were the guns generally used in bringing vessels to.[4] "She was scarcely clear of the ground when a telegram was flashed to Liverpool, advising the Confederate agent at that port" that she had sailed;[5] and about 8 or 9 o'clock that evening a screw-steamer, called the Laurel, "nearly new-built, very strong, and admirably adapted for a privateer,"[6] left Liverpool, clearing for Matamoras, via Nassau, taking a "score or more of natives of the South, who had staked life and fortune on the hazard of a desperate game," among whom were "several old Confederate States navy officers, who had served on board the Sumter, Alabama and Georgia."[7] The Laurel took out as cargo "cases marked as machinery, but in reality containing guns and gun-carriages, such as are

---

[1] Dudley to Seward, Vol. III, page 319.
[2] Dudley to Seward, Vol. III, page 319; Vol. VI, page 560.
[3] Cruise of the Shenandoah, page 10.
[4] Temple's affidavit, Vol. III, page 478; Vol. VI, page 709.
[5] Cruise of the Shenandoah, page 11.
[6] Dudley to Adams, Vol. III, page 316; Vol. VI, page 556.
[7] Cruise of the Shenandoah, page 16. See also Vol. III, page 318.

used in war vessels."[1] Mr. Dudley, the Consul at Liverpool, from the number of guns and the number of men, drew the correct conclusion that they were shipped in order to be transferred to some other vessel.[2] The officers in Her Majesty's service, by the exercise of due diligence, might have arrived at the same conclusion, and might have detained both ships.

The appointed place of meeting was the harbor of Funchal, in the island of Madeira. The Laurel arrived there two days in advance of the Sea King.[3] The latter vessel had enlisted its crew "for a voyage to Bombay or any port of the Indian Ocean, China Seas, or Japan, for a term not to exceed two years."[4] She "went down the English Channel under steam and sail, and when off Land's End she was put under reefed canvas," and so continued to Madeira. She was fully rigged for sailing, and her steam was intended only as an auxiliary.

The Sea King arrived off Funchal the night of the 19th.[5] The Laurel, on the morning of the 20th, came out to meet her, "with a full head of steam on;" signaled her to round the Desertas, a barren rocky island lying near Madeira: and proceeded to the place of rendezvous, the Sea King following in the wake.[6]

"Tackles were at once got aloft on both vessels, and they commenced operations by first transferring from the Laurel to the Sea King the heavy guns." "At the expiration of thirty-six hours the transfer was effected, and the munitions of war, clothing, and stores, with which the Laurel had been laden, were piled in utter confusion on the decks and in the hold of the Sea King, which was to bear that name no more."[7] They "took in from the Laurel eight cannon, *viz.* six large and two small, with their carriages, (the guns were called 68-pounders:) a quantity of powder, muskets, pistols,

---

[1] Dudley to Seward, Vol. III, page 317; Vol. VI, page 556.
[2] Dudley to Seward, Vol. III, page 318; Vol. VI, page 557.
[3] Cruise of the Shenandoah, page 19.
[4] Ellison's affidavit, Vol. III, page 359; Vol. VI, page 580.
[5] Harris's affidavit, Vol. III, page 363; Vol. VI, page 584.
[6] Cruise of the Shenandoah, pages 19, 20.
[7] Cruise of the Shenandoah, page 21.

shot, and shell; clothing, and a quantity of other stores, and also a quantity of coals."[1]

Corbett then came forward and announced a pretended sale of the vessel, (the real sale having taken place in London,) and tried to induce the men who had enlisted to sail in the Sea King to continue their contract in the Shenandoah. The conduct of this person was so palpably a violation of the Foreign Enlistment Act that the British Consul at Funchal sent him home as a prisoner, accompanied by depositions to prove his guilt.[2] Captain Waddell, the new commander in the place of Corbett, made a speech, "which was received with but little enthusiasm by the majority of those who listened to him."[3] "Out of eighty twenty-three only cast in their lots with the new cruiser."[4] When the Shenandoah left the Laurel her "officers and crew only numbered forty-two souls, less than half her regular complement."[5] This obliged her "to depend upon her auxiliary engine."

When the news of these proceedings was fully known in London, Mr. Adams brought the subject to the notice of Earl Russell.[6] In a subsequent note he referred to this fact in the following language:[7]

"On the 18th of November, 1864, I had the honor to transmit to your Lordship certain evidence which went to show that on the 18th of October preceding a steamer had been dispatched, under the British flag, from London, called the Sea King, with a view to meet another steamer, called the Laurel, likewise bearing that flag, dispatched from Liverpool on the 9th of the same month, at some point near the island of Madeira. These vessels were at the time of sailing equipped and manned by British subjects; yet they were sent out with arms, munitions of war, supplies, officers, and

---

[1] Vol. III, page 363; Vol. VI, page 580. See also the other affidavits which follow this.
[2] Vol. VI, page 572.
[3] Cruise of the Shenandoah, page 22.
[4] Cruise of the Shenandoah, page 23.
[5] Cruise of the Shenandoah, page 24.
[6] Adams to Russell, Vol. III, page 323.
[7] Same to same, Vol. III, page 377.

enlisted men, for the purpose of initiating a hostile enterprise to the people of the United States, with whom Great Britain was at the time under solemn obligations to preserve the peace.

"It further appears that, on or about the 18th of the same month, these vessels met at the place agreed upon, and there the British commander of the Sea King made a private transfer of the vessel to a person of whom he then declared to the crew his knowledge that he was about to embark on an expedition of the kind described. Thus knowing its nature, he nevertheless went on to urge these seamen, being British subjects themselves, to enlist as members of it.

"It is also clear that a transfer then took place from the British bark Laurel of the arms of every kind with which she was laden, for this same object; and, lastly, of a number of persons, some calling themselves officers, who had been brought from Liverpool expressly to take part in the enterprise. Of these last a considerable portion consisted of the very same persons, many of them British subjects, who had been rescued from the waves by British intervention at the moment when they had surrendered from the sinking Alabama, the previous history of which is but too well known to your Lordship.

"Thus equipped, fitted out, and armed from Great Britain, the successor to the destroyed corsair, now assuming the name of the Shenandoah, though in no other respects changing its British character, addressed itself at once to the work for which it had been intended. At no time in her later career has she ever reached a port of the country which her commander has pretended to represent. At no instance has she earned any national characteristic other than that with which she started from Great Britain. She has thus far roamed over the ocean, receiving her sole protection against the consequences of the most piratical acts from the gift of a nominal title which Great Britain first bestowed upon her contrivers, and then recognized as legitimating their successful fraud."

It is not necessary to follow in detail the cruise of the Shenandoah from Madeira to Melbourne. It is enough to say that it lasted ninety days,[1] during which time several vessels of the merchant marine of the United States were destroyed, with valuable cargoes. On the 25th of January, 1865, she "dropped anchor off Sandridge, a small town about two miles from Melbourne."[2]

"The November mail from Europe, which arrived at Melbourne about the middle of January, had brought the news that the Sea King had left England with the intention of being converted into a war vessel to cruise against the commerce of the United States."[3] Suspicions were at once aroused that the newly-arrived man-of-war under the insurgent flag was no other than the Sea King; suspicions which were confirmed by the statements of the prisoners from the captured vessels, and by others.[4]

The Consul of the United States appears to have acted with both courtesy and vigor. He placed before the authorities all the information in his possession, tending to show the illegal origin of the vessel, and the liabilities which she was imposing upon Great Britain by her depredations on the commerce of the United States.[5] He told the Governor that the "Shenandoah, alias Sea King," had never "entered a port of the so-styled Confederate States for the purposes of naturalization, and consequently was not entitled to belligerent rights;"[6] and that the table-service, plate, &c., on the vessel all bore the mark of "Sea King." He earnestly urged that "after the severest scrutiny it should be determined if this vessel and crew are entitled to the rights of belligerency, or whether the vessel should not be detained until the facts can be duly investigated."[7] When he found that, in spite

---

[1] Cruise of the Shenandoah, page 93.
[2] Cruise of the Shenandoah, page 94.
[3] Blanchard to Seward, Vol. III, page 384; Vol. VI, page 586.
[4] See depositions in Vol. III, on pages 399, 401, 402, 405, 407, and 417. The same depositions may be found in Vol. VI. This point appears to have been settled beyond doubt. See extract from Melbourne Herald, Vol. VI, page 650.
[5] See Mr. Blanchard's dispatch to Mr. Seward, Vol. III, page 384.
[6] Vol. III, page 394; Vol. VI, page 598.
[7] Blanchard to Darling, Vol. III, page 395; Vol. VI, page 598.

of his remonstrances and of the proof of her character, it had been decided that the Shenandoah should be repaired, and should be allowed to take in supplies and coals, he protested "in behalf of his Government against the aid, comfort, and refuge" extended to her.[1] When he was informed that the Governor had come to the decision "that whatever may be the previous history of the Shenandoah, the Government of the Colony is bound to treat her as a ship of war belonging to a belligerent Power," he protested afresh, and notified the Governor "that the United States will claim indemnity for the damages already done to its shipping by said vessel, and also which may hereafter be committed if allowed to depart from this port."[2] He placed in the hands of the Attorney General conclusive "evidence to establish that the Shenandoah is in fact the Sea King."[3] When it came to his knowledge that Waddell was enlisting a crew in Melbourne for the Shenandoah, he put the proof of it at once into the hands of the Governor.[4] When he heard that she was taking coal on board he communicated that fact also.[5] From the beginning of the visit of the Shenandoah at Melbourne to the hour of her departure, the officer was constant in his vigilance, and in his efforts to aid the British authorities in the performance of their duties, as the representatives of a neutral nation.

As soon as she arrived, almost before her anchor was dropped, her commander wrote to the Governor for permission to "make the necessary repairs and obtain a supply of coals."[6]

This letter was officially answered the next day, after the twenty-four hours allowed by the instructions of January, 1862, for his stay had expired. He was told that directions had been given to enable him to make the necessary repairs and to coal his vessel, and he was asked, at his earliest convenience, to intimate the nature and extent of his require-

---

[1] Blanchard to Darling, Vol. III, page 397; Vol. VI, page 600.
[2] Blanchard to Darling, Vol. III, page 398; Vol. VI, page 602.
[3] Vol. III, pages 403 and 404, 405 and 407. See also Vol. VI.
[4] Vol. III, pages 414, 420, 423, 427, 428. See also Vol. VI.
[5] Vol. III, page 425; Vol. VI, page 630.
[6] Waddell to Darling, Vol. V, page 599.

ments as regards repairs and supplies.[1] This was the official answer. The real answer had been given the previous night to Waddell's messenger, who was dispatched on shore "as soon as practicable the afternoon of arrival, to confer with the authorities and obtain permission for the ship to remain and procure some "necessary repairs." "He returned *before midnight, having succeeded in his mission.*"[2]

Two days were taken to reply to the question as to the nature and extent of the needed repairs and supplies. Waddell then stated, as a reason why he could not yet report, that the mechanics had not reported to him. He spoke generally about the condition of his propeller shaft, and the bearings under water, and, he added, "*the other repairs are progressing rapidly.*"[3] It thus appears that he had been at that time three days in port, had made no official statement of the supplies or the necessary repairs, and that he had a force at work upon his vessel, without any report to the Governor showing the necessity.

The next day he was asked to furnish a list of supplies required for the immediate use of his vessel.[4] He appears to have furnished such a statement, but it has not been printed in any document within the control of the United States. As the list is in the possession of Great Britain, it will doubtless be produced, if it tends to release that Government from responsibility.

On the following day, being the fifth day after he arrived in port, the fourth day after he received permission to make his repairs, and the third or fourth day after the repairs were commenced, he reported to the Governor that the lining of the outer sternback (probably meaning the outer sternbush) was entirely gone, and that in order to replace it the Shenandoah must go into the Government slip for about ten days.[5]

---

[1] Francis to Waddell, Vol. V, page 599; Vol. VI, page 639.
[2] Cruise of the Shenandoah, page 97.
[3] Vol. V, page 600; Vol. VI, page 640.
[4] Francis to Waddell, Vol. V, page 600; Vol. VI, page 641.
[5] Waddell to the Commissioner of Trade, Vol. V, page 600; Vol. VI, page 641.

On the 1st of February the Governor assented to the making of these repairs[1] and the time named for them.

On the 7th of February, through his Secretary he called upon Captain Waddell "to name the day when he would be prepared to proceed to sea."[2] Waddell said that he could not name a day; and he gives excuses why his vessel was not yet on the slip; a fact which furnishes the evident reason for the letter of the Governor's Secretary.[3]

On the 14th of February, a week later, inquiry is again made whether he is "in a position to state more definitely when the Shenandoah will be in a position to proceed to sea."[4]

The reply shows that the Shenandoah was then on the slip, and was to be launched the next day. He thought he could proceed to sea by the 19th, though he had yet to take in all his stores and coals.[5]

The next correspondence between Waddell and the Governor's Secretary furnishes the solution of the delay in the original report upon the repairs, the delay in the getting the vessel into the slip, the delay in getting her out of it, and the unreasonable time required "to take in stores, coals, and to swing the ship." During all this time Waddell had been enlisting men for the Shenandoah out of the streets of Melbourne, and had protracted his repairs as an excuse for delay, while he filled up the thin ranks of his crew.

The arrival of this vessel at Melbourne had produced a profound sensation. An inquiry was made of the Government in the Legislature to know if Her Majesty's Proclamation had not been violated by the Shenandoah. The member making the inquiry called attention to the news of the departure of the Sea King from London for the purpose of being converted into a cruiser, and he showed that the Sea King and the Shenandoah were the same vessel. The House was opposed to him, and he was called to order as he did this. The

---

[1] Francis to Waddell, Vol. V, page 602; Vol. VI, page 644.
[2] Francis to Waddell, Vol. V, page 602; Vol. VI, page 643.
[3] Waddell to Francis, Vol. V, page 602; Vol. VI, page 644.
[4] Francis to Waddell, Vol. V, page 602; Vol. VI, page 644.
[5] Waddell to Francis, Vol. V, page 602; Vol. VI, page 644.

Chief Secretary replied, not so much calling in question the identity of the Sea King with the Shenandoah, as doubting the propriety of accepting the fact on the evidence quoted by the former speaker; and he added that, "in dealing with this vessel, they had not only to consider the terms of the proclamation referred to, *but also the confidential instructions from the Home Government.*"[1]

Here the United States learned for the first time that, in addition to the published instructions which were made known to the world, there were private and confidential and perhaps conflicting instructions on this subject. It is beyond their power to furnish to this Tribunal copies of these confidential instructions. Should their production be deemed important by Her Majesty's Government or should they tend to relieve Great Britain from liability to the United States, they will, undoubtedly, be furnished to the Tribunal.

The Consul of the United States at Melbourne penetrated the reasons for Waddell's delay, and supplied the Colonial Authorities with evidence that men were being enlisted at Melbourne for the Shenandoah. His first letter to the Governor on this subject was dated the 10th of February. In it he called attention "to the shipment of men on board said Shenandoah in this port."[2] Again, on the 14th of February, he transmitted to the Governor further proof on the same subject.[3]

The affidavits furnished by the Consul showed that an enlistment on a large scale was going on. The affidavit of Wicke, for instance, spoke of a cook named "Charley," and ten men;[4] the affidavit of Behucke, of "about ten men concealed in said Shenandoah."[5]

The authorities proceeded against "Charley" only. They

---

[1] Vol. V, page 611; Vol. VI, page 660, et seq. It was in consequence of these doubts expressed by the Chief Secretary that the Consul furnished the evidence of the identity of the two vessels. Vol. III, page 386; Vol. VI, page 590.
[2] Blanchard to Darling, Vol. III, page 420; Vol. VI, page 625.
[3] Blanchard to Darling, Vol. III, page 414; Vol. VI, page 619.
[4] Vol. III, page 421; Vol. VI, page 625.
[5] Vol. III, page 422; Vol. VI, page 626.

carefully let alone Captain Waddell and his officers, who had been violating Her Majesty's proclamation and the laws of the Empire,[1] and they aimed the thunders of the law against an assistant cook. When the officer arrived at the vessel to serve the warrant for Charley's arrest, he was informed that no such person was on board. On expressing a wish to ascertain this fact for himself, his request was refused.[2] The next day he went again, and Captain Waddell "stated, on his honor and faith as a gentleman and an officer, that there was no such person as Charley on board."[3] On the evening of the same day Charley and three other men who had been enlisted in Melbourne were arrested as they left the Shenandoah by the water police,[4] thus showing that they must have been there all the while.

In consequence of this the permission to make repairs was suspended; but it was soon restored. The reason given for the restoration was that, Charley being taken, Waddell was "in a position to say, as commanding officer of the ship, that there were no persons on board except those whose names are on the shipping articles, and that no one has been enlisted in the service of the Confederate States since arrival in this port."[5] It does not appear that Waddell made any such commitment; on the contrary, he said that he considered "the tone of the letter remarkably disrespectful and insulting."

The Melbourne authorities did not insist upon having such an assurance. The Secretary of the Governor had said that

---

[1] The second section of the Foreign Enlistment Act of 1819 made it illegal to procure any person to engage to enlist as a sailor in sea service under any person assuming to exercise any powers of government, or to agree to go from any part of Her Majesty's dominions for the purpose of being so enlisted; and persons committing that offense were to be deemed guilty of a misdemeanor, and to be punished, on conviction, by fine or imprisonment, or both. It would be difficult to describe what Captain Waddell actually did at Melbourne in more accurate language than this.
[2] Vol. V, page 618; Vol. VI, page 665.
[3] Vol. V, page 618; Vol. VI, page 665.
[4] Francis to Waddell, Vol. V, page 605; Vol. VI, page 647.
[5] Ibid., Vol. V, page 605.

Waddell was in a position to give the assurance; that was enough. The Chief Secretary said in the Assembly, speaking of the enlistment of "Charley," "it appears to me and to the Government that if anything can be a violation of strict neutrality, this is it;"[1] but he added, in a few moments, (his attention being called to the fact that there were still persons on board who had joined the ship at Melbourne,) "The particular warrant that was issued for this particular individual (Charley) was satisfied; and if further warrants are issued for other persons who may be on board, *the position of the Government will be altered.* It may be that there are other persons on board."[2]

There were other persons on board whose presence was a violation of British neutrality, and whose exposure would "alter the position of the Government"—some fifty in all; but no warrant was issued, and "the position of the Government" was not "altered." The Shenandoah took on board her coal (three hundred tons in all) and her supplies, the character of which is not known to the United States, for the reasons already given.

The United States Consul to the last did his duty. On the 17th, the day before she sailed, he informed the Governor that "the Shenandoah was taking in three hundred tons of of coal, in addition to the quantity she had on board when she came into this port—about four hundred tons; and added, "The Shenandoah is a full-rigged sailing vessel; steam is only auxiliary with her; and I cannot believe Your Excellency is aware of the large amount of coal now being furnished said vessel."[3] This coal was dispatched from Liverpool in a vessel called the John Fraser. The earmarks were on the transaction in the very name of the transport.

On the same day the Consul also lodged with the Governor the affidavit of one Andrew Forbes, to show that six persons, residents of Melbourne, whom he named, were to join the Shenandoah outside, she being then ready to sail.

---

[1] Vol. V, page 619; Vol. VI, page 666.
[2] Vol. V, pages 620 and 667.
[3] Blanchard to Darling, Vol. III, pages 425, 426; Vol. VI, page 630.

As time was of importance, and a day's delay might be too late, the Consul went with his witnesses to the office of the Crown Solicitor, to whom the Attorney General had previously directed him to communicate such information. He found that officer leaving for his dinner. He told him "his business was urgent," and that he had "come as the representative of the United States to lay before him, as Crown Solicitor, the evidence that a large number of men were about violating the neutrality laws."[1] The Solicitor said he must go to his dinner, and passed on. The Consul then went to several other officers in order to secure immediate action on his complaint. Among others, he went to the Attorney General, who sent him to another Solicitor; but he could get no one to attend to it, and the Shenandoah left early in the morning of the 18th without further British interference.

The attention of the Tribunal of Arbitration is invited to the fact that a sworn list of the crew of the Shenandoah is attached to an affidavit made in Liverpool by one Temple ten months after the vessel left Melbourne.[2] Forbes in his affidavit, which was submitted to the Governor and laid before the Attorney General, gave the names of five persons who he had reason to believe were about to join the vessel from Melbourne. Temple's affidavit shows that at least three of those persons did join and did serve, viz.: "Robert Dunning, an Englishman, captain of the foretop;[3] Thomas Evans, Welchman;[4] and William Green, an Englishman."[5] This corroborative, independent piece of testimony establishes the truthfulness of Forbes's affidavit. This affidavit, so summarily rejected by the Crown Solicitor, was the specific evidence of the commission of a crime which Her Majesty's Government required to be furnished by the United States. When produced the British authorities declined to act upon it.

The United States assert, without fear of contradiction, that there was no time during the stay of the Shenandoah

---

[1] Lord to Blanchard, Vol. III, page 429; Vol. VI, page 635.
[2] Vol. III, page 477; Vol. VI, page 709.
[3] Vol. III, page 488; Vol. VI, page 719.
[4] Vol. III, page 489; Vol. VI, page 727.
[5] Vol. III, pages 489, 490; Vol. VI, page 721.

in Melbourne, when it was not notorious that she was procuring recruits. She went there for that purpose. Her effective power as a man-of-war depended entirely upon her success in obtaining a new crew. When she left the Laurel she had but twenty-three men besides her officers. With every capture between there and Melbourne great efforts were made to induce the captured seamen to enlist; and those who would not enlist were compelled to work as sailors in order to avoid being put in irons. The author of the "Cruise of the Shenandoah" says that fourteen were enlisted in this way—ten from the Alines and the Godfrey,[1] two from the Susan,[2] and two from the Stacey.[3] Temple in his affidavit gives the names of three from the Alina, five from the Godfrey, one from the Susan, two from the Stacey, and one from the Edward.[4] It is probable that Temple's statement is correct. Of the twelve whom he names, two appear to have left the vessel at Melbourne, viz.: Bruce, of the Alina; and Williams, of the Godfrey. It would therefore appear that, had the Shenandoah received no recruitment of men at Melbourne, her force on leaving would have been thirty-three marines, firemen, and ordinary seamen. One officer and two petty officers were discharged there, which reduced the number of officers to twenty, and her whole force to fifty-three. She was a full-rigged ship, 220 feet in length and 35 feet beam, and carried royal-studding sails, and required double or treble that number of men to make her effective as a man-of-war.[5] The Tribunal will see how important it was to recruit men at Melbourne.

She took in there, according to the account given by the author of the Cruise of the Shenandoah, forty-five men.[6] Temple, in his affidavit, gives the names of forty-three, divided as follows: one officer, twelve petty officers, twenty seamen, seven firemen, and three marines. The United States complain of this act, not alone as a technical violation of

---

[1] Cruise of the Shenandoah, page 42.
[2] Ibid., page 47. [3] Ibid., page 43.
[4] Vol. III, pages 487—491; Vol. VI, page 718, et seq.
[5] Cruise of the Shenandoah, page 23.
[6] Ibid., page 113.

the duties as a neutral, as laid down in the second rule of the Treaty, but as a great injury to them, from which flowed the subsequent damages to their commerce from the Shenandoah. This recruitment might have been stopped by the exercise of the most ordinary diligence. It ought to have been stopped after the Consul's letter of the 10th of February. It ought to have been stopped after his letter of the 14th. The authorities should have detained the Shenandoah on the information he communicated on the 17th. Most of the men went on board that night. It was a great negligence not to have prevented this. When the Shenandoah sailed on the morning of the 18th, the whole community knew that she had more than doubled her force in Melbourne. The newspapers of the next day were full of it. The Herald said: "Rumors are afloat that the Shenandoah shipped or received on board somewhere about eighty men."[1] The Argus said: "It is not to be denied that during Friday night a large number of men found their way on board the Shenandoah, and did not return on shore again."[2] And the Age said: "It is currently reported that she shipped some eighty men."[3] It is not probable—it may indeed be said to be most improbable—that a shipment of half that number of men could have been made without complicity of the authorities. Mr. Mountague Bernard intimates that they could not have come there without the knowledge of Captain Waddell."[4] A similar train of reasoning will convince the Tribunal of Arbitration that the least measure of "diligence" would have discovered the fact to the local authorities.

The permitting a shipment of three hundred tons of coal at Melbourne was also a violation of the duties of a neutral. The Shenandoah was a sailing vessel. Her steam-power was auxiliary. From early in December until two days before her arrival at Melbourne, some seven weeks in all,[5] she was under sail, without using her steam; she went from Land's

---

[1] Vol. III, page 435; Vol. VI, page 683.
[2] Vol. III, page 436; Vol. VI, page 684.
[3] Vol. III, page 436; Vol. VI, page 685.
[4] Bernard's Neutrality, page 434.
[5] Cruise of the Schenandoah, pages 63—94.

End to Madeira in the same way.[1] She took on board, when she left London, a supply of coal for twelve months. Four hundred tons of it remained when she reached Melbourne. She required no fresh supply to enable her to return to an insurgent port, and she sought it only for the purpose of cruising against the commerce of the United States, thus making Melbourne a base of the insurgent naval operations. The United States are of the opinion that it was a breach of the duties of an impartial neutral to permit unlimited supplies of coal to be furnished to the Shenandoah in a British port, under circumstances similar to those in which like supplies had been refused to the vessels of the United States; and that it was a still greater violation to permit the supply to be furnished from the insurgent transport John Fraser, dispatched from Liverpool for that purpose, while the United States were forbidden to supply their vessels in like manner.

When the Shenandoah left London she took general supplies for a year; yet she was allowed to replenish at Melbourne within less than six months from the time of leaving London. It must be concluded from the declarations of the author of the Cruise of the Shenandoah, that when this was done she had enough supplies on board for the subsistence of the crew to the nearest insurgent port. The addition obtained at Melbourne enabled her to continue her hostile cruise and to light up the icy seas of the north with the fires of American vessels, long after the military resistance to the United States had ceased.

The United States further insist that when the authorities at Melbourne permitted the Shenandoah to make repairs to her machinery in that port, a still greater violation of the duties of Great Britain as a neutral was committed.

It has just been shown that this vessel was under no necessity of using her steam; that she had gone to Madeira under sail; that she had come from the Cape of Good Hope to Melbourne under sail. For many days before arriving at Melbourne "a heavy and continuous gale" prevailed.[2] At

---

[1] Schulcher's affidavit, Vol. III, page 365; Vol. VI, page 580.
[2] Cruise of the Shenandoah, page 66.

its height it was "sublime beyond description," and the Shenandoah "drove before it at the rate of eleven knots an hour, under close-reefed topsails and reefed foresail."[1] Yet the author of the Cruise of the Shenandoah makes no mention of any injury to the vessel, or of any leak, and there is nothing to show that the hull needed repairs, or that anything was done to it except that "a gang of calkers were procured and went to work upon the decks with pitch and oakum."[2] The United States are convinced that no other repairs were necessary for the hull, and that if the departure of the vessel was delayed for the ostensible purpose of further repairs to the vessel itself, the pretense was made solely for the purpose of delay.

The repairs to the machinery, as distinguished from the hull, were made with the object of enabling the Shenandoah to go to the Arctic Ocean, there to destroy the whalers of the United States, in accordance with Bullock's instructions to Waddell before he left Liverpool.[3] It is evident, not only from the absence of any mention of injury to the hull by the author of the cruise of the Shenandoah, but also from the statement of experts of the repairs which the machinery required, that the hull was sound and seaworthy, and that the Shenandoah as a sailing vessel, without steam, could at once have proceeded to sea, and have made her way to the insurgent ports.[4] When Captain Boggs, of the United States Navy, two months later, (after the surrender of Lee,) asked permission to remain at Barbadoes "a few days, for the purpose of overhauling the piston and engine," he was required, as a preliminary to the permission, to "give a definite assurance of his inability to proceed to

---

[1] Ibid., page 67. [2] Ibid., page 104.
[3] Vol. III, page 461; Vol. VI, page 705.
[4] It is true that the Insurgents had no ports at that time which the Shenandoah could enter. Wilmington, the last of their ports, was closed by the capture of Fort Fisher. This, however, was an additional reason why the Shenandoah should not have been allowed to leave Melbourne, carrying a flag that had no port to receive it. See the correspondence between the United States and Portugal referred to ante, page 82.

sea."[1] As a man of honor and truth he could not do this, and he went to sea without his repairs. The same rule applied to the Shenandoah would have produced the same result, supposing Captain Waddell to have been as honorable and as truthful a man as Captain Boggs.

Twenty-four hours elapsed before any questions were put to Captain Waddell by the local authorities. Then he was told to state what repairs he wanted, in order that the Governor might know how long he was to enjoy the hospitalities of the port. He delayed for two days to answer this question, going on, however, in the meanwhile with some of his repairs. He then reported the repairs already begun as "progressing rapidly," and added that Langland Brothers & Co. were to examine the propeller and bracings (probably a misprint for "bearings") under water; that a diver had that day examined them; and that "so soon as Messrs. Langland Brothers & Co. should hand in their report" he would inclose it.

Two days later, on the 30th, Langland Brothers & Co. made their report, "after inspection by the diver," saying that "the lining of the outer sternback" (probably a misprint for "sternbush") is entirely gone, and will have to be replaced; that "three days will elapse before she is slipped," and that they "will not be able to accomplish the repairs within ten days from date."[2]

The Tribunal will observe that it was proposed that two kinds of repairs should be made.

The first class did not require the vessel to go into the slip. These included the calking referred to by the author of the Cruise of the Shenandoah,[3] and perhaps also repairs of a general character, which all steam machinery requires after having been run for any length of time, such as refitting of brasses, packing stuffing-boxes, examining and readjusting of working parts, &c., &c. All these repairs could have gone on simultaneously. Such coal as might be allowed

---

[1] Walker to Boggs; Vol. VI, pages 178—9.
[2] Waddell to Francis, Vol. V, page 600; Vol. VI, page 640.
[3] Cruise of the Shenandoah, page 77.

within the construction of the instructions of January 31, 1862, as those instructions were applied to the vessels of the United States, and such supplies as were legally permitted, could also be taken on, and the vessel could be ready to go to sea again in from two to four days after her arrival in port. Or, should it be necessary for the vessel to go into a slip for the purpose of repairing the propeller, this class of repairs might also be going on in the slip, at the same time with the others.

The other class of repairs were those which Langland Brothers & Co. were to report upon—repairs to the propeller. It appears from the report made by these mechanics on the 30th of January, that they founded their estimate upon the report of a diver. Mechanics ordinarily have to depend upon such a report, and to found their estimates upon it. The examination of the propeller of a screw-steamer, and of its bearings below the water-line, is a simple matter, and takes but a short time. It is confined to the stern of the vessel. A practiced expert can go down, satisfy himself of the extent of the injury, and return and report in a few minutes. Had the Governor treated Captain Waddell as Captain Boggs was treated, the examination could easily have been made on the morning of the 26th, and the whole extent of the injury could have been reported to the Governor on the afternoon of the same day within twenty-four hours after the arrival of the vessel in port. Captain Waddell, however, was not required to move so rapidly. He did not send his diver down until the 28th; he did not get the official report of his mechanics until the 30th. Thus he spent five days in doing what could have been done in five hours. There must have been a motive for that delay; the United States find that motive in his necessity to enlist a crew.

The Tribunal will also observe that his own report on the 28th of the extent of his injuries differs from that made by his mechanics on the 30th. He reported that "the composition castings of the propeller-shaft were entirely gone, and the bracings (probably a misprint for "bearings") under water were in the same condition. This was a more serious injury than the one reported by his mechanics two days later, namely, the necessity of giving the shaft a new outer sternbush. The latter would, it is true, require the docking of the ship to admit of the removal of the shaft. But when the ship was once in the slip, the propeller could be easily hoisted, being a movable one;[1] and then the renewal of the lignumvitæ lining, technically known as the sternbush, the only repairs which the experts reported to be necessary, could be completed two or three days after the ship should be on the slip. If the vessel was necessarily longer on the slip she must have received more repairs than are described in the official report of the Langlands, which embraced all for which the permission was granted.

It therefore appears that, on the supposition that the authorities at Melbourne could, under the circumstances, without violating the duty of Great Britain as a neutral, permit the repairs reported by Langlund Brothers & Co. to be made, the Shenandoah should have gone to sea in ten days after her arrival. This estimate gives the extreme time for every requisite step, viz.: one calendar day for the examination of the diver, excluding the day of arrival; three days (the estimate of the Langlands) for putting the vessel in the slip; three days for the repairs by the Langlands; one day for getting her out of the slip; and two days for reloading and getting to sea, which was the time actually taken; but as, during this time, she unwarrantably took on board three hundred tons of coal, this is probably too large an estimate. Instead of requiring these repairs to be completed in ten days, the Melbourne authorities allowed the Shenandoah to stay there twenty-four days. The extra fourteen days were occupied in the recruitment of the forty-three men whom she carried away with her. It is difficult, under the circumstances, to resist the conclusion that the repairs were dawdled along for the purpose of securing the recruits, and that the authorities, to say the least, shut their eyes while this was going on; especially if it be true, as said by Temple, that the Government engineer was on board three or four times

---

[1] Wilson's affidavit, Vol. III, page 325; Vol. VI, page 566.

a day while they were undergoing repairs, and assisted them with his opinion and advice.[1] It is fair to say that this fact is doubted by the Governor of the Colony.[2] If the Government engineer was not there, however, he should have been, in order to see that Waddell was not violating British neutrality.

Leaving Melbourne, the Shenandoah went through the Pacific Ocean to the Arctic Seas, via Behring's Straits, under the instructions issued by Bullock, in Liverpool, for the purpose of destroying the whalers of the United States. How successful she was in her attacks upon these intrepid and daring navigators is shown by the long list of captured vessels, for whose destruction the United States claim compensation.

On the cruise to those seas she used her sails only. After arrival there she commenced steaming on the 25th of June, and "from that time till she left the Arctic seas she made comparatively little use of her sails."[3] Many of the most valuable vessels were destroyed after that time. Temple names, in his affidavit, fifteen that were destroyed after Waddell knew of the suppression of the insurrection.[4] Bullock wrote him a letter, instructing him "to desist from any further destruction of United States property,"[5] and Earl Russell undertook to send the letter "through the British Consuls at the ports where the ship may be expected." It was not until the 17th day of October, 1865, that she ceased to be officially registered as a British vessel. Waddell arrived at Liverpool with the Shenandoah on the 6th of the following November, and wrote Earl Russell that the destructions committed on the 28th of June—when Temple said that he knew of the surrender of Lee—were committed "in ignorance of the obliteration of the Govern-

---

[1] Temple's affidavit, Vol. III, page 481; Vol. V, page 712.
[2] Darling to Cardwell, Vol. III, page 506.
[3] Cruise of the Shenandoah, page 187.
[4] Vol. III, pages 482, 483; Vol. VI, page 709, et seq. This statement by Temple is confirmed by Hathaway's affidavit, Vol. VII, page 95.
[5] Vol. III, page 458; Vol. VI, page 698.

ment." He said that he received his first intelligence on the 2d of August. The author of the Cruise of the Shenandoah says that they received, on the 28th of June, while burning the whalers, the news of the assassination of Mr. Lincoln.[1] This event took place a week after the surrender of Lee. The affidavits of Temple and Nye in Vol. VII indicate still earlier knowledge. It would seem, therefore, that Waddell's statements to Earl Russell could not have been correct.

"The re-appearance of the Shenandoah in British waters" was regarded as "an untoward and unwelcome event." The Times reminded the public that "in a certain sense it was doubtless true that the Shenandoah was built and manned in fraud of British neutrality."[2] Great Britain dealt with the "untoward" question as it had dealt with others during the contest—by evading it. The vessel was delivered to the United States. The men who had been preying upon the commerce of the United States for months without a semblance of authority behind them, most of whom were British subjects, with unmistakable British bearing and speech, were called before an officer of the British Navy to be examined as to their nationality, they understanding in advance that it was a crime for British subjects to have served on the Shenandoah. "Each one stated that he belonged to one or the other of the States of America,"[3] and they were discharged without further inquiry.

On the 28th of December, 1865, Mr. Adams, commenting upon these proceedings, wrote to Earl Clarendon as follows:[4] "I trust it may be made to appear—

"1. That the Sea King did depart from a British port armed with all the means she ever had occasion to use in the course of her cruise against the commerce of the United States; and that no inconsiderable portion of her hostile career was passed while she was still registered as a British vessel, with a British owner, on the official records of the Kingdom.

---

[1] Cruise of the Shenandoah, page 206.
[2] London Times, November 8, 1865; Vol. III, page 449.
[3] Cheek to Paynter, Vol. III, page 505.
[4] Vol. III, page 475.

"2. That the commander had been made fully aware of the suppression of the rebellion the very day before he committed a series of outrages on innocent, industrious, and unarmed citizens of the United States, in the Sea of Okhotsk.

"3. The list of the crew, with all the particulars attending the sources from which the persons were drawn, is believed to be so far substantially correct as to set at rest the pretense of the officer sent on board that there were no British subjects belonging to the vessel."

The United States confidently insist that they have incontestably established the points there claimed by Mr. Adams; and further,

"4. That the Shenandoah was fitted out and armed within British jurisdiction, namely, at London, for the purpose of cruising against the United States; that Great Britain had reasonable ground to believe that such was the case, and did not use due diligence to prevent it.

"5. That she came again within British jurisdiction, where all these facts were open and notorious, and the British authorities exercised no diligence to prevent her departure, but claimed the right to treat her as a commissioned man-of-war, and to permit her to depart as such.

"6. That twice within British jurisdiction she received large recruitments of men, without due diligence being used to prevent it: 1st. At Liverpool, from whence the men were forwarded by the Laurel; and, 2d, at Melbourne.

"7. That she was allowed to make repairs and to receive coal and supplies which were denied to vessels of the United States in similar circumstances."

The subsequent career of the steamer Laurel, which, with the Shenandoah, formed the hostile expedition against the United States, throws additional light on the sincerity of the British neutrality in the case of the Shenandoah. On the 7th of March, 1865, Mr. Adams wrote as follows to Earl Russell:

"I am pained to be obliged once more to call your attention to the proceedings of the vessel called the steamer Laurel.

"This is the vessel concerning which I had the honor to

make a representation, in a note dated the 10th November last, which appears to have proved, in substance, correct.

"Her departure from Liverpool on the 9th October, laden with men and arms destined to be placed on board of the steamer Sea King, her meeting with that vessel at Porto Santo, in the Madeira Islands, her subsequent transfer of her freight to that steamer, which thereupon assumed the name of the Shenandoah, and proceeded to capture and destroy vessels belonging to the people of the United States, are all facts now established by incontestable evidence.

"It now appears that this steamer Laurel, having accomplished her object under British colors, instead of immediately returning to this Kingdom, made her way through the blockade to the port of Charleston, where she changed her register and her name, and assumed to be a so-called Confederate vessel. In this shape she next made her appearance at the port of Nassau as the 'Confederate States.' From that place she cleared, not long since, to go, via Madeira, to the same port of Liverpool, from whence she had originally started.

"It further appears that, notwithstanding the assumption of this new character, this vessel carried out from Nassau a ship mail, made up at the post office of that port, and transported the same to Liverpool. I have the honor to transmit a copy of a letter from the postmaster at that place establishing that fact.

"Under these circumstances, I have the honor to inform your Lordship that I am instructed by my Government to remonstrate against the receipt and clearance with mails of this vessel from Nassau, and to request that such measures may be adopted in regard to her as may prevent her from thus abusing the neutrality of Her Majesty's territory, for the purpose of facilitating the operations of the United States."[1]

To this Earl Russell replied "that Her Majesty's Government are advised, that although the proceedings of the steamer Confederated States, formerly Laurel, may have

---

[1] Vol. III, page 339.

rendered her liable to capture on the high seas by the cruisers of the United States, *she has not, so far as is known, committed any offense punishable by British law.*"[1]

From all these various facts, the United States ask the Tribunal of Arbitration to find and certify as to the Shenandoah, that Great Britain has, by its acts and by its omissions, failed to fulfill its duties set forth in the three rules of the Treaty of Washington, or recognized by the principles of law not inconsistent with such rules. Should the Tribunal exercise the power conferred upon it by the seventh article of the Treaty, to award a sum in gross to be paid to the United States, they ask that, in considering the amount to be awarded, the losses in the destruction of vessels and their cargoes by the Shenandoah, and the expense to which the United States were put in the pursuit of it, may be taken into account.

Summary.

In the course of the long discussions between the two Governments, which followed the close of the insurrection, it became the duty of Mr. Adams to make a summary of the points which he maintained had been established by the United States. This he did in the following language, addressed to Earl Russell:[2]

"It was my wish to maintain—

"1. That the act of recognition by Her Majesty's Government of insurgents as belligerents on the high seas before they had a single vessel afloat was precipitate and unprecedented.

"2. That it had the effect of creating these parties belligerents after the recognition, instead of merely acknowledging an existing fact.

"3. That this creation has been since effected exclusively from the ports of Her Majesty's Kingdom and its dependencies, with the aid and co-operation of Her Majesty's subjects.

---

[1] Vol. III, page 341.   [2] Vol. III, page 533.

SUMMARY OF THE POINTS ESTABLISHED. 287

"4. That during the whole course of the struggle in America, of nearly four years in duration, there has been no appearance of the insurgents as a belligerent on the ocean excepting in the shape of British vessels, constructed, equipped, supplied, manned, and armed in British ports.

"5. That during the same period it has been the constant and persistent endeavor of my Government to remonstrate in every possible form against this abuse of the neutrality of this Kingdom, and to call upon Her Majesty's Government to exercise the necessary powers to put an effective stop to it.

"6. That although the desire of Her Majesty's Ministers to exert themselves in the suppression of these abuses is freely acknowledged, the efforts which they made proved in a great degree powerless, from the inefficiency of the law on which they relied, and from their absolute refusal, when solicited, to procure additional powers to attain the objects.

"7. That, by reason of the failure to check this flagrant abuse of neutrality, the issue from British ports of a number of British vessels, with the aid of the recognition of their belligerent character in all the ports of Her Majesty's dependencies around the globe, has resulted in the burning and destroying on the ocean of a large number of merchant vessels, and a very large amount of property belonging to the people of the United States.

"8. That, in addition to this direct injury, the action of these British built, manned, and armed vessels has had the indirect effect of driving from the sea a large portion of the commercial marine of the United States, and to a corresponding extent enlarging that of Great Britain, thus enabling one portion of the British people to derive an unjust advantage from the wrong committed on a friendly nation by another portion.

"9. That the injuries thus received by a country which has meanwhile sedulously endeavored to perform all its obligations, owing to the imperfection of the legal means at hand to prevent them, as well as the unwillingness to seek for more stringent powers, are of so grave a nature as in reason and justice to constitute a valid claim for reparation and indemnification."

The United States, with confidence, maintain that every point thus asserted by Mr. Adams has been established by the proof hereinbefore referred to. In leaving in the hands of the Tribunal this part of their Case, they think it no impropriety earnestly to call attention to the magnitude of the issues to be decided.

Many a vindictive and bloody war has grown out of less provocation than the United States thus suffered from a nation with which they supposed that they were holding friendly relations. On the 4th of July, 1777, during the war of the American Revolution, Lord Stormont was instructed to say to the French Ministers that "the shelter given to the armed vessels of the rebels, the facility they have of disposing of their prizes by the connivance of the Government, and the conveniences allowed them to refit, are such irrefragable proofs of support, that scarcely more could be done if there was an avowed alliance between France and them, and that we were in a state of war with that Kingdom." He was also directed to say that however desirous of maintaining the peace, His Britannic Majesty could not, "from his respect to his honor and his regard to the interest of his trading subjects, submit to such strong and public instances of support and protection shown to the rebels by a nation that at the same time professes in the strongest terms its desire to maintain the present harmony subsisting between the two Crowns."[1]

The injuries inflicted upon the United States during the insurrection, under the cover of professions of friendship, are well described in this language of the Ministers of George III, except that the insurgents were allowed to burn, instead of assisted to dispose of their prizes. But the United States, although just emerging from a successful war, with all the appliances of destruction in their grasp, preferred to await a better state of feeling in Great Britain, rather than follow the example of that Government in resorting to war. The time came when Her Majesty's Government felt that it would not be derogatory to the elevated position of their Sovereign, to express regret for the escape of the cruisers and for the

---

[1] Vol. III, page 599.

depredations which they committed. The United States, receiving this expression of regret in the spirit in which it was made, stand before this Tribunal of Arbitration to abide its judgment.

If the facts which they bring here constitute, in the opinion of the Tribunal, no just cause for claim against Great Britain, they must bow to the decision. But if, on the other hand, Great Britain shall not be able to explain to their complete satisfaction the charges and the proof which they present, the United States will count upon an award to the full extent of their demand. They feel that it is their duty to insist before this August Body, not only in their own interest, but for the sake of the future peace of the world, that it is not a just performance of the duties of a neutral to permit a belligerent to carry on organized war from its territories against a Power with which the neutral is at peace.

If this Tribunal shall hold that combined operations like those of Bullock, Fraser, Trenholm & Co., Huse, Heyliger, and others, (which in the judgment of the United States constituted an organized war,) are legitimate, their decision will, in the opinion of the United States, lay the foundation for endless dissensions and wars.

If wrongs like those which the United States suffered are held by this Tribunal to be no violation of the duties which one nation owes to another, the rules of the Treaty of Washington can have little effective force, and there will be little inducement for nations in future to adopt the peaceful method of arbitration for the settlement of their differences.

If it was right to furnish the Nashville at Bermuda with a full supply of coal, sufficient to carry her to Southampton, instead of what might be necessary for her to return to Charleston, the United States and the other maritime nations must accept the doctrine in the future.

If there was no violation of international duty in receiving the Sumter at Trinidad, and in supplying her with the fuel necessary to enable her to continue her career of destruction, instead of giving her what was requisite, with her sailing power, to enable her to return to New Orleans or Galveston, it is important that the maritime Powers should know it.

If recognized vessels of war, like the Sumter and the

Georgia, may be lawfully sold in a neutral port during time of war, the United States, as a nation whose normal condition is one of neutrality, accept the doctrine.

If the duties of a neutral in preventing, within its territory, the construction, arming, equipping, or fitting out of vessels by one belligerent, which may be intended to cruise against the other belligerent, or the furnishing of arms or military supplies to such vessel, or the recruitment of men for such belligerent, are to be limited to the exercise of the powers conferred upon the neutral Government by municipal law, the United States, with their extended frontier on both oceans, have more interest than any other maritime Power in recognizing that fact.

If the recognition of belligerency by a neutral, in favor of an organized insurrection, authorizes a so-called Government of insurrectionists to issue commissions, which are to protect vessels that may have violated the sovereignty of the neutral from examination, inquiry, or punishment by the neutral authorities when again within their jurisdiction, the United States, and other nations here represented, must hold themselves at liberty in future to conform to such measure of duty, in that respect, as may be indicated by this Tribunal.

If Georgias, Alabamas, Floridas, and Shenandoahs may be allowed to go out from neutral ports without violations of international duty, to prey upon the commerce of friendly nations; if it be no offense to recruit men for them and to send the recruits to join them in Alars, Bermudas, Bahamas, and Laurels, the United States as a neutral will be relieved, when other States are at war, from a great part of the difficulties they encounter in watching a long line of coast.

If Tallahassees and Chickamaugas may be constructed in neutral territory, without violation of international duty; to serve as it may suit the pleasure of a belligerent, alternately either as blockade-runners or as men-of-war, those maritime nations whose normal condition is one of neutrality need not regret such a doctrine, when viewed, not in the light of principle, but as effecting their pecuniary interests.

And if it be no offense, as in the case of the Retribution, to take a captured cargo into a neutral port, and there to dispose of it with the knowledge and without the interference of the local magistracy, the maritime Powers, knowing that such buccaneering customs are to be permitted, will be the better able to guard against them.

It will depend upon this Tribunal to say whether any or all of these precedents are to be sanctioned and are to stand for future guidance.

The conduct of other nations contrasted with that of Great Britain. The United States, in closing this branch of the Case, desire to call the attention of the Tribunal to the fact that they came out from this long and bloody contest without serious cause of complaint against any nation except Great Britain.

The Executives of other nations issued notices to their citizens or subjects, enjoining upon them to remain neutral in the contest.

Belgium issued a notice on the 25th of June, 1861, warning Belgians against engaging as privateers.[1] The United States had never any cause of complaint in this respect against Belgium.

The Emperor of the French, on the 10th of June, 1861, issued a proclamation commanding his subjects to "maintain a strict neutrality in the struggle entered upon between the Government of the Union and the States which pretended to form a separate confederation."[2] The United States refer to the foregoing recital of the proceedings against Mr Arman's vessels, as a proof of the fidelity with which the Imperial Government maintained the neutrality which it imposed upon its subjects.

The Government of the Netherlands forbade privateers to enter its ports, and warned the inhabitants of the Netherlands and the King's subjects abroad not to accept letters of marque.[3] The United States have no knowledge that these directions were disobeyed.

---

[1] Vol. IV, page 3. [2] Vol. IV, page 4.
[3] Vol. IV, page 6.

The Government of Portugal shut the harbors of the Portuguese dominions against privateers and their prizes.[1] Of this the United States had no complaint to make. At a later period that Government went so far "as to forbid the coaling of any steamer designing to violate the blockade," and to "require a bond to be given, before allowing coals to be furnished at all, that the ship receiving the supply will not run the blockade."[2] When the insurgent iron-clad Stonewall came into Lisbon Harbor in March, 1865, it was ordered to leave in twenty-four hours.[3] The United States bear willing testimony to this honorable conduct of Portugal.

The Prussian Government announced that it would not protect its shipping or its subjects who might take letters of marque, share in privateering enterprises, carry merchandise of war, or forward dispatches.[4] The United States have no reason to suppose that the subjects of the King of Prussia departed from the line of duty thus indicated.

The Russian Government ordered that even "the flag of men-of-war belonging to the seceded States must not be saluted."[5]

Spain followed France in the track of England,[6] but care was taken to avoid, in the Royal Proclamation, the use of the word "belligerents."[7] It has been seen with what fidelity and impartiality the authorities at Cardenas carried out the letter and the spirit of this proclamation, when the Florida arrived there from Nassau, in the summer of 1862.

The Emperor of Brazil required his subjects to observe a strict neutrality; and his Government informed them what acts of the belligerents would forfeit the right of hospitality. It was ordered that "a belligerent who has once violated neutrality shall not be admitted into the ports of the Empire;" and that "vessels which may attempt to violate neutrality

---

[1] Vol. IV, page 7.
[2] Mr. Harvey to Mr. Seward, Diplomatic Correspondence, 1864, part 4, page 296.
[3] Same to same, Diplomatic Correspondence, 1865, part 3, page 109.
[4] Vol. IV, page 8.   [5] Vol. IV, page 9.
[6] Vol. IV, page 10. [7] Vol. IV, page 9.

shall be compelled to leave the maritime territory immediately, and they shall be allowed to procure no supplies." These rules were enforced. The Alabama was refused the hospitality of Brazilian ports in consequence of violations of the neutrality which the Emperor had determined to maintain. When the Tuscaloosa came to St. Catharine's from Simon's Bay, in November, 1863, she was refused supplies and ordered to leave, because she was a tender and prize of the Alabama, and was tainted by the acts of that vessel. The commander of the Shenandoah boarded a vessel between Cardiff and Bahia, opened the manifest, and broke the seal of the Brazilian Consul: for this act his vessel, and any vessel which he might command, were excluded from Brazilian ports.[1] The Imperial Government, in all these proceedings, appeared desirous of asserting its sovereignty, and of maintaining an honest neutrality.

Mr. Fish, in one of his first utterances after he became Secretary of State, expressed the sense which the United States entertained of this difference between the conduct of Great Britain and that of other nations. "There were other Powers," he said, "that were contemporaneous with England in similar concessions; but it was in England only that that concession was supplemented by acts causing direct damage to the United States. The President is careful to make this discrimination, because he is anxious, as much a possible, to simplify the case, and to bring into view these subsequent acts, which are so important in determining the question between the two countries."[2]

---

[1] Vol. VI, page 588.
[2] Mr. Fish to Mr. Motley, May 15, 1869, Vol. VI, page 4.

PART VI.

THE TRIBUNAL SHOULD AWARD A SUM IN GROSS TO THE UNITED STATES.

Offer of the American Commissioners in the Joint High Commission. In the opening conference of the Joint High Commission relating to the Alabama Claims, the American Commissioners stated the nature of the demands of the United States. They said that there were "extensive direct losses in the capture and destruction of a large number of vessels with their cargoes, and in the heavy national expenditures in the pursuit of the cruisers, and indirect injury in the transfer of a large part of the American commercial marine to the British flag, in the enhanced payments of insurance, in the prolongation of the war, and in the addition of a large sum to the cost of the war and the suppression of the rebellion." They further said that the amount of the direct losses to individuals "which had thus far been presented, amounted to about fourteen millions of dollars, without interest, which amount was liable to be greatly increased by claims which had not been presented;" and that the direct loss to the Government "in the pursuit of cruisers could easily be ascertained by certificates of Government accounting officers." They added that "in the hope of an amicable settlement, no estimate was made of the indirect losses, without prejudice, however, to the right of indemnification on their account in the event of no such settlement being made."[1]

---

[1] Ante, pages 2.

A SUM IN GROSS SHOULD BE AWARDED. 295

Rejection of the offer by the British Commissioners. Terms of the submission by the Treaty.
The British Commissioners declined to make the "amicable settlement" which was proposed on the part of the United States. The Joint High Commission then entered into negotiations which resulted in an agreement "in order to remove and adjust all complaints and claims on the part of the United States, and to provide for the speedy settlement of such claims," that all the claims "growing out of the acts committed by the several vessels which have given rise to the claims generically known as the Alabama Claims," should be referred to this Tribunal of Arbitration. It was further agreed that this Tribunal, should it find that Great Britain had, by any act or omission, failed to fulfill any of the duties set forth in the rules in the sixth article of the Treaty, or recognized by principles of International Law not inconsistent with such rules, might then "proceed to award a sum in gross to be paid by Great Britain to the United States for all the claims referred to it."

General statement of the claims.
The claims as stated by the American Commissioners may be classified as follows:

1. The claims for direct losses growing out of the destruction of vessels and their cargoes by the insurgent cruisers.

2. The national expenditures in the pursuit of those cruisers.

3. The loss in the transfer of the American commercial marine to the British flag.

4. The enhanced payments of insurance.

5. The prolongation of the war and the addition of a large sum to the cost of the war and the suppression of the rebellion.

So far as these various losses and expenditures grew out of the acts committed by the several cruisers, the United States are entitled to ask compensation and remuneration therefore before this Tribunal.

Claims growing out of destruction of vessels and cargoes.
The claims for direct losses growing out of the destruction of vessels and their cargoes may be further subdivided into: 1. Claims for destruction of vessels and property of the Government of the

United States. 2. Claims for the destruction of vessels and property under the flag of the United States. 3. Claims for damages or injuries to persons, growing out of the destruction of each class of vessels. In the accompanying Volume, VII, the Tribunal will find ample data for determining the amount of damage which should be awarded, in consequence of the injuries inflicted by reason of the destruction of vessels or property, whether of the Government or of private persons.

Government vessels. The Government vessels destroyed were of two classes—those under the charge of the Treasury Department, and those in charge of the Navy Department. The Tribunal of Arbitration will find in Volume VII detailed statements of this class of losses, certified by the Secretary of the Navy, or by the Secretary of the Treasury, as the case may be.

The United States reserve, however, as to this and as to all other classes of claims, the right to present further claims and further evidence in support of these and such further claims, for the consideration of this Tribunal; and also similar rights as to all classes of claims, in case this Tribunal shall determine not to award a sum in gross to the United States.

Merchant vessels. The United States, with this reservation, present a detailed statement of all the claims which have as yet come to their knowledge, for the destruction of vessels and property by the cruisers. The statement shows the cruiser which did the injury, the vessel destroyed, the several claimants for the vessel and for the cargo, the amounts insured upon each, and all the other facts necessary to enable the Tribunal to reach a conclusion as to the amount of the injury committed by the cruiser. It also shows the nature and character of the proof placed in the hands of the United States by the sufferers. The originals of the documents referred to are on file in the Department of State at Washington, and can be produced if desired. The United States only ask a reasonable notice, giving them sufficient opportunity to produce them.

Injuries to persons. It is impossible, at present, for the United States to present to the Tribunal a detailed statement of the damages or injuries to persons growing out of the destruction of each class of vessels. Every vessel had its officers and its crew, who were entitled to the protection of the flag of the United States, and to be included in the estimate of any sum which the Tribunal may see fit to award. It will not be difficult, from the data which are furnished, to ascertain the names and the tonnage of the different vessels destroyed, and to form an estimate of the number of hardy, but helpless, seamen who were thus deprived of their means of subsistence, and to determine what aggregate sum it would be just to place in the hands of the United States on that account. It cannot be less than hundreds of thousands, and possibly millions of dollars.

Expenditures in pursuit of the cruisers. The United States present to the Tribunal a detailed statement of the amount of the national expenditure in the pursuit of the insurgent cruisers, verified in the manner proposed by the American members of the Joint High Commission. The aggregate of this amount is several millions of dollars.

Transfer of vessels to the British flag. The United States ask the Tribunal of Arbitration to estimate the amount which ought to be paid to them for the transfer of the American commercial marine to the British flag, in consequence of the acts of the rebel cruisers.

On the 13th of May, 1864, Mr. Cobden warned the House of Commons of the great losses which the United States were suffering in this respect. He said:[1]

"You have been carrying on hostilities from these shores against the people of the United States, and have been inflicting an amount of damage on that country greater than would be produced by many ordinary wars. It is estimated that the loss sustained by the capture and burning of American vessels has been about $15,000,000, or nearly £3,000,000 sterling. But that is a small part of the injury which has been inflicted on the American marine. We have rendered the rest of her vast mercantile property for the present valueless. Under the system of free trade, by which the com-

---

[1] Hansard, 3d series, Vol. 175, pp. 496—500; Vol V, page 589.

merce of the world is now so largely carried on, if you raise the rate of insurance on the flag of any Maritime Power you throw the trade into the hands of its competitors, because it is no longer profitable for merchants or manufacturers to employ ships to carry freights when those vessels become liable to war risks. I have here one or two facts which I should like to lay before the honorable and learned gentleman, in order to show the way in which this has been operating. When he has heard them, he will see what a cruel satire it is to say that our laws have been found sufficient to enforce our neutrality. I hold in my hand an account of the foreign trade of New York for the quarter ending June 30, 1860, and also for the quarter ending June 30, 1863, which is the last date up to which a comparison is made. I find that the total amount of the foreign trade of New York for the first-mentioned period was $92,000,000, of which $62,000,000 were carried in American bottoms and $30,000,000 in foreign. This state of things rapidly changed as the war continued, for it appears that for the quarter ending June 30, 1863, the total amount of the foreign trade of New York was $88,000,000, of which amount $23,000,000 were carried in American vessels and $65,000,000 in foreign, the change brought about being that while in 1860 two-thirds of the commerce of New York were carried on in American bottoms, in 1863 three-fourths were carried on in foreign bottoms. You see, therefore, what a complete revolution must have taken place in the value of American shipping; and what has been the consequence? That a very large transfer has been made of American shipping to English owners, because the proprietors no longer found it profitable to carry on their business. A document has been laid on the table which gives us some important information on this subject. I refer to an account of the number and tonnage of United States vessels which have been registered in the United Kingdom and in the ports of British North America between the years 1858, and 1863, both inclusive. It shows that the transfer of United States shipping to English capitalists in each of the years comprised in that period was as follows:

"In 1858, vessels 33, tonnage 12,684.
"In 1859, vessels 49, tonnage 21,308.
"In 1860, vessels 41, tonnage 13,638.
"In 1861, vessels 126, tonnage 71,673.
"In 1862, vessels 135, tonnage 64,578.
"In 1863, vessels 348, tonnage 252,579.[1]

"I am told that this operation is now going on as fast as ever. Now, I hold this to be the most serious aspect of the question of our relations with America. I care very little about what newspapers may write, or orators may utter, on one side or the other. We may balance off an inflammatory speech from an honorable member here against a similar speech made in the Congress at Washington. We may pair off a leading article published in New York against one published in London, but little consequence, I suspect, would be attached to either. The two countries, I hope, would discount these incendiary articles, or these incendiary harangues, at their proper value. But what I do fear in the relations between these two nations of the same race, is the heaping up of a gigantic material grievance, such as we are now accumulating by the transactions connected with these cruisers; because there is a vast amount of individual suffering, personal wrong, and personal rancor arising out of this matter, and that in a country where popular feeling rules in public affairs. I am not sure that any legislation can meet this question. What with the high rate of Insurance, what with these captures, and what with the rapid transfer of tonnage to British capitalists, you have virtually made valueless that vast property. Why, if you had gone and helped the Confederates by bombarding all the accessible sea-port towns of America, a few lives might have been lost which, as it is, have not been sacrificed, but you could hardly have done more injury in destroying property than you have done by these few cruisers."

Enhanced rates of insurance. With the reservations already stated, the United States present the amount, so far as

---

[1] In the year 1864 one hundred and six vessels were transferred to the British flag, with an aggregate tonnage of 92,052 tons.

it has come to their knowledge, of the enhanced payments of insurance, caused by the acts of the insurgent cruisers. All of these cruisers came from England; and should the Tribunal find Great Britain responsible for the injuries caused by their acts, it cannot be denied that the war risk was the result of their dispatch from British ports. The amount of this injury, so far as yet known to the United States, appears in Vol. VII.

Prolongation of the war. It is impossible for the United States to determine, it is perhaps impossible for any one to estimate with accuracy, the vast injury which these cruisers caused in prolonging the war.

The great exertions which were made in the months of April, May, and June, 1863, to secure arms and ammunition for immediate use in Richmond have already been noted. Letter followed letter in rapid succession, urging Walker to forward the desired articles without delay. The energetic measures which Walker took to obtain coal to enable him to comply with his instructions have been commented on. The insurrection was at that moment gathering itself up for a blow which was intended to be final and decisive.

On the 29th of April in that year Grant, having taken an army past the fortifications of Vicksburg, began the attack upon Grand Gulf, and from that day conducted his operations with such vigor, that, by the 21st of May he had defeated the armies of the insurgents in five pitched battles, and had commenced the investment of Vicksburg. In the Atlantic States the fortunes of the United States had been less favorable. The army of the Potomac under Hooker had met with a decided reverse at Chancellorsville, and was resting inactive after the failure.

The military authorities at Richmond, having received the supplies which Walker had forwarded, selected this moment for a blow in Pennsylvania, which was intended at once to relieve Vicksburg, and decide the contest. History tells how utterly they failed. After three days of bloody fighting, Lee retired from Gettysburg discomfited. The same day Grant entered Vicksburg and opened the Mississippi.

The 4th day of July, 1863, saw the aggressive force on

hind of the insurrection crushed. From that day its only hope lay in prolonging a defense until, by the continuance of the permitted violations of British neutrality by the insurgents, the United States should become involved in a war with Great Britain. The insurgents had, at that time, good reason to look for that result. The Florida, the Alabama, and the Georgia had left British ports for the purpose of carrying on war against the United States, and were, nevertheless, received with unusual honors and hospitality in all the colonial ports of Great Britain. Only ten days before the battle of Gettysburg, the judge who presided at the trial of the Alexandra had instructed the jury that no law or duty of Great Britain had been violated in the construction and dispatch of the Alabama. About three months before that time Her Majesty's Government had decided that they would not recommend Parliament to enact a more effective law for the preservation of neutrality. Laird was constructing the rams in Liverpool under the existing interpretation of the law, and the British Government was refusing to interfere with them. The Chancellor of the Exchequer, five days before the battle of Gettysburg, had declared in the House of Commons, speaking not individually, but in the plural, "We do not believe that the restoration of the American Union by force is attainable." Under these circumstances the insurgents made great exertions to keep the Florida, the Alabama, and the Georgia afloat, and to stimulate their officers and crews to renewed destruction of the commerce of the United States. They counted, not without reason, upon inflaming popular passion in the United States by the continuance of these acts, until the people should force the Government into a retaliation upon Great Britain, the real author of their woes. In pursuance of this policy they withdrew their military forces within the lines of Richmond, and poured money into Bullock's hands to keep afloat and increase his British-built navy, and to send it into the most distant seas in pursuit of the merchant marine of the United States.

Thus the Tribunal will see that, after the battle of Gettysburg, the offensive operations of the insurgents were conducted only at sea, through the cruisers; and observing that the war was prolonged for that purpose, will be able to determine whether Great Britain ought not, in equity, to reimburse to the United States the expenses thereby entailed upon them.

On all these points evidence is presented which will enable the Tribunal to ascertain and determine the amount of the several losses and injuries complained of. To the amount *Interest claimed to the date of payment.* thus shown should be added interest upon the claims to the day when the award is payable by the terms of the Treaty, namely, twelve months after the date of the award. The usual legal rate of interest in the city of New York, where most of the claims of individuals are held, is seven per cent. per annum. In some of the States it is greater: in few of them less. The United States make a claim for interest at that rate. The computation of the interest should be made from an average day to be determined. The United States suggest the 1st day of July, 1863, as the most equitable day.

Reasons why a gross sum should be awarded. They earnestly hope that the Tribunal will exercise the power conferred upon it, to award a sum in gross to be paid by Great Britain to the United States. The injuries of which the United States complain were committed many years since. The original wrongs to the sufferers by the acts of the insurgent cruisers have been increased by the delay in making reparation. It will be unjust to impose further delay, and the expense of prosecuting claims to another Tribunal, if the evidence which the United States have the honor to present for the consideration of these Arbitrators shall prove to be sufficient to enable them to determine what sum in gross would be a just compensation to the United States for the injuries and losses of which they complain.

Above all it is in the highest interest of the two great Powers which appear at this bar, that the causes of difference which have been hereinbefore set forth should be speedily and forever set at rest. The United States entertain a confident expectation that Her Majesty's Goverment will concur with them in this opinion.

INDEX.

	Page.
ADAMS, CHARLES FRANCIS:	
day of probable arrival in London known in advance	31
arrives in London	32
comments on negotiations regarding declaration of Paris	45
complains of doings at Nassau	143
complains of insurgent operations in British jurisdiction	151
says insurgent government is interested in blockade-running	176—178
further representations as to blockade-running	180
representations as to the Honduras	180
notifies Earl Russel that sale of Sumter will not be recognized	203
informs Earl Russel of the character of the Florida	210
brings to Earl Russell's notice treatment of Florida in colonies	226
calls Earl Russell's attention to the Alabama	230
sends Earl Russell affidavits regarding Alabama	234
confers with Earl Russell about the Alabama	235
complains to Earl Russell of the Georgia	249
complains to Earl Russell of enlistments for the Georgia	251, 252
complains to Earl Russell of the Georgia	254, 255
complains to Earl Russell about the Shenandoah	265, 283
complains to Earl Russell about the Laurel	284
ADAMS, JOHN QUINCY:	
correspondence regarding claims of Portugal	84— 87
ADMIRALTY AND COLONIAL INSTRUCTIONS:	
of January 31, 1862, unfriendly to United States	141
abstract of those instructions	144
AGRIPPINA, THE:	
takes stores and coal to Alabama at Terceira	237
takes coal to same at Martinique	240

	Page.
AJAX, THE:	
inquires as to	196
ALABAMA, THE:	
short sketch of	150
Lord Russell thinks it a scandal to British laws	158
discription of	229
built for Insurgent man-of-war	229
contracted for by Bullock	229
crew of, wages paid by Fraser, Trenholm & Co	230
customs officers report her a man-of-war	231
attention of Liverpool collector called to her	232
he sees nothing wrong in her	232
Mr. R. P. Collier's opinion taken as to	232
affidavits as to character of, obtained and officially communicated to British government	233
these affidavits remain a week unacted upon	234
orders then given to detain	234
orders revealed and Alabama escapes	235
goes to Moelfra Bay and the Hercules follows next day with crew	236
gross inefficiency, or worse, of the collector	236
the Alabama proceeds to Terceira	237
receives arms, stores, and coal from Bahama and Agrippina	237
was adapted for warlike purposes when she left Liverpool	238
was fitted out there, at least in part	239
Semmes's opinion of the vessel	239
she receives coal from Agrippina at Martiniquo	240
is received at Jamaica as a man-of-war	240
goes to Brazil and the Cape of Good Hope	240
Mr. Adams complains to Earl Russell	240
her tender, the Tuscaloosa, (see *Tuscaloosa*)	242, 245
she coals at Singapore	242
coals again at Table Bay	242
is sunk off Cherbourg by the Kearsarge	243
reasons why Great Britain is liable for her acts	244
ALAR, THE:	
takes arms and stores to the Georgia	249
ALEXANDRA, THE:	
ruling of the court in the case of	98
seizure, trial, and acquittal	160
ruling of the court in, emasculated the foreign enlistment act of 1819	162
AMENDMENTS:	
of municipal laws may be asked by a belligerent	83
of law of 1819 asked by United States and refused	156, 156

AMPHION, THE:	Page
Inquiries as to .	186
ARCHER, THE:	
career of	228
ARMAN. (See *Bullock; France*.)	
when arming a vessel is a violation of neutrality.	87
should be prevented by due diligence	130
AYLIFFE:	
views as to diligence and negligence. . . note	92
BAHAMA:	
takes out Florida's armament	210
arrival at Nassau	212
arms and crew from, for Alabama	237
BARBADOES:	
a base of hostile operations	224
DARING, THOMAS:	
speech on the Georgia	252
BELGIUM:	
course of the government of, contrasted with that of the British government	291
BELLIGERENTS, (see *Blockade; Russell*:)	
insurgents recognized as	25
recognition determined upon before May 1, 1861 .	27
France consulted as to recognition	28
answer of the French government	29
President's proclamation not then received	29
privateering of, legalized by Queen's proclamation	32
right to issue such proclamation not denied	35
it was an unfriendly act	36
and issued with an unfriendly purpose	36
may ask to have defective neutrality laws amended	88
BENJAMIN, JUDAH P.:	
sends agent of insurgent war department to Nassau	138
BERMUDA:	
(steamship) runs blockade with arms, &c	136
(island) well adapted as a depot of insurgent supplies	138
an insurgent depot established there	147
BERNARD, MR. MONTAGUE:	
computes amount of cotton in 1861 . . . . note	135
statement regarding Fraser, Trenholm & Co. . note	136
describes Nassau . . . . note	138
describes the Alexandra . . . . note	160
gives list of vessels detained by Great Britain	185
his criticism on Mr. Fish's dispatch not sustained	187
his statement concerning the Florida . . . . note	216
his statement as to prosecutions for offenses against foreign enlistment act	251

	Page
BLACKSTONE, SIR WILLIAM:	
defines extent and force of law of nations	71
BLOCKADE:	
notice of by proclamation	24
proclamation of, when news of received in England	25
an imperfect copy submitted to law officers for opinion	27
BLOCKADE-RUNNERS:	
general character of determined by insurgent government	138
converted into men-of-war, and *vice versa*	260
BLOCKADE-RUNNING:	
operations in 1862	146
operations in 1863	171
insurgent government interested in	174
complaints thereof to British government	176
answer that it is no offense	176
further proof of insurgent interest in	178
BLUNTSCHLI, DR.:	
definition of neutrality	73
criticism on the Alabama	105
BRAZIL:	
course of the government of, contrasted with that of the government of Great Britain	292
BRIGHT, MR.:	
views as to the Queen's proclamation	35
speech of, March 13, 1865	51
BULLOCK, JAMES DUNWOODY:	
sent to England by the insurgents	134
arrives there in the summer of 1861	149
has an office with Fraser, Trenholm & Co	149
contracts for Florida and Alabama	149, 229
superintends construction of rams	162
contracts for construction of men-of-war in France	166
remittances to	168
writes Waddell to stop destruction by Shenandoah	282
BURDEN OF PROOF:	
thrown upon Great Britain to show that it exercised diligence	200
CAIRNS, LORD:	
definition of due diligence	96
comment on the word "escape"	note 133
CALVO:	
collects authorities defining neutrality	74
CAMPBELL, LORD:	
views as to effect of Queen's proclamation	33
was Lord Chancellor when proclamation issued	57

INDEX. 307

	Page
CANNING, MR.:	
his opinion regarding conduct of United States as a neutral	62
CAPE TOWN, (see *Tuscaloosa:*)	
Alabama at	242
Georgia at	252
CHICKAMAUGA:	
description of and her career	260
shifts from blockade-runner to man-of-war	260
reasons why Great Britain is liable for acts of	261
CLAIMS OF THE UNITED STATES:	
general statement of, by American commissioners	2, 295
rejection of, by British commissioners	3, 295
detailed statement of, where to be found and should be met by award of a gross sum	295, 302
CLARENCE, THE:	
career of	228
COAL, (see *Alabama; Georgia; Florida; Shenandoah:*)	
great need of insurgents of, at Bermuda, in 1863	173
what is a just rule regarding supplies of . . . note	204
permission refused to United States to deposit at Nassau	206
COCKBURN, SIR ALEXANDER:	
charge to jury in Highatt's case	248
COBDEN, RICHARD:	
says Great Britain has recognized duty to detain vessels coming within its jurisdiction	100, 102
comments on loss of mercantile marine of United States	297
COLLIER, R. P.:	
solicitor general in 1863, and now attorney general	232
his opinions in the Alabama matter	232, 233
COMMISSION:	
as man-of-war, effect of on offending vessel	125
how regarded by France, Great Britain, Spain, and Portugal	129
COMMON LAW OF ENGLAND:	
international law is part of	35, 70
COMPENSATION FOR INJURIES:	
when it should be made	82, 104
CONFEDERATE STATES. (See *Insurrection.*)	
CONNECTICUT.	
repairs refused to, at Barbadoes	224, 278
CONTRABAND OF WAR:	
a ship constructed in a neutral port for the use of.	
a belligerent not to be confounded with	119
opinion of Ortolan, as to	120

20*

	Page
CONTRABAND OF WAR.	
opinion of Heffter, as to	121
opinion of Chief Justice Marshall, as to	124
dealings in, in what the trade at Nassau differed from	142
fraudulently cleared at Nassau for St. John's	146
COTTON:	
furnished means for carrying on the war	134
amount unexported in April, 1861 . . . note	135
CRIMEAN WAR:	
Course of Great Britain toward Prussia during	63
DACOTAH, THE:	
treatment of at Bermuda	221
DALLAS, MR.:	
interview with Lord John Russell, April 9, 1861	24
interview with same, May 1, 1861	25
DAVIS, JEFFERSON, (see *Insurrection:*)	
chosen president of insurgent government	10
his speech acknowledging the same	10
DEPOSIT OF OFFENSE:	
cannot be made fraudulently	129, 131
DILIGENCE:	
what is due	91
correlative with negligence	91
necessary extent of, in order to escape responsibility	92
definition of term due diligence	97
duty of a neutral to exercise	130, 131
abandonment of, in advance by Great Britain	159, 199
DROUYN DE LHUYS:	
his note to Mr. Dayton, concerning iron-clads	166
DUDLEY, CONSUL:	
his energetic action regarding the Alabama	232
ENGLAND. (See *Great Britain.*)	
EQUIPPING:	
when equipping a vessel is an offense	97
defined in the Alexandra case	99
defined in the British act of 1870 . . . note	99
should be prevented by due diligence	130
EVIDENCE, (see *Treaty of Washington:*)	
of the United States, how cited and arranged	14
FAWCETT, PRESTON & Co.:	
contract for the Florida	149, 208
FISH, MR.:	
his instructions to Mr. Motley	187, 203
the allegations in those instructions sustained	187
contrasts the course of Great Britain with that of other powers	203

INDEX.   309

	Page
FITTING OUT:	
of a vessel, when a violation of duties of a neutral should be prevented by due diligence	97
	131
FLORIDA, THE:	
construction of, advanced in November, 1861	149
sketch of proceedings as to	150
money sent to Nassau for, through J. Fraser & Co	153
proceedings at Nassau as to	153
Lord Russell thinks it a scandal to British laws	158
Bullock makes contract for	208
coals at Liverpool and registers as a British vessel	209
armament for, shipped in the Bahama	209
clears for Palermo and Jamaica	211
customs officers report to be a man-of-war	211
arrives at Nassau	211
proceedings against, at Nassau	212
complaints as to, disregarded	214
civil authorities neglect duty in proceedings against	215
judge disregards law and evidence in decision as to	217
crew enlisted for, at Nassau	218
clearance of, for St. John's a fraud	218
receives arms and stores in British waters	218
attempts to elude Spanish laws and fails	220
enters and leaves Mobile	220
coals and provisions in excessive quantities at Nassau	220
receives fresh supplies at Barbadoes in one month thereafter	223
protest of Admiral Wilkes as to	223
receives repairs at Bermuda	224
goes to Brest	225
receives crew, armament, and machinery from Liverpool	225
receives repairs and supplies at Bermuda	226
these repairs of, and supplies excessive	226
termination of cruise at Bahia	227
career of tenders of	228
reasons why Great Britain is liable for acts of	228
FOREIGN ENLISTMENT ACT OF 1819:	
is founded on the United States laws	62
intended to aid in performances of international duties	63
duties recognized by it	65
commission to revise	67
report of commissioners as to	68
object of proposed commission	69
inefficiency of the act	155
propositions for amendment of	156, 157
declined by Great Britain	156, 157

	Page
FOREIGN ENLISTMENT ACT OF 1819:	
emasculated by ruling in Alexandra case	160
FOREIGN ENLISTMENT ACT OF 1870:	
provisions of	69
judicial construction of	69
its object, to enable Great Britain to fulfill international duties	69
FRANCE:	
joint action of, invited and secured	24
how regards the effect of a commission on a cruiser illegally fitted out	129
detains vessels constructed by Arman	106
course of, contrasted with Great Britain's	291
FRASER, TRENHOLM & Co.:	
firm of, when founded in Liverpool	135
treasury depositaries insurgents	136
insurgent remittances to Bullock through	168
supply Walker with coal at Bermuda	174
pay wages of Alabama crew	230
GENET, (see *Washington:*)	
commissions French privateers in United States in 1793	76
Jefferson's rebuke of	77
GEORGIA, THE:	
sketch of career	159
built for insurgents, description of	246
crew for, engaged and shipped in Liverpool	247
registered as a British vessel	247
armed from the Alar	249
negligence of British government as to	250
complaints of enlistments for	251
returns to Liverpool	252
her career sketched by Mr. Thomas Baring	252
goes into dock at Liverpool	255
captured by the Niagara	255
reasons why Great Britain liable for acts of	255
GEORGIANA, THE:	
inquiries as to	185
GETTYSBURG:	
preparations for the battle of	166, 173
GLADIATOR, THE:	
insurgents contract in London to purchase	139
arrives in Nassau with arms and munitions of war	139
gets permission to break bulk and transship	140
GLADSTONE, RIGHT HON. W. E.:	
declines to consider effect of Queen's proclamation on privateering	37

INDEX.   311

	Page
GLADSTONE, RIGHT HON. W. E.:	
speech of October 7, 1862	52, 132
speech of June 30, 1863	55
GRAN PARA, THE:	
opinion of the court in the case of	124, 126
GRANVILLE, LORD:	
definition of due diligence	96
GREAT BRITAIN, (see *United States; Crimean war:*)	
friendly relations of, with United States before 1860	15
various treaties with	15, 16, 17
early informed of views of Mr. Lincoln's Government	22
joint action of, with France	24
invitation of, for such joint action unfriendly	24
law of nations part of law of	54, 70
conduct in Trent affair	47
cabinet of, personally unfriendly to United States	55
people of, with some exceptions, unfriendly	57
possible reasons for such unfriendliness	58
action of, influenced by it	60
its neutrality laws	64–70
proclamation of its neutrality	32, 73
instructions to officials of, during insurrection	75
minister of, intervenes against course of Genet	77
reply of Mr. Jefferson to	77
duties recognized in its correspondence with United States	84
branches of insurgent government established in	148
admiralty instructions of, unfriendly to the United States	187
the base of the insurgent naval operations	194
the arsenal of the insurgents	194
the systematic operations of the insurgents is a violation of its international duties	195
its neutrality partial and insincere	196
hostile and unfriendly acts tolerated in	196
abandons all diligence in advance	198
confidential instructions of, supposed to conflict with published instructions of January 31, 1862	271
course of, contrasted with the course of other Powers	283
GROSS SUM:	
reasons for awarding a, to the United States	2 294
HAMMOND, MR.:	
British minister to United States in 1793	77
complains of acts of Mr. Genet	77
receives Mr. Jefferson's reply	77
HARDWICK, LORD:	
views as to privateering	31

HAUTEFEUILLE:
  definition of neutrality 74
  his views regarding construction of a vessel of war
    on belligerent account in neutral territory. 105
HAWK, THE:
  a blockade-runner, inquiries as to 185
HECTOR, THE:
  built for Great Britain 185
HEFFTER:
  on contraband of war and the illegal construction of
    ships of war. 121
HEYLIGER, LEWIS:
  appointed agent at Nassau for disposal of insurgent
    cotton, and for shipment of arms and supplies. . 139
  has confidential relations with colonial authorities . 141
  operations of, in 1862, reviewed 147
  takes charge of Florida and Bahama at Nassau . . 211
HERCULES, THE, (see *Alabama:*)
  inquiries as to 186
HICKLEY, CAPTAIN, R. N.:
  his opinion of the Florida at Nassau 212
HUSE, CALEB:
  sent to England by the insurgents 134
  ships arms and munitions thence in 1861 136
  ordered to ship purchases to West India Islands. . 145
  operations of, in 1862, reviewed 147
INSURGENTS:
  government interested in blockade-running. 176
  make Great Britain the base of their naval operations 194
INSURRECTION, (see *Belligerents:*)
  secession of South Carolina and other States . . . 18
  election of president and vice-president 19
  a large party in the South opposed to 20
  letters of marque authorized 24
  would have succumbed earlier but for aid from Great
    Britain 195
INTERNATIONAL, THE:
  decision as to under foreign enlistment act of 1871 69
INTERNATIONAL LAW:
  a part of the common law of England 34, 70
IRON CLADS, (see *Lairds' rams:*)
  insurgents' contract for six, in 1862 151
JACQUEMYNS. (See *Rolin.*)
JAMAICA:
  the Alabama at 240
JAY'S TREATY. (See *United States.*)

	Page
JEFFERSON, MR.:	
reply to Mr. Hammond's representations	77
his views of the duty of a neutral nation	80
JOINT HIGH COMMISSION:	
meeting at Washington	1
protocol of conferences	2
JONES & CO.:	
ship crew for Georgia in Liverpool	247
trial of members of, before Sir Alexander Cockburn	248
KLINGENDEN, M. G. & Co.:	
connected with Fraser, Trenholm & Co . . . note	202
purchase the Sumter at Gibraltar	202
and pay the wages of Alabama crew . . . . note	202
LAIRD, JOHN:	
speech of, April 27, 1863	53
& Son's contract for Alabama	149
and accompany her as far as the buoy when she sails	236
LAIRDS' RAMS:	
contract for and construction	162
various representations by Mr. Adams, as to	164
Lord Russell refuses to interfere with	164, 165
the seizure and detention of, not an abandonment of previous lax rule by British government	165
LAUREL, THE:	
takes arms and crew to Shenandoah	263
Mr. Adams complains of	284
LEWIS, SIR GEORGE CORNWALL:	
says a proclamation will be issued by the Queen	31
opinion as to the duties of neutrals	34
LINCOLN, PRESIDENT. (See *United States; Blockade:*)	
elected President	18
inaugurated	22
convenes Congress, and calls out militia	24
LIVERPOOL:	
branches of insurgent government established at	136
collector of, notified as to Alabama	232, 233
LOUISA ANN FANNY, THE:	
inquiries as to	186
LYNDHURST, LORD:	
views as to law of England and duties of neutrals	34
MAFFITT, COMMANDER:	
arrives in Nassau	140
sends to Bullock men discharged from Florida	168
ships crew for Florida at Nassau	218
MANSFIELD, LORD:	
opinion in case of Russian ambassador	71

	Page
MARSHALL, CHIEF JUSTICE:	
opinion in the Gran Para case. 124,	126
on the effect of a commission upon a man-of-war .	126
MAURY, THE BARK:	
seized by request of British minister at Washington	81
seizure without cause and discharged	81
MELBOURNE. (See *Shenandoah*.)	
MERCANTILE TRADING COMPANY;	
form partnership with insurgent government	174
MONROE, JAMES:	
correspondence regarding claims of Portugal	83
MUNICIPAL LAWS:	
designed to aid in performance of international duty	62
international obligation not dependent upon them 62,	130
an evidence of the nation's sense of its duties . . .	62
neutral bound to enforce	130
belligerent may require enforcement of	130
and enactment of new, if existing laws insufficient .	130
Great Britain held legal proof of violation of, to be necessary before its action as a neutral could be required	232
MUNICIPAL PROCLAMATION:	
the United States had a right to expect the enforcement of.	81
NASHVILLE, THE:	
escapes from Charleston	206
receives excessive supply of coal at Bermuda . . .	206
burns the Harvey Birch	207
arrives at Southampton	207
proceeds to Bermuda and coals there	207
reasons why Great Britain should be held responsible for acts of.	207
NASSAU:	
well adapted for a depot of insurgent supplies . . .	138
made an insurgent depot and base of operations, note 138,	139
Mr. Adams complains of, to Lord Russell	143
made depot for quartermaster's stores	175
civil authorities of, act in interest of insurgents . .	214
NETHERLANDS:	
course of government of, contrasted with that of Great Britain	291
NEUTRALITY:	
definitions of, by Phillimore, Bluntschli, Hautefeuille and Lord Stowell 73,	74
duty to observe	120
failure to observe as to San Jacinto and Honduras .	180

INDEX. 315

	Page
NEUTRALITY LAWS, (see *Foreign Enlistment Act:*)
  of United States enacted at request of Great Britain ... 80
NEUTRALS, (see *Paris*; *Belligerents*; *Treaty of Washington:*)
  duties of, as defined in the treaty of Washington . 9, 32
  duties and rights of, as defined in the declaration of
    Paris 39
  animus of the sole criterion according to Lord Westbury ... 59
  bound to enforce municipal laws in belligerent's
    favor 63, 130
NEUTRALS:
  duties of, recognized in the Queen's proclamation . 73, 74
  bound to enforce municipal proclamations ... 81, 130
  bound to use all the means in its power to prevent
    violations of their neutrality 82, 131
  when liable to make compensation 82, 131
  should amend defective neutrality laws when requested
    by belligerents 88, 130
  when should institute proceedings to prevent violations
    of neutrality 88
  should detain offending vessels coming within their
    jurisdiction 100, 130
  should not permit their ports to be made the base
    of hostile operations 102, 131
  summary of the duties of, as applicable to this case 129--131
  obligations of, as to an offending vessel, not dis-
    charged by commission as man-of-war 131
  nor by evasion of municipal law 131
  when they may not set up a deposit of the offense 131
NORTH:
  sent to England by the insurgents 134
  Miss, names the Virginia, (or Georgia) 246
ORETO. (See *Florida*.)
ORTOLAN, THEODORE:
  views of, as to construction of men-of-war for belli-
    gerents in neutral ports 111
  says such vessel not to be confounded with ordinary
    contraband of war 118
PALMER, SIR ROUNDEL:
  his definition of due diligence 96
  his statement of the opinions of British lawyers . note 100
  his views as to the effect of a commission upon an
    offending vessel 124
  his speech on the Georgia 254
PALMERSTON, LORD:
  thinks separation must take place 31
  awaiting opinion of law officers 31
  speech of, March 27, 1863 55

316   INDEX.

	Page
PALMERSTON, LORD:	
speech of, June 30, 1863	56
speech of, July 23, 1863	63
minatory conversation with Mr. Adams	145
PAMPERO, THE:	
seizure of, and trial	162
PARIS, DECLARATION OF:	
unfriendly course of Great Britain as to, detailed	37—47
PHANTOM, THE:	
a blockade-runner	185
PHILLIMORE, SIR R. J.:	
decision in the case of the International	69
definition of neutrality	73
PIERANTONI:	
criticism on the Alabama	113
PORTUGAL:	
abstract of correspondence between, and the United States	82—88
principles recognized by, in that correspondence	88
recognizes International duty to make compensation for injuries committed by cruisers fitted out in neutral port	104
how regards effect of commission on such cruiser	129
course of government of, contrasted with that of British government	291
PRIOLEAU, CHARLES K.:	
managing member of Fraser, Trenholm & Co.	136
becomes naturalized as British subject	136
PRIVATEERING:	
declaration of congress of Paris, as to	39
Great Britian willing to legalize with Insurgents	42
but not with the United States	44
PROCLAMATION:	
announcing blockade. (See *Blockade*.)	
recognizing insurgents as belligerents. (See *Belligerents*.)	
the Queen's, a recognition of the international duties of Great Britain	61
such duties recognized by it defined	73, 75
PROSECUTIONS. (See *Bernard*.)	
PRUSSIA:	
course of government of, contrasted with that of British government	292
RAMS. (See *Lairds' rams*.)	
RAPPAHANNOCK:	
short sketch of	182
is detained by French authorities	182

	Page
RAPPAHANNOCK:	
course of French government as to, contrasted with conduct of British officials	185
REGRET. (See *Treaty of Washington*.)	
RETRIBUTION, THE:	
built at Buffalo, captured by rebels	245
turned into a cruiser	245
her career	245, 246
ROLIN, JACQUEMYNS:	
views as to the Queen's proclamation	36
views as to British neutrality	51
criticism on Mr. Bernard's book	103
RULES, (see *Treaty of Washington; Neutrals:*)	
the principles stated in these rules in force before the Treaty of Washington	89
RUSSELL, LORD JOHN, (see *Russell, Earl, where references to are indexed:*)	
created Earl Russell during insurrection	57
RUSSELL, EARL, (see *Dallas; Adams, Charles Francis:*)	
promises to await Mr. Adams's arrival	28
discusses independence with insurgent commissioners	28
calls the United States the Northern portion of the late Union	30
is doubtful June 1, 1861, whether there is a war	32
speech of, October 14, 1861	51
speech of, February 5, 1863	52
speech of, June 9, 1864	56
says the insurgents build ships of war in Great Britain because they have no ports of their own	132
reply to Mr. Adams's complaints regarding Nassau	143
declines to act on Mr. Adams's complaints regarding insurgent operations in February, 1863	155
declines to advise amendment of foreign enlistment act	156, 157
says the Alabama and Oreto are a scandal to British laws	158
thinks the interest of the insurgent government in blockade-runners should not be interfered with	176, 177, 181
letter to Mason, Slidell, and Mann	193
reply to Mr. Adams's note regarding sale of Sumter	202
sends Mr. Adams the report of customs officers on the Florida	211
reply to Mr. Adams regarding treatment of Florida at Bermuda	227
tells Mr. Adams to refer evidence about Alabama to Liverpool collector	230
conference with Mr. Adams after escape of Alabama	235

RUSSELL, EARL, (see *Dallas; Adams, Charles Francis:*) Page
   says Alabama was partly fitted out in Great Britain . 239
   reply to Mr. Adams's complaints about Georgia . . 249
   forwards Bullock's letter to Waddell 281
   reply to Mr. Adams's complaints regarding Laurel . 285
RUSSIA:
   course of the government of, contrasted with that of
      Great Britain 292
RUSSIAN AMBASSADOR:
   arrest of, in time of Queen Anne 71
SALDANHA'S EXPEDITION:
   arrest of at Terceira 112
SALISBURY, MARQUIS OF:
   speech of, when Lord Robert Cecil 58
SAN JACINTO:
   how treated at Barbadoes 223
SANTISIMA TRINIDAD:
   opinion in case of 121
SEA-KING, THE: (See *Shenandoah*.)
SEMMES, RAPHAEL, (See *Alabama:*)
   his opinion of the Alabama 239
SEWARD, MR.:
   instructs Mr. Adams to complain of insurgent operations
      made from British jurisdiction 154
SHIPS. (See *Vessels*.)
SHENANDOAH, THE; OR SEA-KING:
   short sketch of 183
   built in Clyde, and attracted Dudley's attention . . 262
   description of 262
   sold to father-in-law of Prioleau 262
   sails armed, and under command of Corbett, a well-
      known blockade-runner 263
   her officers and crew sail from Liverpool in the Laurel 263
   is armed from the Laurel at Madeira 264
   is short of men 265
   arrives at Melbourne 267
   her transfer to the insurgents known there in advance
      of her arrival 267
   representations as to, by United States consul to
      authorities 267
   captain of, asks permission to coal and make repairs 268
   permission granted 268
   delay in reporting what repairs were necessary . . 269
   report as to repairs made five days after arrival . . 269
   permission to repair again granted 270
   captain is requested to name day when he can go
      to sea 270

INDEX.

	Page
SHENANDOAH, THE; OR SEA-KING:	
many men are illegally enlisted for crew of	210
proceedings as to, in colonial legislature	211
correspondence with colonial authorities regarding enlistments for	271
enlistments continue; repairs suspended	272
repairs resumed and completed	273
three hundred tons of coal taken from a transport sent for the purpose from Liverpool	273
consul furnishes proof of illegal enlistments to colonial authorities	273
no action taken thereon	274
number and notoriety of enlistments	275—276
no supplies or coal needed for	277
repairs prolonged to enlist men	277
no repairs needed	278
critical examination of report of repairs	278—282
returns to Liverpool	282
violations of neutrality by	283
reasons for holding Great Britain liable for acts of	286
SINGAPORE:	
Alabama coals at	242
SLAVERY:	
opposition to the limitation of, the cause of secession	19
SPAIN:	
recognizes international duty to make compensation for injuries by cruisers fitted out in violation of international duty	104
how, regards the effect of a commission on such cruisers	129
course of the government of, contrasted with that of the British government	292
STOERKODDER, THE; OR STONEWALL:	
short sketch of career of	167
STORY, MR. JUSTICE:	
definitions of diligence	93, 95
opinion in the case of the Santisima Trinidad	121
STEPHENS, ALEXANDER H.:	
vice-president of insurgent government	19
his views as to slavery	20
his speech against secession	20
SUMTER:	
proceedings at Gibraltar as to	152
proceedings at Trinidad as to	153
coals at Trinidad	200
arrives at Gibraltar	201
shut up there by Kearsage	201

320 INDEX.

	Page
SUMTER:	
sold under protest of United States consul	201
treatment of, a partiality toward insurgents	202
reasons why Great Britain liable for acts of	205
SUMTER, FORT:	
surrender of	23
SWEDISH VESSELS:	
the case of	115
TACONY, THE:	
career of	223
TALLAHASSEE, THE:	
fitted out in London as a' privateer	258
her career	258
what was done at Halifax as to	259
reasons why Great Britain liable for acts of	259
TENTERDEN, LORD:	
memorandum on neutrality laws	62
says privateering was suppressed by reason of the course adopted by Washington	79
TERCEIRA, (see *Saldanha's expedition*:)	
Alabama arrives there	237
TRANSSHIPMENT OF CONTRABAND OF WAR:	
the permission in colonial ports a failure to perform the duties of a neutral	140
injurious to the United States	140
TREATY OF WASHINGTON:	
expresses regret at escape of the cruisers	6
terms of submission of claims of the United States	6
meeting of the arbitrators, provisions for	7
time for delivery of cases and evidence	8
time for delivery of counter cases and evidence	8
when originals must be produced	9
duties of agents of each government	9
counsel may be heard	9
rules applicable to the case, (see *Neutrals*)	9, 96
award, when and how made	10
board of assessors, how constituted and duties of	11
the first clause in the first rule to be found in United States neutrality law of 1794	91
what is due diligence	91—97
fitting out, arming, or equipping, each an offense	97
reasons for words "specially adapted," &c.	97
continuing force of second clause of first rule	100
limitation and explanation of second rule	102
recognizes obligation to make compensation for injuries	104
TREATY OF 1794. (See *United States*.)	

INDEX.   321

TRENHOLM, GEORGE A.:   Page
    principal member of firm of Fraser, Trenholm & Co.,
    and secretary of insurgent treasury   135
TRENT. (See *Great Britain.*)
TRINIDAD:
    The Sumter at 153, 202
TUSCALOOSA, OR CONRAD:
    a prize captured by the Alabama   168
    claims to be received at Cape Town as a tender .   168
    is seized, then released, and received as man-of-war 169
    this decision reversed in London   170
    comes again to Cape Town and is seized   170
    this act disapproved in London   171
TWENTY-FOUR HOURS' RULE:
    contained in admiralty and colonial instructions . . 144
UNITED STATES, (see *Great Britain; Washington:*)
    relations with Great Britain before 1860 friendly .   15
    various treaties with Great Britain . . . . . .   15—16
    number of States and Territories in 1860 . note   17
    election of Mr. Lincoln as President   18
    secession of South Carolina and other States . . .   18
    cause of secession   19
    neutrality law of 1818 . . . . note   65
    had no municipal law in 1793 to aid in performance
       of international duties   76
    course during President Washington's administration   76
    treaty of 1794   79
    construction thereof by commissioners   79
    enact neutrality laws at request of Great Britain .   80
    correspondence with Portugal . . . . 82—   88
    principles recognized by that correspondence . . .   88
    what they regard as due diligence   91
    seizure of Spanish gun-boats in 1869   98
    character of southern blockaded coast   137
VESSELS OF WAR, (see *Commission; Contraband; Neutrals:*)
    of belligerents, sale of in neutral ports 202
VIRGINIA, THE:
    inquiries as to   166
WACHUSETT:
    treatment of, at Bermuda   221
WALKER, NORMAN S.:
    made insurgent agent at Bermuda   147
    his urgent demand for coal   173
    is supplied with coal by Fraser, Trenholm & Co. .   173
WASHINGTON, PRESIDENT:
    his course towards Mr. Genet   77,   79

WASHINGTON, PRESIDENT:
    determines to restore prizes captured by privateers
        fitted out in United States   79
    his course suppressed privateering   79

WESTBURY, LORD:
    appointed Lord High Chancellor, June, 1861 . . .   57
    regards animus of neutral as sole criterion   59
    says United States may use Queen's proclamation to
        prove animus   59
    says ship should not be built in neutral port by bel-
        ligerent with view to war 114

WILKES, ADMIRAL:
    correspondence with governor of Bermuda 223

www.ingramcontent.com/pod-product-compliance
Lightning Source LLC
Chambersburg PA
CBHW021204230426
43667CB00006B/550